# MASTERING THE THIRTY AIRES

by Scott Michael Stenwick

Volume III of the Mastering Enochian Magick Series

PENDRAIG PUBLISHING INC

Copyright © 2022 Scott Stenwick

ISBN: 978-1-936922-96-3

All rights reserved.
No part of this book may be reproduced in any form or by any electronic or mechanical means, including information storage or retrieval systems, without permission in writing from the publisher, except by reviewers, who may quote brief passages in a review.

The opinions stated in this book are those of the author and may not represent the opinions of the publisher.

Cover Art by Scott Stenwick
Cover design by Ted Venemann
Book Design and Layout by Nord Compo

Printed and bound in USA
First Printing _____ 2022

Published by Pendraig Publishing Inc
PO Box 8427
Green Valley Lake CA 92341
Visit www.pendraigpublishing.com

*For Michele Montserrat, Thomas Brenden, and Maurine Stenwick, all of whom joined with me in the Thirty Aires workings that led to the writing of this book. May you all accomplish the Great Work and attain the Summum Bonum, True Wisdom, and Perfect Happiness!*

*Thanks once again to Joseph H. Peterson for his wonderful Enochian artwork, used here with his permission.*

# Contents

1. Introduction ... 1
2. Renaissance Astrology ... 5
3. The Thirty Aires ... 29
4. The Parts of the Earth ... 37
5. The Temple Arrangement ... 107
6. Thirty Aires Ritual Template ... 119
7. Opening the Temple ... 123
8. Preliminary Invocations ... 129
9. The Angelic Keys ... 133
10. Tuning the Space ... 145
11. Thirty Aires Conjurations ... 157
12. The Charge ... 175
13. Scrying the Aethyrs ... 183
14. Closing the Temple ... 193

15. Conclusion                                                          195

**Appendix A: Basic Ritual Forms**                                      197

**Appendix B: Comselh Ananael Thirty Aires Evocation Ritual**           225

**Bibliography**                                                        233

**Index**                                                               235

# 1
# Introduction

> "It's far too late for anything but magick,
> as the future is clearly up for grabs."
>
> —Antero Alli, <u>The Akashic Record Player</u>[1]

MASTERING THE THIRTY AIRES took me far longer to write than I ever expected. Back in the late 1990's, I set out to write a book that I planned on calling *The Enochian Universe*. My plan was to cover the magical system of John Dee and Edward Kelley using the attributions of the system as they would have understood it, and with that rather than the Golden Dawn magical system as a starting point, I would go on to develop a system of magick that could be easily integrated with modern ritual forms and techniques. If you have read the first two books in this series, I am sure that you recognize the methodology.

Essentially, the material I hoped to include in *The Enochian Universe* is the same material found in these three volumes of the *Mastering Enochian Magick* series. In writing this would-be *magnum opus* of mine, I got as far as assembling all the material for my version of the Heptarchial and Great Table work. The reason I never published it, though, is that I got bogged down in putting together all the material for the Thirty Aires. This meant that for the first two books in the series, I was able to go back and rework my almost-complete material from *Enochian Universe*, but for this one I had to pull all the supporting material together before I could even start writing.

---

1 Antero Alli, *The Akashic Record Player: A Non-Stop Geomantic Conspiracy* (Tempe, AZ: New Falcon, 1988), 6.

According to Dee and Kelley's system, the magick of the Thirty Aires concerns itself with zodiacal and political forces. I never expected to be publishing this book into what has turned out to be the current political climate in the United States, but day after day, it seems that the leading quote from Anterro Alli could not be more appropriate. Our current politics are polarized, chaotic, and volatile—exactly the sort of situation in which magick is most effective. The idea that magician and occultists somehow secretly rule the world is laughable, and yet, depending on how things pan out we may find ourselves in a position that will allow us a great deal of influence over the sweep of history. Let's make the most of it.

Backing up a bit, one of the criticisms leveled at the first book in this series, *Mastering the Mystical Heptarchy*, was that the term "Mastering" in the title was misleading. Many books on Enochian magick engage in detailed textual breakdowns of Dee's spirit diaries, complex linguistic analysis of Angelic words, involved applications of gematria, and so forth. If this is what the word "Mastery" implies to you, then the truth is that you probably are looking for a different book than one of mine. While I have explored most of the subjects outlined above during my own study of the Enochian system from 1992 onward, my intent with this series is to distill the system down into the basic components that make for effective magical work.

Mastery, to my way of thinking, is not something that you can obtain by reading a book, or for that matter a whole library. Mastery is obtained by doing the work, day in and day out. It is obtained by sticking with your daily practices over an extended period and building up your spiritual body. It is obtained by using practical magick to improve your daily life. And, it is obtained by contacting and forging relationships with the various entities that populate the magical universe, whether you are working with Enochian angels, planetary spirits, or Goetic demons. One difficulty of doing this with Enochian magick is that the complexity of the system as commonly taught makes it hard to determine even a starting point, let alone a comprehensive set of practices that will lead you to eventual mastery of its intricacies.

The entire point of this series is to lay out just such an approach. The methods contained here have been tested for many years and found highly effective by myself and the members of my magical working group. The daily practice regimen that I lay out will enhance both your understanding of the system and your personal magical power over time. The practical techniques I recommend will allow you to shape your life in such a way that it will support both your ongoing spiritual realization and your control over the events that surround you. Even though mastery as such may not be contained between the covers of this book or the others in the series, a workable path to mastery is. You just need to start in on the work and keep at it.

This third volume of the *Mastering Enochian Magick* series covers the Thirty Aires, the final piece of John Dee and Edward Kelley's Enochian magical system. The Aires are conceptualized as thirty concentric spheres radiating out from the Great Table. These Aires contain magical representations of the ninety-one parts of the Earth and their twelve zodiacal governors. Thus, as the Mystical Heptarchy is attributed to the planetary realm and the Great Table is attributed to the elemental realm, the Thirty Aires are attributed to the zodiacal realm. The foundational symbol set of the Western Esoteric Tradition spans these same three realms, making Dee and Kelley's system of magick complete on its own.

These three facets of the Enochian system come together to create a comprehensive system of magical arts that span the whole of creation, and it is perhaps this essential completeness that provides the system with its reputed strength and intricate beauty. If we are indeed going to engage in magical work to shape the future into the best of all possible worlds, with liberty, justice, and realization for all, it seems to me that we could not pick a better system with which to do it. The angels spoke over and over to Dee and Kelley of a "golden age" to come, and perhaps for us that moment has arrived at last.

Scott Michael Stenwick<br>Minneapolis, Minnesota

# 2
# Renaissance Astrology

THE THREE PRIMARY SETS of correspondences employed by most Western magicians are the elements, planets, and signs of the zodiac. The Enochian magick of John Dee and Edward Kelley incorporates all three. The material found in the *Heptarchia Mystica* represents the activity of the seven ancient planets in the form of Kings and Princes of the days of the week. The four quadrants of the Great Table represent the action of the four elements and the "black cross," which binds them together and is often attributed to the "fifth element," akasha or spirit. Finally, the twelve signs of the zodiac are attributed to the divisions of the Thirty Aires, the final portion of the Enochian system to be received.

As the Thirty Aires represent the astrological portion of the Enochian magical system, some understanding of the worldview associated with Renaissance astrology is necessary. One of Dr. John Dee's many professions was that of astrologer, and it is in that capacity he became familiar with Queen Elizabeth. He cast her chart when she was imprisoned by her sister, but he was able to accurately predict that Mary would soon die unexpectedly and make Elizabeth Queen. Dee went on to serve as her royal astrologer for the duration of her reign.

Many modern astrologers treat the system as form of psychology, in which the various planetary positions represent aspects of the personality. This is the approach on which pop-culture astrology is based. The Sun sign is seen as the sign most associated with a person's basic nature, and for many people this is all they know about their astrological chart. The statement "I'm a Taurus" is shorthand for all the personality traits associated with the sign Taurus. However, this modern methodology is not how Dee approached the discipline.

In Renaissance astrology, the interpretation of not only the Sun sign but all chart information is quite different. Rather than representing facets of personal psychological topography, the planets and signs are thought to represent forces acting upon the individual in the various aspects of life as determined by their House placement. Using the previous example, a Taurus Sun may not indicate Taurus personality traits in the individual at all, but rather the individual's relationship with his or her father. A well-aspected Sun would indicate a positive relationship, while a poorly-aspected Sun could indicate a negative or contentious one.

Renaissance astrology is a complex topic, and this chapter provides only a brief overview. However, understanding Dee's worldview can help provide some insight into how he saw the zodiacal elements of the Enochian magical system. The Angels explained to Dee and Kelley that the Parts of the Earth associated with the Thirty Aires could be used to influence the decisions of Kings and Princes and conquer countries without armies. This sounds like a tall order, but in fact from the standpoint of Renaissance astrology it was not at all unthinkable that setting in motion a force corresponding with the sign related to a nation or region could shift its destiny in a new direction.

**Signs:** The twelve signs of the zodiac have a long history, dating back at least as far as the Babylonians. The same signs are also employed in the Vedic astrology of India, suggesting that the assignment of their characteristics could prove as old as human civilization. Note that the seasonal descriptions given here are specific to the northern hemisphere. In the southern hemisphere they are reversed, so that for example Leo is during the winter and Aquarius is during the summer.

**Aries** – Cardinal, fire, masculine, spring season. Hot and dry at new beginning season of year. Cardinal, which means quick acting but not sustained. Good at starting but not continuing. Aries is fire so planets here are active, and not necessarily thoughtful or reflective. Aries is not a sign that is generally sensitive to others.

**Taurus** – Fixed, earth, feminine, spring—a cold, dry element in a warm moist season. I think of this as like the moist and fertile spring soil at the time plants are really starting to grow from the increasing warmth of the season. Sustained, stable earth plus fixed mode emphasizes its heaviness, stability, reliability, passivity, and stubbornness.

**Gemini** – Mutable, air, masculine, spring—mutable air in the spring or air season, so air scattered in all directions. Air doesn't get any airier than this. Mercury is ruler—very strong and 'in his element' but not necessarily most useful or practical. Mercury likes to connect with others in this air element but being mutable it can fly off in all directions.

**Cancer** – Cardinal, water, feminine, summer—water that is warm, moving, outgoing, so it has an active, nurturing quality. This is the first sign of the season of summer, when growth really kicks into overdrive. The sign is a cold, wet element in the hot, dry season of summer, so there are some contradictory qualities here. Cancer can be outgoing and nurturing, but also withdrawing and protective. The cardinal quality of Cancer works with the hot quality of the season to make this the most initiating and moving of the water signs. Cancer is rushing water, streams at full strength moving swiftly.

**Leo** – Fixed, fire, masculine, summer. This is a hot and dry sign in a hot and dry season, so it comes on very strong. Leo is a fixed sign which is sustained more than Aries, so it stays very strong. This is the peak of the summer—fixed, dry, relentless, steady, and unending heat. The Sun is the ruler of this sign and is hotter and stronger here than anywhere else. This is also the sign in which the Sun is the most visible and prominent.

**Virgo** – Mutable, earth, feminine, summer. Virgo falls at the beginning of the harvest season. This is a mutable sign, a transition, in which summer is starting to fall apart and you sense the first signs of approaching autumn. Change is in the air, and things are not stable. Like other mutable signs, Virgo has a self-reflective quality—you can think of it as an inner equivalent of separating out the wheat from the chaff during harvest.

**Libra** – Cardinal, air, masculine, autumn. This is the first of the two seasons where cold dominates, and where the night is longer than the day, the beginning of the decline of the Sun. This is the peak of harvest time, and also the season when the leaves in temperate climates turn their brightest and most brilliant before they fade and fall from the trees. Venus is the ruler of this sign. This is sensitive, reflective Venus in a warm and moist air sign, and I think this is where we associate most of the meaning of Libra as having to do with relationship, communication, and awareness of the needs of others.

**Scorpio** – Fixed, water, feminine, autumn. This is a cold wet sign in a cold dry season. Scorpio is the 'driest' of the water signs, partly from being fixed, partly from the season associated with cold, dry earth. The season is cold and dry, the sign is cold, wet and fixed. This is the time of year when the leaves are brown and fallen, the trees are bare, and the nights are getting longer. With all that cold and fixed energy being emphasized, this sign is more internal, less outgoing. Also, an inner movement is shown in the withdrawing of life from seasonal plants, being drawn down inward and into the earth as leaves are shed, plants die, turn brown, wither, and start to decay.

**Sagittarius** – Mutable, fire, masculine, autumn. This is the most mutable, reflective, and intellectual of the fire signs. Late autumn is not a time for active physical striving, so here fire expresses as aspiration, ideals, and striving to attain those ideals. The meaning of Sagittarius is largely colored by Jupiter being the ruler of the sign. There is an association with law, philosophy, benevolent optimism, striving after ideals. Jupiter has a mental quality—mix that with fire, and you get much of Sagittarius.

**Capricorn** – Cardinal, earth, feminine, water. Cardinal starts it, earth can keep it going once in motion. Here is a case where you have to think in terms of planet taking priority over sign. Saturn is the ruler of Capricorn. Saturn is cold, dry reserved, and practical, in a cold winter sign. I think this emphasizes what can be the shyness and reserve associated with this sign. Saturn is not particularly outgoing or ambitious, so Capricorn can be cautious, guarded, practical, but not necessarily striving for earthly accomplishment.

**Aquarius** – Fixed, air, masculine, winter—this is a warm moist sign, in a cold moist season, but fixed. Air is intellect, but the fixity adds stubbornness. In traditional astrology Aquarius is ruled by Saturn. If there is idealism (air) to this sign it also has rigidity, a lack of receptivity or flexibility. People devoted to an ideal can be very intolerant of those who do not share that ideal, and I think that is related to the sign being ruled by Saturn. Also, Saturn adds to the impersonal and group-oriented flavor of the sign.

**Pisces** – Mutable, water, feminine, winter—a cold wet sign in a cold wet season—it is mutable, so it has no fixity or structure. This is the most watery of the water signs—hard to pin down, flexible, receptive, emotional. It doesn't get any wetter than this. If Cancer is a cardinal running river and Scorpio is fixed ice, then Pisces is the mutable ocean—universal, moving outward in all directions, emphasizing the lack of boundaries often associated with this sign. Also, as with other mutable signs, there is an introspective, self-conscious, inward-turned reflective quality to the sign.[2]

One of the differences between Vedic and European astrology is the use of tropical rather than sidereal sign positions. The sidereal system is based on the actual position of the individual constellations in the sky, whereas the tropical system keeps the signs lined up with the seasons as described above. The procession of the Earth's axis means that over long periods of time the constellations slowly shift with respect to the seasons. European astrologers may have adopted the tropical system because European seasons are much more pronounced that those in India, which is nearer to the equator.

As an aside, while little scientific evidence for astrology has been compiled, at least one recent study suggests that birth season may play a role in brain development and be related to certain personality traits.[3] If this finding holds up to replication and peer review, it may provide some evidence that traits associated with "birth sign" could be based at least in part on accurate naturalistic observation of individuals born at different times throughout the year. This, in turn, would support the use of the tropical system over the sidereal, as it maintains the seasonal relationships between the signs.

---

2 Charles Obert, *Introduction to Traditional Natal Astrology* (Minneapolis, MN: Almuten Press, 2015), 86-93.
3 Christian Jarrett, *How Your Season of Birth is Etched in Your Brain* (Wired, 3/5/2014. Retrieved 8/26/2015 from http://www.wired.com/2014/03/season-birth-etched-brain/).

**Planets:** Planetary rulership of signs during the Renaissance was that same as that used by modern astrologers before the discovery of the outer planets. As such, only the seven ancient planets are employed, which excludes Uranus, Neptune, and Pluto. The Sun and Moon rule one sign each, while the other five planets each rule two. While today's modern astrologers have assigned Uranus as the ruler of Aquarius, Neptune as the ruler of Pisces, and Pluto as the ruler of Scorpio, the original system dates to ancient times and is quite elegant.

The following chart shows the signs, their planetary rulers, the corresponding days of the week, and the Sect of the sign.

| Sign | Ruler | Day | Sect |
| --- | --- | --- | --- |
| Aries | Mars | Tuesday | Diurnal |
| Taurus | Venus | Friday | Nocturnal |
| Gemini | Mercury | Wednesday | Diurnal |
| Cancer | Moon | Monday | Nocturnal |
| Leo | Sun | Sunday | Diurnal |
| Virgo | Mercury | Wednesday | Nocturnal |
| Libra | Venus | Friday | Diurnal |
| Scorpio | Mars | Tuesday | Nocturnal |
| Sagittarius | Jupiter | Thursday | Diurnal |
| Capricorn | Saturn | Saturday | Nocturnal |
| Aquarius | Saturn | Saturday | Diurnal |
| Pisces | Jupiter | Thursday | Nocturnal |

*Table 1. Signs, Rulers, and Sects*

The term **Sect** may be unfamiliar to those who work with modern astrology. Each sign is assigned to the **Diurnal** or **Nocturnal** sect, beginning with Aries as diurnal and from there alternating through the signs. The Sun, as ruler of the Day or Diurnal Sect, rules the diurnal sign, Leo. The Moon, as ruler of the Night or Nocturnal Sect, rules the nocturnal sign Cancer. The other planets rule one diurnal and one nocturnal sign each, which is why assigning the outer planets as sign rulers disrupts the classical system.

If Uranus is assigned as the ruler of Aquarius, Saturn is left with only one sign to rule, the nocturnal sign Capricorn. If Neptune is assigned as ruler of Pisces, Jupiter is left with only the diurnal sign Sagittarius. And, if Pluto is assigned as the ruler of Scorpio, Mars is left with only the diurnal sign Aries. However, Mercury still rules both Gemini and Virgo, and Venus still rules Taurus and Libra. The symmetry is thus broken, or at best incomplete.

The Renaissance system also makes use of the other standard dignities and debilities of the planets. In addition to the dignity of **Rulership**, planets also acquire the dignity of **Exaltation**, and the debilities of **Detriment** and **Fall**, when they are in certain signs.

These are shown in the following table.

| **Planet** | **Rulership** | **Exaltation** | **Detriment** | **Fall** |
|---|---|---|---|---|
| Sun | Leo | Aries | Aquarius | Libra |
| Moon | Cancer | Taurus | Capricorn | Scorpio |
| Mercury | Gemini, Virgo | Virgo | Sagittarius, Pisces | Pisces |
| Venus | Taurus, Libra | Pisces | Aries, Scorpio | Virgo |
| Mars | Aries, Scorpio | Capricorn | Taurus, Libra | Cancer |
| Jupiter | Sagittarius, Pisces | Cancer | Gemini, Virgo | Capricorn |
| Saturn | Capricorn, Aquarius | Libra | Cancer, Leo | Aries |

*Table 2. Planetary Dignities and Debilities*

A planet in Rulership is said to be competent, in control, and positively disposed. A planet in its Exaltation is likewise positively disposed, but at the same time not ultimately in control of its circumstances. Such a planet may be thought of as an honored and welcome guest in the house of the sign's ruler. Also, some astrologers have noted that while both Rulership and Exaltation bring good fortune to planets so disposed, there can be an illusionary quality associated with Exaltation. With Rulership, this is usually not the case.

A planet is in Detriment when it is in the sign opposite its Rulership. Likewise, a planet is in Fall when it is in the sign opposite its Exaltation.

Rulership denotes competence; it is the state in which the planet is both positively disposed and in control. Detriment is the opposite of Rulership, denoting incompetence and an inability to hold things together. Exaltation denotes a state in which the planet is positively disposed, prominent, and paid attention to, though not actually in control of the situation. Fall is the opposite of Exaltation, in which the planet is ignored and paid no respect. Rulership is the most positive dignity, followed by Exaltation. Detriment is the most negative debility, followed by Fall.

**Houses:** Modern astrology makes use of many different House systems. A House corresponds to certain areas of life and can be mapped by starting with the sign rising at the moment the chart is cast and from there dividing the whole of the ecliptic into twelve parts, one for each House. Renaissance astrology makes use of whole sign houses, which means that each sign in the chart maps to exactly one house. In my own Natal Chart, I have Cancer rising, making the whole of Cancer the First House in the Renaissance system. The whole of Leo is then the Second House, the whole of Virgo the Third House, and so forth.

I have heard a rumor to the effect that Dee may have employed the Placidus house system at some point, which is used by many modern astrologers, but I have not been able to track down any hard evidence of this. The Placidus technique was mentioned in the works of Ibn Ezra, who predated Dee by centuries, but it is believed that the first European publication of the system was in 1602. While it is possible that Dee, who died in 1608, might have made use of it, he would most likely have done so at the very end of his life, decades after his work with Edward Kelley.

The following list of traits generally describes the nature of each House, from the first to the twelfth. In modern astrology, each House is also associated with a sign, but in Renaissance astrology, these attributions are not used. Rather, the sign of each House in the chart will determine how the people, places, things, and events associated with the House will be expressed.

**First** – Body, appearance, main character, temperament, personality, quality of mind, how one communicates.

**Second** – Money, small belongings, material assets, livelihood, material fortune. Partners & associates (next to 1st).

**Third** – Siblings, immediate neighbors, and environment, day to day associates. Short journeys. Communication, writing, learning, religion and spirituality, education.

**Fourth** – Ancestors in general, father. Earth, land and property, house and residence. End of life, endings.

**Fifth** – Children. Pleasure, amusement, entertainment, the arts, sex. Gambling as amusement, games of chance.

**Sixth** – Health problems, illness. Nurses and health workers. Lack of recognition, unrewarding work. Slaves and servants. Small animals. Averse from Ascendant.

**Seventh** – One on one relationships. Marriage, partners, opponents, open enemies. Other party in a business transaction or horary.

**Eighth** – Death, fear, anxiety, lack of control. Also called an "idle" house. Spouse's money, legacies (2nd from 7th). Averse from Ascendant. Hard for planets here to be seen or act effectively. If 8th has an occult connotation, as necromancy, communication with the world of the dead.

**Ninth** – Long journeys, travel, foreign lands. Religion, spirituality, astrology, omens, dreams, divination. Learning and places thereof. Universities, churches.

**Tenth** – Dignity, public reputation, fame, eminence. Most public house. Career as what you are known for. Superior or boss at work.

**Eleventh** – Friends, good fortune in general, money from superiors (2nd from 10th). Hope, trust, confidence.

**Twelfth** – Hidden enemies, prison, confinement, self-undoing, illness, death. Large animals. Averse from Ascendant.[4]

---

[4] Charles Obert, *Introduction to Traditional Natal Astrology* (Minneapolis, MN: Almuten Press, 2015) 113-114.

The use of whole signs makes the houses much easier to calculate than with Placidus or any other modern system. It also makes the relationship between the signs and houses much clearer when reading the chart.

House position affects the strength of the planets relative to each other. If you are attempting to strengthen the planetary ruler of a sign, in addition to the day and hour you can pick a time in which the planet's house position is particularly favorable. From strongest (1) to weakest (12), the houses are ordered thus:

1. First
2. Tenth
3. Seventh
4. Fourth
5. Eleventh
6. Fifth
7. Second
8. Ninth
9. Eighth
10. Third
11. Twelfth
12. Sixth

**Aspects:** Planets form aspects when they are at certain angles to each other in a chart. The signs do not change in relation to each other, but the planets move freely from sign to sign across the ecliptic. As they move at different rates, they constantly form aspects with each other. Rather than looking at exact degrees, Renaissance astrology primarily makes use of whole sign aspects, such that, for example, two planets in Aries may be considered as forming a conjunction by sign, even if one is at the beginning of the sign and the other at the end.

The standard aspects are as follows:

**Conjunction** – This aspect describes an angle of 0 degrees. It indicates a union of the characteristics of the planets in question.

**Opposition** – This aspect describes an angle of 180 degrees. It often indicates conflict between the planets in question in which they hinder or oppose each other but can occasionally indicate situations in which the planets complement each other and thus can work together.

**Trine** – This aspect describes an angle of 120 degrees. It indicates that the characteristics of the planets in questions are working together in a smooth, harmonious fashion.

**Square** – This aspect describes an angle of 90 degrees. It indicates that the characteristics of the planets in question are not working well together, producing stress and conflict that demands attention.

**Sextile** – This aspect describes an angle of 60 degrees. This aspect indicates that the characteristics of the planets in question are cooperating, but not as smoothly as in a Trine. The sextile is considered a positive aspect, but it is generally viewed as weaker than the others.

**Aversion** – This is not technically an aspect, but rather the absence of one. From any given sign there are four other signs that are said to be in aversion. The first two are the signs directly adjacent. If a planet is in Aries, any other planet in Taurus or Pisces is in aversion to it. The other two are the signs are opposite those that are adjacent, in this example Scorpio (opposite Taurus) and Virgo (opposite Pisces). Therefore, any planet in Scorpio or Virgo will also be in aversion to a planet in Aries.

Planets that form aspects are thought of as being able to see each other and interact, even if some kinds of interaction are negative rather than positive. Planets in aversion, however, have difficulty being aware of each other and have trouble interacting in any way. Under some circumstances, this can be useful, as in a magical operation that seeks to remove the influence of a certain planet, but under other circumstances, it can prove challenging as planets in aversion only rarely can meaningfully communicate.

**Electional Techniques:** Electional astrology is a means by which astrological operations can be timed to produce the most effective result. The simplest electional method employs aspects formed by the Moon. Because the Moon is the fastest-moving of all the heavenly bodies, it makes a complete cycle around the zodiac every month. As such, it constantly forms aspects with the other planets as it moves through the signs.

Like planetary hours, these electional methods can be used with any system of magick, not just the Enochian Parts of the Earth. They can be used to substantially increase your magical results in general by bringing your operations into greater harmony with the celestial forces that are all around us, all the time.

When the Moon enters a sign, it begins "working on" the next aspect that it will form in that sign. Once it makes that aspect, it moves on to the next. Finally, once it has made all the aspects it can in the sign, it becomes **Void of Course** until it enters the next sign. The first rule derived from this process is that no magical operation should ever be started on a void of course Moon. This is because when the Moon is void of course the operation is very likely to fail, or at best accomplish nothing particularly worthwhile.

The second rule is to look at the Moon's final aspect and when you are planning your ritual. The final aspect is the last aspect the Moon makes before going void of course. If the final aspect is negative—an opposition or square—you should find another time to perform your operation, even if all the other factors line up. On the other hand, if the final aspect is positive—a conjunction, trine, or sextile—you are good to go. Astrological calendars are available that include this information, so you can see it at a glance without having to consult an ephemeris.

One special case with this electional method is when the final aspect is to one of the malefic planets, Mars or Saturn. For most operations, this is still considered negative, even if the final aspect is a trine or conjunction. However, if your operation involves Mars, Saturn, or one of the signs ruled by those planets—Aries, Scorpio, Capricorn, and Aquarius—it can still be considered a positive result as the operation will be working with the qualities associated with the planet or planets in aspect.

A more involved electional technique for working with signs involves looking at the condition of the sign's planetary ruler, which you can find in the preceding tables. The first thing to look for is whether the planet is dignified or debilitated in the sign that it currently occupies. You will want to time your operation so that at the very least the planet is not debilitated. Preferably the planet should be in rulership or exaltation, but you can still go forward if it is neither dignified nor debilitated.

The next thing to check is the ruling planet's next aspect. While natal Renaissance astrology makes use of whole sign houses to form aspects, electional astrology looks at the exact degrees. Furthermore, in electional astrology, an aspect is only in play so long as it is culminating—that is, while the planets involved are moving closer to each other. As soon as the planets begin to separate, the aspect is said to be past and no longer in effect for electional purposes. If you are working with Gemini but Mercury is forming a square with another planet, you can wait until just after the moment the aspect peaks and start your ritual then.

This electional method employs an orb of five degrees or so for aspects to the sign ruler, meaning that even culminating aspects do not come into play until they are approximately five degrees from their peak. Outside that range, they are not treated as functional and should not be relevant to magical operations. This also goes for positive aspects, which can no longer be employed once they have passed their peak. Much like catching a bus, either you are there at the proper time and able to get on, or you miss it and have to wait for the next one.

**The Chart Victor:** I originally learned how to perform this calculation from Benjamin Dykes, who found it in among the works of Abraham ibn Ezra. Dykes' book, *The Search of the Heart*[5], goes into great detail regarding the application of the method and includes never-before-translated astrological material from the twelfth century. This section will cover the calculation and briefly discuss its basic application for zodiacal operations, but if you want to know more, I highly recommended picking up a copy of the book for yourself.

The magical application of this method for zodiacal operations has to do with the dignities or debilities acquired by the Chart Victor when it is in the sign with which you are working. Ideally, you want to perform a zodiacal operation for a particular sign when the Chart Victor is the ruler of the sign, or exalted in it. Rulership is the most favorable dignity, followed

---

5  Benjamin Dykes, *The Search of the Heart* (Golden Valley, MN: The Cazimi Press, 2012)

by Exaltation. You should always avoid performing an operation for a particular sign when the Chart Victor is debilitated in the sign by Detriment or Fall.

Like electional techniques, the Chart Victor method can be used with any system of magick, not just the Enochian Parts of the Earth. When working with other systems, you can identify the planet or planets most associated with the work you are doing and time your operation so that one of more of those planets will be the Chart Victor.

To calculate the Chart Victor, you will also need either an ephemeris or some sort of astrology software to generate the chart. I usually just use Astrolog[6], a freeware astrology program available for most desktop platforms. The website is extremely dated, but the program has been around a long time and does everything you need it to do. You start with a calculation grid, which looks like this:

|  | Saturn | Jupiter | Mars | Sun | Venus | Mercury | Moon |
|---|---|---|---|---|---|---|---|
| Degree of Sun |  |  |  |  |  |  |  |
| Degree of Moon |  |  |  |  |  |  |  |
| Degree of Ascendant |  |  |  |  |  |  |  |
| Degree of Lot of Fortune |  |  |  |  |  |  |  |
| Degree of Prenatal Lunation |  |  |  |  |  |  |  |
| Ruler of the Day |  |  |  |  |  |  |  |
| Ruler of the Hour |  |  |  |  |  |  |  |
| Houses |  |  |  |  |  |  |  |
| Superiors |  |  |  |  |  |  |  |

*Table 3: Chart Victor Calculation Grid*

Next, you cast the chart. This example is for Monday, January 9th, 2017, in Minneapolis, Minnesota at 7:00 AM. Running it in Astrolog, you get the chart shown below.

---

6  http://www.astrolog.org/astrolog.htm

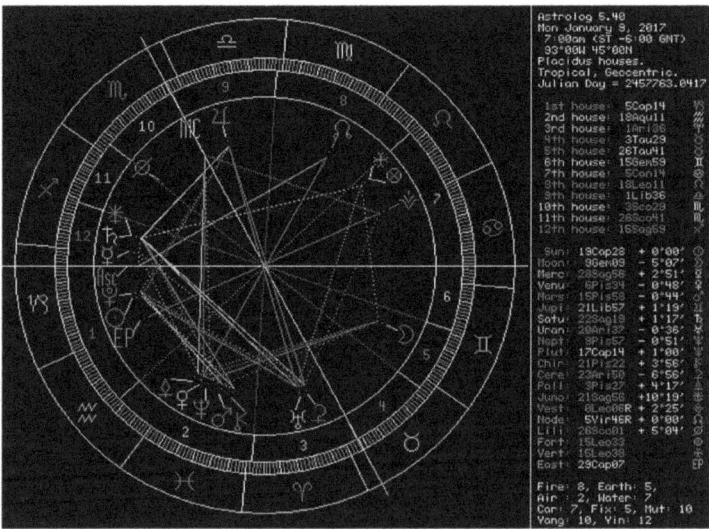

*Figure 1. Chart with Minors*

Make a note of the degree of the Lot of Fortune (Fort), which for this chart is 15 Leo. Then, go up to the menu, click **Setting**, and uncheck **Include Minors**. That gives you the chart shown below. Again, you can click to enlarge. Aside from the Part of Fortune, we are only concerned with the seven ancient planets shown on the grid and the Ascendant.

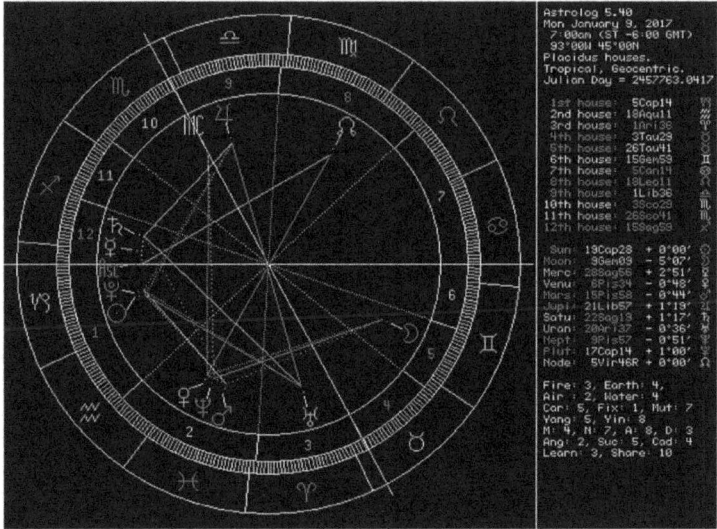

*Figure 2. Chart without Minors*

The Degree of the Sun is 19 Capricorn. The Degree of the Moon is 9 Gemini. The Degree of Ascendant ("1st House") is 5 Capricorn. We already made a note of the Degree of Lot of Fortune, which is 15 Leo. The Prenatal Lunation is the most difficult of these points to figure out. The Degree of Prenatal Lunation is the degree of the most recent Full or New Moon. Astrolog has a feature that lets you progress the chart backward that I usually use to figure this out. For this chart, it was a New Moon, with a degree of 7 Capricorn. You don't need to worry about minutes, just degrees.

The planetary day is the day of the week, with the day beginning at sunrise, not midnight. Today is a Monday, but it's before sunrise, so the ruler of the day is the Sun, not the Moon. Magically, until the Sun rises, it is still Sunday.

To calculate the planetary hour, divide the time between sunrise and sunset into twelve equal parts to get the hours of the day, and the time between sunset and sunrise into twelve equal parts to get the hours of the night. Days begin at sunrise. The first hour of the day is attributed to the planet ruling the day, and the subsequent hours are assigned according to the Chaldean Order.

**Saturn → Jupiter → Mars → Sun → Venus → Mercury → Moon**

Following the hour of the Moon, the order starts over again with Saturn. While it seems complicated at first, once you do it a bunch, you'll find that it is relatively easy. At this point, I can almost do it in my head. There are also software programs that you can download to do the calculation for you and even some websites that will tell you the hours.

Looking at ChronosXP[7], my planetary hours program, I can see that at 7:00 this morning we are in the hour of Mercury. This lets you fill in the first column of the grid, like so:

|  | Saturn | Jupiter | Mars | Sun | Venus | Mercury | Moon |
|---|---|---|---|---|---|---|---|
| Degree of Sun 19 Capricorn |  |  |  |  |  |  |  |
| Degree of Moon 9 Gemini |  |  |  |  |  |  |  |

---

7  http://chronosxp.sourceforge.net/en/

|  | Saturn | Jupiter | Mars | Sun | Venus | Mercury | Moon |
|---|---|---|---|---|---|---|---|
| Degree of Ascendant 5 Capricorn | | | | | | | |
| Degree of Lot of Fortune 15 Leo | | | | | | | |
| Degree of Prenatal Lunation 7 Capricorn | | | | | | | |
| Ruler of the Day Sun | | | | | | | |
| Ruler of the Hour Mercury | | | | | | | |
| Houses | | | | | | | |
| Superiors | | | | | | | |

*Table 4. Chart Victor Calculation Grid with Degrees*

Now we can begin assigning points to the seven ancient planets. To get the Chart Victor, we go through this process several times, ascribing points to each planet based on the values that we just determined. First off, we assign 7 points to the Ruler of the Day and 6 points to the Ruler of the Hour. Then, for each of the listed positions, we assign 5 points to the ruling planet, and 4 to the exalted planet for that sign.

These dignities can be determined by referencing **Table 2**. This is how you determine the condition of the Chart Victor in the context of your operation. For example, if you are doing an Aries working, you would not want your Chart Victor to be Venus or Saturn because those two planets are debilitated by detriment and fall, respectively, in Aries.

So as an example, for the first line, Degree of Sun, you allocate 5 points to Saturn, the sign ruler, and 4 points to Mars, the exalted planet. You repeat for the other sets of degrees, yielding this:

|  | Saturn | Jupiter | Mars | Sun | Venus | Mercury | Moon |
|---|---|---|---|---|---|---|---|
| Degree of Sun 19 Capricorn | 5 | | 4 | | | | |
| Degree of Moon 9 Gemini | | | | | | 5 | |

|  | Saturn | Jupiter | Mars | Sun | Venus | Mercury | Moon |
|---|---|---|---|---|---|---|---|
| Degree of Ascendant 5 Capricorn | 5 |  | 4 |  |  |  |  |
| Degree of Lot of Fortune 15 Leo |  |  |  | 5 |  |  |  |
| Degree of Prenatal Lunation 7 Capricorn | 5 |  | 4 |  |  |  |  |
| Ruler of the Day Sun |  |  |  | 7 |  |  |  |
| Ruler of the Hour Mercury |  |  |  |  |  | 6 |  |
| Houses |  |  |  |  |  |  |  |
| Superiors |  |  |  |  |  |  |  |

*Table 5. Chart Victor Calculation Grid with Dignities*

Next, you look at the Triplicity Lords, which are derived from the sign's element and whether the Sun is above (day) or below (night) the horizon in the chart. Since our example is before sunrise, the chart is considered nocturnal. For each of the sets of degrees, you allocate three points to the planet that is the appropriate Triplicity Lord. This is derived from the following table:

| Triplicity | Primary/Day | Secondary/Night |
|---|---|---|
| Fire | Sun | Jupiter |
| Air | Saturn | Mercury |
| Water | Venus | Mars |
| Earth | Venus | Moon |

*Table 6. Triplicity Lords*

This lets us fill in points for the Triplicity Lords, yielding the grid shown below. Remember that more than one number can be placed in a given square, and when the final calculation is made, those numbers are added together. For example, Capricorn in the first line is an Earth sign, and this is a nocturnal chart, so for that line the 3 points are given to the Moon.

|  | Saturn | Jupiter | Mars | Sun | Venus | Mercury | Moon |
|---|---|---|---|---|---|---|---|
| Degree of Sun 19 Capricorn | 5 |  | 4 |  |  |  | 3 |
| Degree of Moon 9 Gemini |  |  |  |  |  | 5, 3 |  |
| Degree of Ascendant 5 Capricorn | 5 |  | 4 |  |  |  | 3 |
| Degree of Lot of Fortune 15 Leo |  | 3 |  | 5 |  |  |  |
| Degree of Prenatal Lunation 7 Capricorn | 5 |  | 4 |  |  | 3 |  |
| Ruler of the Day Sun |  |  |  | 7 |  |  |  |
| Ruler of the Hour Mercury |  |  |  |  |  | 6 |  |
| Houses |  |  |  |  |  |  |  |
| Superiors |  |  |  |  |  |  |  |

*Table 7. Chart Victor Calculation Grid with Triplicities*

Next are the Egyptian Bounds, which are derived based on the degree of each sign. For each line, 2 points are awarded to the Bound Lord, according to the following table.

| Aries | 0 - Jupiter | 6 - Venus | 13 - Mercury | 21 - Mars | 25 - Saturn |
|---|---|---|---|---|---|
| Taurus | 0 - Venus | 8 - Mercury | 14 - Jupiter | 22 - Saturn | 27 - Mars |
| Gemini | 0 - Mercury | 6 - Jupiter | 12 - Venus | 17 - Mars | 24 - Saturn |
| Cancer | 0 - Mars | 7 - Venus | 13 - Mercury | 19 - Jupiter | 26 - Saturn |
| Leo | 0 - Jupiter | 6 - Venus | 11 - Saturn | 18- Mercury | 24 - Mars |
| Virgo | 0 - Mercury | 7 - Venus | 17 - Jupiter | 21- Mars | 28 - Saturn |
| Libra | 0 - Saturn | 6 - Mercury | 14 - Jupiter | 21 - Venus | 28 - Mars |
| Scorpio | 0 - Mars | 7 - Venus | 11 - Mercury | 19 - Jupiter | 24 - Saturn |
| Sagittarius | 0 - Jupiter | 12 - Venus | 17 - Mercury | 21 - Saturn | 26 - Mars |
| Capricorn | 0 - Mercury | 7 - Jupiter | 14 - Venus | 22 - Saturn | 26 - Mars |

| Aquarius | 0 - Mercury | 7 - Venus | 13 - Jupiter | 20 - Mars | 25 - Saturn |
| Pisces | 0 - Venus | 12 - Jupiter | 16 - Mercury | 19 - Mars | 28 - Saturn |

*Table 8. Egyptian Bounds*

For example, for our first line, the Degree of Sun is 19 Capricorn. Looking across the Capricorn line, we see that 19 falls between 14 and 22, making Venus the Bound Lord. Filling in 2 points each for the Bound Lords yields the following:

| | Saturn | Jupiter | Mars | Sun | Venus | Mercury | Moon |
|---|---|---|---|---|---|---|---|
| Degree of Sun 19 Capricorn | 5 | | 4 | | 2 | | 3 |
| Degree of Moon 9 Gemini | | 2 | | | | 5, 3 | |
| Degree of Ascendant 5 Capricorn | 5 | | 4 | | | 2 | 3 |
| Degree of Lot of Fortune 15 Leo | 2 | 3 | | 5 | | | |
| Degree of Prenatal Lunation 7 Capricorn | 5 | 2 | 4 | | | 3 | |
| Ruler of the Day Sun | | | | 7 | | | |
| Ruler of the Hour Mercury | | | | | | 6 | |
| Houses | | | | | | | |
| Superiors | | | | | | | |

*Table 9. Chart Victor Calculation Grid with Egyptian Bounds*

Next are the Decan Lords, derived again from the degree of the sign. 0-9 is First Decan, 10-19 is Second Decan, and 20-29 is Third Decan. The Decan Lords each get 1 point, and are derived from the following table:

| Sign | First Decan | Second Decan | Third Decan |
|---|---|---|---|
| Aries | Mars | Sun | Venus |
| Taurus | Mercury | Moon | Saturn |

| Sign | First Decan | Second Decan | Third Decan |
|---|---|---|---|
| Gemini | Jupiter | Mars | Sun |
| Cancer | Venus | Mercury | Moon |
| Leo | Saturn | Jupiter | Mars |
| Virgo | Sun | Venus | Mercury |
| Libra | Moon | Saturn | Jupiter |
| Scorpio | Mars | Sun | Venus |
| Sagittarius | Mercury | Moon | Saturn |
| Capricorn | Jupiter | Mars | Sun |
| Aquarius | Venus | Mercury | Moon |
| Pisces | Saturn | Jupiter | Mars |

*Table 10. Decan Lords*

For example, for the first line, 19 Capricorn is Second Decan, so Mars is the Decan Lord. Filling the rest in yields the following:

| | Saturn | Jupiter | Mars | Sun | Venus | Mercury | Moon |
|---|---|---|---|---|---|---|---|
| Degree of Sun 19 Capricorn | 5 | | 4, 1 | | 2 | | 3 |
| Degree of Moon 9 Gemini | | 2, 1 | | | | 5, 3 | |
| Degree of Ascendant 5 Capricorn | 5 | 1 | 4 | | | 2 | 3 |
| Degree of Lot of Fortune 15 Leo | 2 | 3, 1 | | 5 | | | |
| Degree of Prenatal Lunation 7 Capricorn | 5 | 2, 1 | 4 | | | 3 | |
| Ruler of the Day Sun | | | | 7 | | | |
| Ruler of the Hour Mercury | | | | | | 6 | |
| Houses | | | | | | | |
| Superiors | | | | | | | |

*Table 11. Chart Victor Calculation Grid with Decans*

Next, we need to allocate points to the planets based on house position. This requires a bit of explanation. In Medieval astrology, whole sign equal houses are used. That is, with the Ascendant in Capricorn, all of Capricorn counts as First House, all of Aquarius counts as Second House, all of Pisces counts as Third House, and so forth. At the time this system was developed, house systems such as Placidus were not used. Rather, the sign boundaries also counted as house boundaries.

Points are allocated to each planet according to its house in the chart as follows:

| 1st | 2nd | 3rd | 4th | 5th | 6th | 7th | 8th | 9th | 10th | 11th | 12th |
|---|---|---|---|---|---|---|---|---|---|---|---|
| 12 | 6 | 3 | 9 | 7 | 1 | 10 | 4 | 5 | 11 | 8 | 2 |

*Table 12. Houses*

This yields the following when applied to the grid:

|  | Saturn | Jupiter | Mars | Sun | Venus | Mercury | Moon |
|---|---|---|---|---|---|---|---|
| Degree of Sun<br>19 Capricorn | 5 |  | 4, 1 |  | 2 |  | 3 |
| Degree of Moon<br>9 Gemini |  | 2, 1 |  |  |  | 5, 3 |  |
| Degree of Ascendant<br>5 Capricorn | 5 | 1 | 4 |  |  | 2 | 3 |
| Degree of Lot of Fortune<br>15 Leo | 2 | 3, 1 |  | 5 |  |  |  |
| Degree of Prenatal Lunation<br>7 Capricorn | 5 | 2, 1 | 4 |  |  | 3 |  |
| Ruler of the Day<br>Sun |  |  |  | 7 |  |  |  |
| Ruler of the Hour<br>Mercury |  |  |  |  |  | 6 |  |
| Houses | 2 | 11 | 3 | 12 | 3 | 2 | 1 |
| Superiors |  |  |  |  |  |  |  |

*Table 13. Chart Victor Calculation Grid with Houses*

The last step is to check the positions of Saturn, Jupiter, and Mars in the chart. If one of those planets rises between 15 and 60 degrees ahead of the Sun, that planet is given 3 points. Looking at the chart, Saturn rises about 30 degrees ahead of the Sun, so it gets 3 points. If one of those planets rises between 60 and 90 degrees ahead of the Sun, that planet is given 2 points. Looking at the chart, Jupiter rises a little less than 90 degrees ahead of the Sun, so it gets 2 points. If one of those planets rises between 90 degrees ahead of the Sun and the first retrograde station, it is given 1 point. In this chart Mars rises after the Sun, so it does not receive any points.

Filling in the Superiors line with these values and adding all the columns up yields the following:

|  | Saturn | Jupiter | Mars | Sun | Venus | Mercury | Moon |
| --- | --- | --- | --- | --- | --- | --- | --- |
| Degree of Sun<br>19 Capricorn | 5 |  | 4, 1 |  | 2 |  | 3 |
| Degree of Moon<br>9 Gemini |  | 2, 1 |  |  |  | 5, 3 |  |
| Degree of Ascendant<br>5 Capricorn | 5 | 1 | 4 |  |  | 2 | 3 |
| Degree of Lot of Fortune<br>15 Leo | 2 | 3, 1 |  | 5 |  |  |  |
| Degree of Prenatal Lunation<br>7 Capricorn | 5 | 2, 1 | 4 |  |  | 3 |  |
| Ruler of the Day<br>Sun |  |  |  | 7 |  |  |  |
| Ruler of the Hour<br>Mercury |  |  |  |  |  | 6 |  |
| Houses | 2 | 11 | 3 | 12 | 3 | 2 | 1 |
| Superiors | 3 | 2 |  |  |  |  |  |
| Totals | 22 | 24 | 16 | 24 | 5 | 21 | 7 |

*Table 14. Chart Victor Calculation Grid with Houses*

Therefore, the Chart Victors are Jupiter and the Sun. This is unusual for two planets to come out the same. But if that is the case, either may be treated as the Victor. Not all commercial astrology programs implement the Superiors rule, so if you are using one of those programs to calculate an almuten, those that do not come up with the Sun.

The best astrological operations you could do with a Jupiter Chart Victor would be for Sagittarius, Pisces, and Cancer. The worst would be Gemini, Virgo, and Capricorn. With a Sun Chart Victor, the best operations would be Leo and Aries, and the worst would be Aquarius and Libra. Having two possible Victors gives you some flexibility, so with this chart, the signs come out as shown here.

**Perform these: Aries, Cancer, Leo, Sagittarius, Pisces.**
**Find a better time, if possible: Taurus, Scorpio.**
**Don't perform these: Gemini, Virgo, Libra, Capricorn, Aquarius.**

These methods do add complexity to your ritual timing, particularly if you are also working with methods such as the zodiacal days and hours described in Chapter 10. However, if you can employ them successfully, they provide a means by which you can adjust your magical operations to flow in accordance with the basic spiritual principles with which the stars and other heavenly bodies align. It also should be noted that sometimes everything simply cannot be lined up within a reasonable time frame, so as a magician you must do the best you can with what you have to work with.

# 3
# The Thirty Aires

After receiving the layout of the Great Table, covered in the second book in this series, the Angels presented Dee and Kelley with a diagram showing its four quadrants surrounded by thirty consecutive circles that they called the Aires. Modern magicians often refer to the Aires as the Aethyrs, and in the context of the Enochian system, the two terms are synonymous. Each of the Aires has a three-letter name and is associated with certain parts of the Earth named mostly according to Claudius Ptolemy's geography.

The Thirtieth Aire, TEX, is associated with four Parts of the Earth while the other twenty-nine are associated with three each, for a total of ninety-one Parts. These are named in both English and Angelic, and each is associated with one of the twelve zodiacal governors, called "Angelic Kings" in the Golden Dawn system. Dee's diagram of the Aires shows the Great Table divided into four quadrants at the center, with the Aires themselves rendered as a series of concentric circles surrounding it and expanding outward. The Thirtieth Aire is the inmost, and the First Aire, LIL, is the outermost.

| Number | Aire |
| --- | --- |
| 1 | LIL |
| 2 | ARN |
| 3 | ZOM |
| 4 | PAZ |
| 5 | LIT |
| 6 | MAZ |
| 7 | DEO |
| 8 | ZID |

| Number | Aire |
|---|---|
| 9 | ZIP |
| 10 | ZAX |
| 11 | ICH |
| 12 | LOE |
| 13 | ZIM |
| 14 | VTA |
| 15 | OXO |
| 16 | LEA |
| 17 | TAN |
| 18 | ZEN |
| 19 | POP |
| 20 | CHR |
| 21 | ASP |
| 22 | LIN |
| 23 | TOR |
| 24 | NIA |
| 25 | VTI |
| 26 | DES |
| 27 | ZAA |
| 28 | BAG |
| 29 | RII |
| 30 | TEX |

*Table 15. The Thirty Aires*

The Aires fit neatly into the Renaissance conception of the cosmos, which viewed the Heavens as a series of spheres corresponding to the planets and fixed stars, and the way the angels described them as governing the fate of rulers and nations within the various parts corresponds well with the Renaissance model of astrological influences. The Aires may also be conceptualized as representing the expansion of the individual magician's consciousness outward, a neo-Enochian method pioneered by Aleister Crowley commonly called "Scrying the Aethyrs."

John Dee's original title for the section of the diaries describing the Thirty Aires, *Liber Scientiae Auxilii et Victoriae Terrestris*, translates as "The Book of Knowledge, Aid, and Earthly Victory." When evaluating the function of the Aires in the original system, it is important to note that nothing in the diaries implies that it was intended to be used for operations such as the modern practice of "Scrying the Aethyrs." While Crowley's *The Vision and the Voice* is an impressive work, the operations it details represented a completely new way of working with the system. Crowley likely got the idea from his Golden Dawn training, even though most of the evidence regarding Golden Dawn Enochian operations seems to indicate that they focused their attention on the Great Table rather than the Aires.

What Dee hoped to obtain from the Thirty Aires was not a system of devotional or mystical illumination, but rather a highly practical system of magick that he hoped to use to benefit the fledgling British Empire of the Elizabethan age. The ninety-one Parts of the Earth correspond to the various countries and regions of Dee's time, allowing magicians to target magical operations to particular geographic areas. Most of these represent parts of Europe and the Middle East. A few of the parts seem to correspond to areas in the Americas, but these were not well known, and to some extent, the more familiar Dee and Kelley were with particular regions, the more Parts of the Earth can be found there.

One of the biggest misconceptions that I run into when explaining how the Aires work in the original system is that the Golden Dawn decided that the angelic names of the Parts of the Earth were the "governors" of those parts—that is, they represented the names of particular spirits. While there is some ambiguity in the diaries on this point, the more I have studied it, the more I have become convinced that it is incorrect. In the final table that Dee gives showing the Aires and parts, he does not describe the so-called "governor" name as an entity, but rather as the name of that part in the angelic language. He has another column that shows what he calls the Governors, twelve angels that are associated with the signs of the zodiac. It is through these twelve angels that the zodiacal portions of the original Enochian system may be accessed. Given the nature of Renaissance astrology, it is not at all surprising that a system designed to influence the decisions of rulers and the destinies of nations would be zodiacal.

This perspective is important to keep in mind when working with the angels of the Thirty Aires and the Parts of the Earth. Rather than corresponding to microcosmic traits such as personality types, astrological qualities correspond to large-scale macrocosmic forces that can affect societies and governments.

Likewise, when zodiacal entities are called upon to cause change within the magician's own life, the forces brought to bear are of a mostly external and macrocosmic in nature and can often take longer to manifest than elemental or planetary operations. Nonetheless, the changes that they can set in motion over longer periods of time are that much more profound. The stars may be vast and powerful, but they are also patient. Therefore, to obtain the best results magical operations involving the zodiacal entities should be given a longer time frame in which to operate than those involving planetary or elemental entities.

One of the challenges faced by Dee purists looking over the diaries was how to attribute the twelve zodiacal governors. As the governors are attributed by Dee to the Tribes of Israel, the challenge becomes how to arrange the tribes and associate them with the signs. Most modern Enochian magicians use the following set of attributions, which were assembled by S. Liddell MacGregor Mathers and were taught in the original Golden Dawn order.

| "Angelic King" | Tribe | Zodiacal Sign |
| --- | --- | --- |
| Olpaged | Gad | Aries |
| Ziracah | Ephraim | Taurus |
| Hononol | Manasseh | Gemini |
| Zarnaah | Issachar | Cancer |
| Gebabal | Judah | Leo |
| Zurchol | Naphthali | Virgo |
| Alpudus | Asshur | Libra |
| Cadaamp | Dan | Scorpio |
| Zarzilg | Benjamin | Sagittarius |
| Lavavoh | Zebulun | Capricorn |
| Zinggen | Reuben | Aquarius |
| Arfaolg | Simeon | Pisces |

Table 16. The "Kings," Signs, and Tribes of Israel, Mathers Arrangement

The use of these correspondences is not necessarily bad, as there are some ways in which the Mathers arrangement is more logical than some of the other lists that came before it[8]. His system appears to be a straightforward

---

8  David Godwin, *Astrological Attributions of the Twelve Tribes of Israel* (Retrieved 9/29/2015 from http://www.llewellyn.com/journal/article/472).

attempt to clean up some inconsistencies and attribute the tribes to the signs based on shared qualities. However, his arrangement would not have been the set of associations that was familiar to Dee and Kelley. They would have used the correspondences from Agrippa's *Three Books of Occult Philosophy*, which are as follows:

| Tribe | Zodiacal Sign |
|---|---|
| Dan | Aries |
| Ruben | Taurus |
| Judah | Gemini |
| Manasseh | Cancer |
| Asher | Leo |
| Simeon | Virgo |
| Issachar | Libra |
| Benjamin | Scorpio |
| Naphthalin | Sagittarius |
| Gad | Capricorn |
| Zabulon | Aquarius |
| Ephraim | Pisces |

*Table 17. The Tribes of Israel and the Signs, Agrippa Arrangement*

The origin of Agrippa's arrangement is unclear, but as Agrippa was one Dee's main sources, it stands to reason that this would be his understanding of the relationship between the tribes and signs. Furthermore, many of the Parts of the Earth are likewise named in Agrippa's *Three Books of Occult Philosophy*, a point recorded by Dee in the diaries, which argues for his use and acceptance of the Agrippa arrangement. Finally, these same attributions support the arrangement of the Governors and Signs that has attracted the most support from modern magicians seeking to divine Dee's intent from the diaries.

Dee includes a diagram in *Liber Scientiae* described as "Ordo Dispersi Israelis" which allocates the twelve zodiacal governors to the tribes. Dee numbers each of the governors from one to twelve, which likely would have implied the order of the signs from Aries to Pisces to an astrologer. Furthermore, by checking the number system against the tribe attributions found in Agrippa, they match. So 1 = Dan = Aries, 2 = Ruben = Taurus, 3 = Judah = Gemini, and so forth. To my knowledge, this relationship was first noted in the late 1990's[9], and since then has been adopted by most of the "Dee Purist" Enochian magicians that I know. I find it quite convincing that this represents Dee's intent, as the number system matching Agrippa exactly is very unlikely to be coincidental.

One oddity that I found looking through the various books and sources in which this diagram has already been published is that some add the Twelve Names of God from the Great Table and associate them with the governors. This is not an accurate rendering of the original diagram from Sloane 3191, and there is no evidence in the text of the diaries that Dee ever intended an association of this sort to be made. Rather, it seems as if at some point a modern magician decided that there were twelve of each, so clearly, they needed to be related and added to the diagram. Unfortunately, placing them thus suggests that their inclusion originated with Dee when it is, in fact, a modern invention.

The original *Ordo Dispersi* diagram from Sloane 3191 is reproduced here. It may also be found on page 103 of Geoffrey James' *Enochian Evocation*, though the text is rendered very small.

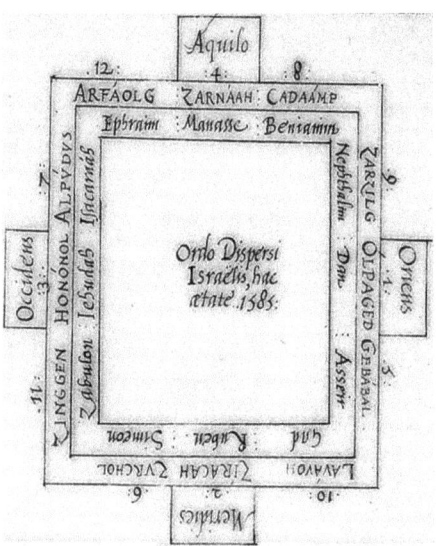

Figure 3. *"Ordo Dispersi" Diagram from Sloane MS 3191*

---

9 Both David Griffin and Aaron Leitch published this arrangement, and despite accusations of plagiarism thrown back and forth it is not clear that either copied from the other. The pattern is pretty obvious once you see it.

Interpreting this diagram along with the Agrippa associations for the tribes and signs yields the following set of attributions:

| Governor | Tribe | Zodiacal Sign |
|---|---|---|
| Olpaged | Dan | Aries |
| Ziracah | Ruben | Taurus |
| Hononol | Judah | Gemini |
| Zarnaah | Manasseh | Cancer |
| Gebabal | Asher | Leo |
| Zurchol | Simeon | Virgo |
| Alpudus | Issachar | Libra |
| Cadaamp | Benjamin | Scorpio |
| Zarzilg | Naphthalin | Sagittarius |
| Lavavot | Gad | Capricorn |
| Zinggen | Zabulon | Aquarius |
| Arfaolg | Ephraim | Pisces |

Table 18. *The Governors, Tribes of Israel, and Signs*

Likely due to attempts to syncretize the zodiacal governors with Twelve Names of God, other modern practitioners have put forth the idea that the order of the governors in this diagram reflects the elemental directional attributions of the Great Table quadrants. But like syncretizing the Twelve Names with the governors, this is also not supported in the diaries and seems to have been arrived upon mostly because the Great Table and "Ordo Dispersi" diagrams both happen to be square and have three associated names per "side." Personally, I reject any such associations in favor of the attributions found in *Mastering the Great Table*, which are instead derived from Kelley's "Golden Talisman" and "Round House" visions.

*Liber Scientia* includes the names and sigils for the various Parts of the Earth, along with their zodiacal governors and other particulars. In 1994, David Allen Hulse published what seemed at first like a brilliant idea to determine the proper lettering for the Great Table. Up until that time, the version of the Great Table that most people knew was from the Golden Dawn tradition and included oddities like multiple letters per square in some cases. This was because there were various versions of the Great Table in use, and the Golden Dawn tablets included every possible letter for each square.

Hulse decided that best way to resolve this would be to take the names of the Parts of the Earth from *Liber Scientia* and generate a version of the tables based on the names. The various sigils fit together like puzzle pieces onto the grid, and therefore they show where each letter goes. *Liber Scientia* was written up by Dee in 1585, so the idea was that whatever went into the text reflected Dee's views of the correct arrangement of letters. The Great Table that Hulse arrived at was published in the Enochian section of *The Key of it All, Book Two*,[10] and it seems reasonable to suggest that the version he arrived at was the most correct rendering as of 1585.

The problem this presents for me is that I use the *Tabula Recensa*, which was reformed in 1587. Dee never recompiled *Liber Scientia* based on this new arrangement of the Great Table, and as far as I know, until now no author has gone through the sigils and adjusted the names appropriately for the 1587 version. This is what I did to generate the names found here for the Parts of the Earth. Most of them are the same, but some differ by multiple letters. In the following chapter, I have included both the *Liber Scientia* and *Tabula Recensa* versions, but the talisman designs that you will find in Chapter 11 use the *Tabula Recensa* names, as that is what I use in my own magical practice. If you wish to use the *Liber Scientia* names instead, I leave it to you to work out the designs. For the ones that are not the same, the only differences will be in the outer ring where the part names corresponding to the Aire are written.

---

10 David Allen Hulse. *The Key of It All, Book Two: The Western Mysteries* (St. Paul, MN: Llewellyn, 1994), 209-212.

# 4
# The Parts of the Earth

THE LOCATIONS OF THE PARTS OF the Earth are mostly derived from Ptolemy's *The Geography*,[11] and as such many of the names are unfamiliar to modern readers. About two-thirds of them can be found in Agrippa's *Three Books of Occult Philosophy*, but the rest seem to refer to locations with which Ptolemy was unfamiliar. The most complete list of the Parts and their locations was assembled by Robin E. Cousins and was first published as part of Robert Turner's *Elizabethan Magic*. More recently, it was included as an appendix in Lon Milo DuQuette's *Enochian Vision Magick*.[12]

While Cousins' list is generally accurate, there are a few discrepancies and omissions. As just one example, the list notes that the Part called Idunia is described in the diaries as "the land beyond Greenland" without explicitly associating it with much of the United States and Canada. Elsewhere in *Enochian Vision Magick*, DuQuette makes a comment about the possible association of the United States with a different Part of the Earth, Marmerica, since it sounds like "America," but this is simply a coincidence. Marmerica was part of North Africa long before the Americas acquired the name of explorer Amerigo Vespucci.

As I mentioned in the previous chapter, this list contains the angelic names of the Parts of the Earth both as derived from the 1587 *Tabula Recensa*, and as found in the 1585 text of *Liber Scientiae Auxilii et Victoriae Terrestris*. I use the *Tabula Recensa* version in my own work, but if you

---

11  Claudius Ptolemy, *The Geography* (New York, NY: Dover Publications, 1991).
12  Lon Milo DuQuette, *Enochian Vision Magick* (San Francisco, CA: Red Wheel/Weiser, 2008), pp 212-223.

prefer to work with the original version of the Great Table, the *Liber Scientia* names are more appropriate.

Most of the maps in this chapter have been adapted from *The Geography* by Claudius Ptolemy, with Ptolemy's locations drawn onto more accurate modern maps. Ptolemy's Roman maps were the actual maps that Dee and Kelley consulted in their conversations with the angels regarding the Parts of the Earth. The maps of the New World are entirely my own, as they were not included in Ptolemy's text.

## Part 1 – LIL (1)

**Mundane Name:** Aegyptus (Egypt)
**Angelic Name:** Occodon
**Governor:** Zarzilg
**Sign:** Sagittarius
**Direction:** East-Northeast
**Sigil:**

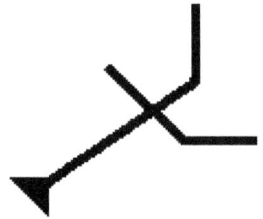

**Location:** In ancient times the land of Egypt was mostly defined by the Nile river valley and delta. This part includes all of Lower Egypt and the current capital of the modern nation, Cairo. It follows the Nile north to Thebaidi (Thebes), Part 10, which represents the area surrounding the modern city of Luxor and the region of Upper Egypt that follows the Nile valley southward from there. Cousins claims that Marmerica, Part 65, extends to the Nile River. However, historically the land of Egypt spanned both sides of the river, so it is more accurate to state that the western edge of the Nile Valley forms the border.

## Part 2 – LIL (1)

**Mundane Name:** Syria
**Angelic Name:** Pascomb
**Governor:** Zinggen
**Sign:** Aquarius
**Direction:** West-Southwest
**Sigil:**

**Location:** Syria south and west of the Euphrates river valley, including the modern capital, Damascus.

## Part 3 – LIL (1)

**Mundane Name:** Mesopotamia
**Angelic Name:** Valgars
**Governor:** Alpudus
**Sign:** Libra
**Direction:** West-Northwest
**Sigil:**

**Location:** Region spanning the Euphrates and Tigris River system in northern and central Iraq, and northeastern Syria.

## Part 4 – ARN (2)

**Mundane Name:** Cappadocia
**Angelic Name (*Tabula Recensa*):** Dongnis
**Angelic Name (*Liber Scientia*):** Doagnis
**Governor:** Zarnaah
**Sign:** Cancer
**Direction:** North
**Sigil:**

**Location:** Central Turkey, between the Black Sea to the north and Cilicia (14) to the south. Modern-day Turkey is something of a mess from the standpoint of the Parts of the Earth. When *The Geography* was written, the region was the seat of the Eastern Roman Empire, and as such Ptolemy documented its parts in great detail. For modern-day political operations, the only part you generally need to work with is Part 89, Phrygia, where the capital city of Ankara is located.

## Part 5 – ARN (2)

**Mundane Name:** Tuscia
**Angelic Name:** Pacasna
**Governor:** Ziracah
**Sign:** Taurus
**Direction:** South
**Sigil:**

**Location:** Tuscany, in central Italy.

## Part 6 – ARN (2)

**Mundane Name:** Parva Asia
**Angelic Name (*Tabula Recensa*):** Dialoia
**Angelic Name (*Liber Scientia*):** Dialiua
**Governor:** Ziracah
**Sign:** Taurus
**Direction:** South
**Sigil:**

**Location:** Eastern or Asiatic Turkey.

## Part 7 – ZOM (3)

**Mundane Name:** Hyrcania
**Angelic Name:** Samapha
**Governor:** Zarzilg
**Sign:** Sagittarius
**Direction:** East-Northeast
**Sigil:**

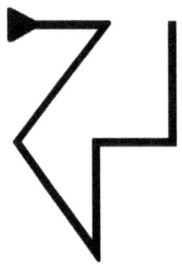

**Location:** Region in modern-day Iran, to the southeast of the Caspian Sea.

## Part 8 – ZOM (3)

**Mundane Name:** Thracia (Thrace)
**Angelic Name (*Tabula Recensa*):** Virooli
**Angelic Name (*Liber Scientia*):** Virochi
**Governor:** Alpudus
**Sign:** Libra
**Direction:** West-Northwest
**Sigil:**

**Location:** Eastern Greece, the European portion of Turkey, and southern Bulgaria.

## Part 9 – ZOM (3)

**Mundane Name:** Gosmam
**Angelic Name:** Andispi
**Governor:** Lavavot
**Sign:** Capricorn

**Direction:** South-Southeast
**Sigil:**

**Location:** Alaska excluding the Lower Peninsula, northern Canada including the Northwest and Yukon territories, and the mainland portion of Nunavut. An earlier version of the North American map published on my blog showed all of Nunavut included in this part, but subsequent research indicates that the "Pole Arctic," Part 48, more likely refers to the island portions of the territory.

## Part 10 – PAZ (4)

**Mundane Name:** Thebaidi
**Angelic Name (*Tabula Recensa*):** Thotant
**Angelic Name (*Liber Scientia*):** Thotanf
**Governor:** Lavavot
**Sign:** Capricorn
**Sigil:**

**Direction:** South-Southeast
**Location:** Upper Egypt, including the city of Thebes.

## Part 11 – PAZ (4)

**Mundane Name:** Parsadal
**Angelic Name (*Tabula Recensa*):** Axxiarg
**Angelic Name (*Liber Scientia*):** Axziarg
**Sigil:**

**Governor:** Lavavot
**Sign:** Capricorn
**Direction:** South-Southeast
**Location:** Ancient Persian city of Pasargadae, in the Fars province of modern Iran. The city is no longer inhabited and is currently an archaeological site containing the tomb of Cyrus the Great.

## Part 12 – PAZ (4)

**Mundane Name:** India
**Angelic Name:** Pothnir
**Governor:** Arfaolg
**Sign:** Pisces
**Direction:** North-Northwest
**Sigil:**

**Location:** Includes modern-day Pakistan and India west of the Ganges River.

## Part 13 – LIT (5)

**Mundane Name:** Bactriane
**Angelic Name:** Laxdizi
**Governor:** Olpaged
**Sign:** Aries
**Direction:** East
**Sigil:**

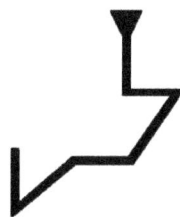

**Location:** Bactriane and Bactriani (Part 87) present a bit of a puzzle. Dee was told that Bactriani alluded to "the people" of Bactriane, which makes this pair of parts stand out from the others that refer to geographical regions. Research into ancient geography shows that Bactria in northern Afghanistan derived its name among the ancient Greeks from its capital city of Bactra. My supposition here is that this part, Bactriane, alludes to the capital city and Bactriana alludes to the region over which it rules.

## Part 14 – LIT (5)

**Mundane Name:** Cilicia
**Angelic Name:** Nocamal
**Governor:** Alpudus
**Sign:** Libra
**Direction:** West-Northwest
**Sigil:**

**Location:** Southeast Turkey along the Mediterranean coast.

## Part 15 – LIT (5)

**Mundane Name:** Oxiana
**Angelic Name:** Tiarpax
**Governor:** Zinggen
**Sign:** Aquarius
**Direction:** West-Southwest
**Sigil:**

**Location:** Area along the Oxus River between northern Afghanistan and Uzbekistan.

## Part 16 – MAZ (6)

**Mundane Name:** Numidia
**Angelic Name:** Saxtomp
**Governor:** Gebabal
**Sign:** Leo
**Direction:** East-Southeast
**Sigil:**

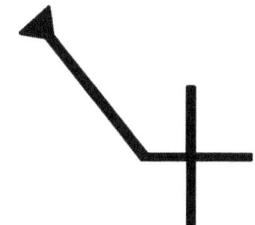

**Location:** Eastern Algerian coastal region in North Africa.

## Part 17 – MAZ (6)

**Mundane Name:** Cyprus
**Angelic Name:** Vauaamp
**Governor:** Arfaolg
**Sign:** Pisces
**Direction:** North-Northwest
**Sigil:**

**Location:** The modern-day island of Cyprus.

## Part 18 – MAZ (6)

**Mundane Name:** Parthia
**Angelic Name:** Zirzird
**Governor:** Gebabal
**Sign:** Leo

**Direction:** East-Southeast
**Sigil:**

**Location:** Northeastern Iran.

## Part 19 – DEO (7)

**Mundane Name:** Getulia
**Angelic Name (*Tabula Recensa*):** Opmacas
**Angelic Name (*Liber Scientia*):** Obmacas
**Governor:** Zarnaah
**Sign:** Cancer
**Direction:** North
**Sigil:**

**Location:** Western Sahara Desert region south of Morocco.

## Part 20 – DEO (7)

**Mundane Name:** Arabia
**Angelic Name (*Tabula Recensa*):** Genadob
**Angelic Name (*Liber Scientia*):** Genadol
**Governor:** Hononol
**Sign:** Gemini
**Direction:** West
**Sigil:**

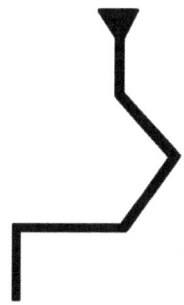

**Location:** Modern-day Saudi Arabia.

## Part 21 – DEO (7)

**Mundane Name:** Phalagon
**Angelic Name:** Aspiaon
**Governor:** Zinggen
**Sign:** Aquarius
**Direction:** West-Southwest
**Sigil:**

**Location:** Modern-day Greenland. An earlier version of the North American map that I published on my blog showed this part corresponding to both Iceland and Greenland. Subsequent research suggests that this part refers to Greenland only, while Iceland corresponds to Part 81.

## Part 22 – ZID (8)

**Mundane Name:** Mantiana
**Angelic Name:** Zamfres
**Governor:** Gebabal
**Sign:** Leo
**Direction:** East-Southeast
**Sigil:**

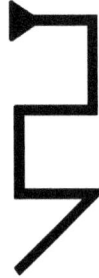

**Location:** Northwestern Iran, roughly corresponding to the portion of Iran that was part of Kurdistan before that region was fractured by colonial borders.

## Part 23 – ZID (8)

**Mundane Name:** Soxia
**Angelic Name:** Todnaon
**Governor:** Olpaged
**Sign:** Aries
**Direction:** East
**Sigil:**

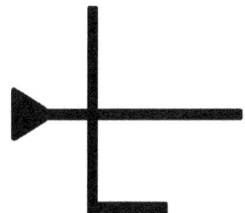

**Location:** North-western China.

## Part 24 – ZID (8)

**Mundane Name:** Gallia
**Angelic Name:** Pristac
**Governor:** Zarzilg
**Sign:** Sagittarius
**Direction:** East-Northeast
**Sigil:**

**Location:** The Roman region of Gaul, which included modern-day France, Switzerland, and a portion of Northern Italy. It extends from the Pyrenees Mountains in the east to the Rhine River in the west, excluding Celtica, Part 56.

## Part 25 – ZIP (9)

**Mundane Name:** Illyria
**Angelic Name:** Oddiorg
**Governor:** Hononol
**Sign:** Gemini
**Direction:** West
**Sigil:**

**Location:** Central and Eastern Austria, Western Hungary, Northern Bulgaria, Romania. It also includes most of the former Yugoslavia except for Macedonia.

## Part 26 – ZIP (9)

**Mundane Name:** Sogdiana
**Angelic Name:** Cralpir
**Governor:** Lavavot
**Sign:** Capricorn
**Direction:** South-Southeast
**Sigil:**

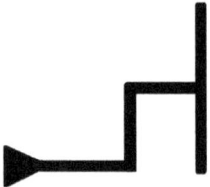

**Location:** Region between the Oxus and Jaxartes Rivers, including Uzbekistan and Tajikstan.

## Part 27 – ZIP (9)

**Mundane Name:** Lydia
**Angelic Name:** Doanzin
**Governor:** Zarzilg
**Sign:** Sagittarius
**Direction:** East-Northeast
**Sigil:**

**Location:** Western Turkey along the Mediterranean Coast.

## Part 28 – ZAX (10)

**Mundane Name:** Caspis
**Angelic Name:** Lexarph
**Governor:** Zinggen
**Sign:** Aquarius
**Direction:** South-Southwest
**Sigil:**

**Location:** Iran to the southwest of the Caspian Sea.

## Part 29 – ZAX (10)

**Mundane Name:** Germania
**Angelic Name:** Comanan
**Governor:** Alpudus
**Sign:** Libra
**Direction:** West-Northwest
**Sigil:**

**Location:** The Roman region of Germania included modern-day Germany, Poland, Czechia, Slovakia, Northern Austria, and Liechtenstein.

## Part 30 – ZAX (10)

**Mundane Name:** Trenam
**Angelic Name:** Tabitom
**Governor:** Zarzilg
**Sign:** Sagittarius
**Direction:** East-Northeast
**Sigil:**

**Location:** Southern coast of West Africa, including Nigeria, Benin, Togo, Ghana, Ivory Coast, Burkina Faso, southern Mali, Liberia, Sierra Leone, Guinea, and Guinea-Bissau. Includes the capital of Mali, Bamako.

## *Part 31 – ICH (11)*

**Mundane Name:** Bithynia
**Angelic Name:** Molpand
**Governor:** Lavavot
**Sign:** Capricorn
**Direction:** South-Southeast
**Sigil:**

**Location:** Region of Northern Turkey on the coast of the Marmara Sea. It includes the Asian portion of Istanbul.

## *Part 32 – ICH (11)*

**Mundane Name:** Graecia
**Angelic Name:** Vsnarda
**Governor:** Zurchol
**Sign:** Virgo
**Direction:** South-Southwest
**Sigil:**

**Location:** The ancient city of Constantinople, which corresponds to the European portion of modern-day Istanbul.

## Part 33 – ICH (11)

**Mundane Name:** Licia
**Angelic Name:** Ponodol
**Governor:** Hononol
**Sign:** Gemini
**Direction:** West
**Sigil:**

**Location:** Region along the southern coast of Turkey.

## Part 34 – LOE (12)

**Mundane Name:** Onigap
**Angelic Name:** Tapamal
**Governor:** Zurchol
**Sign:** Virgo
**Direction:** South-Southwest
**Sigil:**

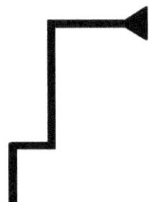

**Location:** Modern-day Mexico, Central America, and South America, excluding Tierra del Fuego and Patagonia. The entire region was claimed by the Iberian Union of the Spanish and Portuguese crowns in the late sixteenth century.

## Part 35 – LOE (12)

**Mundane Name:** India Major
**Angelic Name:** Gedoons
**Governor:** Cadamp
**Sign:** Scorpio
**Direction:** North-Northeast
**Sigil:**

**Location:** India east of the Ganges River, and all of Southeast Asia and Indonesia.

## Part 36 – LOE (12)

**Mundane Name:** Orcheny
**Angelic Name:** Ambriol
**Governor:** Ziracah
**Sign:** Taurus
**Direction:** South
**Sigil:**

**Location:** Region of modern-day Iraq including the lower Tigris and Euphrates rivers.

## Part 37 – ZIM (13)

**Mundane Name:** Achaia
**Angelic Name:** Gecaond
**Governor:** Lavavot
**Sign:** Capricorn
**Direction:** South-Southeast
**Sigil:**

**Location:** Southern Greece, including the modern-day capital, Athens.

## Part 38 – ZIM (13)

**Mundane Name:** Armenia
**Angelic Name:** Laparin
**Governor:** Olpaged
**Sign:** Aries
**Direction:** East
**Sigil:**

**Location:** Modern-day Armenia and Azerbaijan.

## Part 39 – ZIM (13)

**Mundane Name:** Cilicia (Nemrodiania)
**Angelic Name:** Docepax
**Governor:** Alpudus
**Sign:** Libra
**Direction:** West-Northwest
**Sigil:**

**Location:** Northeastern Siberia in the modern-day Russian Federation.

## Part 40 – VTA (14)

**Mundane Name:** Paphlagonia
**Angelic Name (*Tabula Recensa*):** Tedoond
**Angelic Name (*Liber Scientia*):** Tedoand
**Governor:** Gebabal
**Sign:** Leo
**Direction:** East-Southeast
**Sigil:**

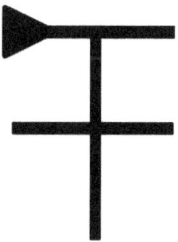

**Location:** Region on the Black Sea coast of Turkey.

## *Part 41 – VTA (14)*

**Mundane Name:** Phasiana
**Angelic Name:** Viuipos
**Governor:** Alpudus
**Sign:** Libra
**Direction:** West-Northwest
**Sigil:**

**Location:** Region of Eastern Turkey that was part of Kurdistan before that region was fractured by colonial borders.

## *Part 42 – VTA (14)*

**Mundane Name:** Chaldei
**Angelic Name (*Tabula Recensa*):** Voanamb
**Angelic Name (*Liber Scientia*):** Ooanamb
**Governor:** Arfaolg
**Sign:** Pisces
**Direction:** North-Northwest
**Sigil:**

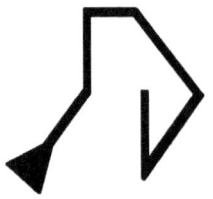

**Location:** Chaldea and Chaldei (Part 72) are the second set of parts in which Dee was told that one alludes to "the people" of another. Using the same logic that I employed with respect to Bactriane and Bactriani, this would imply that Chaldei refers to the Chaldean region while Chaldea alludes to its capital city. This part would allude to southern Iraq and Kuwait, the region in which the Chaldeans settled.

## Part 43 – OXO (15)

**Mundane Name:** Itergi
**Angelic Name (*Tabula Recensa*):** Tahamdo
**Angelic Name (*Liber Scientia*):** Tahando
**Governor:** Zarzilg
**Sign:** Sagittarius
**Direction:** East-Northeast
**Sigil:**

**Location:** Mongolia and Northern China.

## Part 44 – OXO (15)

**Mundane Name:** Macedonia
**Angelic Name (*Tabula Recensa*):** Notiabi
**Angelic Name (*Liber Scientia*):** Nociabi
**Governor:** Lavavot
**Sign:** Capricorn
**Direction:** South-Southeast
**Sigil:**

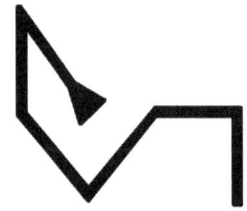

**Location:** Northern Greece, Macedonia, Southern Albania.

## Part 45 – OXO (15)

**Mundane Name:** Garamantica
**Angelic Name (*Tabula Recensa*):** Tastozo
**Angelic Name (*Liber Scientia*):** Tastoxo
**Governor:** Arfaolg
**Sign:** Pisces
**Direction:** North-Northwest
**Sigil:**

**Location:** Garamantes, in the interior of Africa.

## Part 46 – LEA (16)

**Mundane Name:** Sauromatica
**Angelic Name (*Tabula Recensa*):** Cucnrpt
**Angelic Name (*Liber Scientia*):** Cucarpt
**Governor:** Ziracah
**Sign:** Taurus
**Direction:** South
**Sigil:**

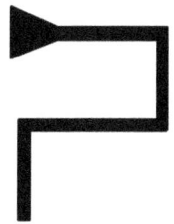

**Location:** European Russia, Estonia, Latvia, Lithuania, Belarus, Ukraine, and Northern Kazakhstan.

## Part 47 – LEA (16)

**Mundane Name:** Aethiopia
**Angelic Name:** Lauacon
**Governor:** Hononol
**Sign:** Gemini
**Direction:** West
**Sigil:**

**Location:** Modern-day Ethiopia and the surrounding region of Africa.

## Part 48 – LEA (16)

**Mundane Name:** Fiacim
**Angelic Name:** Sochial
**Governor:** Arfaolg

**Sign:** Pisces
**Direction:** North-Northwest
**Sigil:**

**Location:** This region consists of the island portions of the Canadian territory of Nunavut. While this was described to Dee and Kelley as the North Pole, they were also told that a great mountain could be found there. While the arctic islands of Nunavut do not correspond to the physical North Pole, they are where the *magnetic* north pole can be found. It was located on Victoria Island in 1590, and since then has moved slightly to the east and north.

The "great mountain" can only be Barbeau Peak on Ellesmere Island, as it is the tallest mountain in all of Eastern North America. My earlier version of the North America map showed these islands as part of Gosmam, Part 9, but subsequent research shows that this part is more likely to be the correct attribution. This also suggests that the description given by the angels was not due to a misunderstanding about the nature of the North Pole as Cousins contends, but rather matches real geography.

## Part 49 – TAN (17)

**Mundane Name:** Colchica
**Angelic Name:** Sigmorf
**Governor:** Ziracah
**Sign:** Taurus
**Direction:** South
**Sigil:**

**Location:** The country of Georgia, on the Black Sea.

## *Part 50 – TAN (17)*

**Mundane Name:** Cireniaca
**Angelic Name:** Aydropt
**Governor:** Olpaged
**Sign:** Aries
**Direction:** East
**Sigil:**

**Location:** Eastern Libya on the Mediterranean coast.

## *Part 51 – TAN (17)*

**Mundane Name:** Nasamonia
**Angelic Name:** Tocarzi
**Governor:** Zarzilg
**Sign:** Taurus
**Direction:** South
**Sigil:**

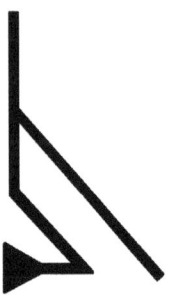

**Location:** North-eastern Libya on the Mediterranean coast.

## *Part 52 – ZEN (18)*

**Mundane Name:** Carthago
**Angelic Name:** Nabaomi
**Governor:** Gebabal
**Sign:** Leo
**Direction:** East-Southeast
**Sigil:**

**Location:** Carthage, located in modern-day Tunisia near Tunis.

## *Part 53 – ZEN (18)*

**Mundane Name:** Coxlant
**Angelic Name:** Zafasai
**Governor:** Alpudus
**Sign:** Libra

**Direction:** West-Northwest
**Sigil:**

**Location:** Modern-day Tibet.

## Part 54 – ZEN (18)

**Mundane Name:** Idumea
**Angelic Name:** Yalpamb
**Governor:** Arfaolg
**Sign:** Pisces
**Direction:** North-Northwest
**Sigil:**

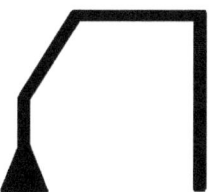

**Location:** Southern region of Israel and Jordan.

## Part 55 – POP (19)

**Mundane Name:** Parstania
**Angelic Name:** Torzoxi
**Governor:** Arfaolg
**Sign:** Pisces

**Direction:** North-Northwest
**Sigil:**

**Location:** Moldavia, between Romania and Russia.

## Part 56 – POP (19)

**Mundane Name:** Celtica
**Angelic Name (*Tabula Recensa*):** Abriond
**Angelic Name (*Liber Scientia*):** Abaiond
**Governor:** Cadaamp
**Sign:** Scorpio
**Direction:** North-Northeast
**Sigil:**

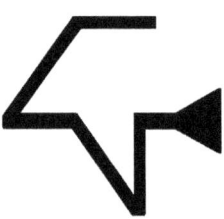

**Location:** The "low countries" - Northeastern France, Belgium, Luxembourg, the Netherlands.

## Part 57 – POP (19)

**Mundane Name:** Vinsan
**Angelic Name:** Omagrap

**Governor:** Zinggen
**Sign:** Aquarius
**Direction:** West-Southwest
**Sigil:**

**Location:** Southeastern Kazakhstan.

## Part 58 – CHR (20)

**Mundane Name:** Tolpam
**Angelic Name:** Zildron
**Governor:** Gebabal
**Sign:** Leo
**Direction:** East-Southeast
**Sigil:**

**Location:** Antarctica and the tip of South America. Cousins includes Australia in this part based on Renaissance maps that show Antarctica extending far northward into the Pacific Ocean, but in my opinion, this is not a good association because Australia extends almost to the equator. While there are enormous parts in the New World like Onigap, Part 34, that spans Mexico and most of South America, the equator is as far from the South Pole as you can get.

## Part 59 – CHR (20)

**Mundane Name:** Carcedonia
**Angelic Name:** Parziba
**Governor:** Hononol
**Sign:** Gemini
**Direction:** West
**Sigil:**

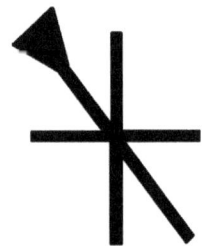

**Location:** Modern-day Tunisia excluding Carthago, Part 52.

## Part 60 – CHR (20)

**Mundane Name:** Italia
**Angelic Name:** Totocan
**Governor:** Alpudus
**Sign:** Libra
**Direction:** West-Northwest
**Sigil:**

**Location:** The Italian Peninsula, excluding the section of North Italy that is part of Gallia (24), along with Tuscia (5) and Apulia (64), and including part of Western Slovenia and Croatia. Includes the modern (and ancient) capital of Italy, Rome.

## Part 61 – ASP (21)

**Mundane Name:** Brytania
**Angelic Name (*Tabula Recensa*):** Chirzpa
**Angelic Name (*Liber Scientia*):** Chirspa
**Governor:** Arfaolg
**Sign:** Pisces
**Direction:** North-Northwest
**Sigil:**

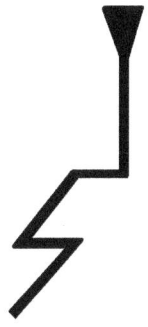

**Location:** The British Isles. Dee and Kelley were told that Brytania could also be used for Denmark, which at the time included Norway via the Kalmar Union. Sweden had withdrawn from the union a little over fifty years prior. This still suggests that Brytania includes not only the British Isles, but Scandinavia as well.

## Part 62 – ASP (21)

**Mundane Name:** Phenices
**Angelic Name:** Toantom
**Governor:** Cadaamp
**Sign:** Scorpio

**Direction:** North-Northeast
**Sigil:**

**Location:** Phoenicia, modern-day Northern Israel and Lebanon.

## Part 63 – ASP (21)

**Mundane Name:** Comaginen
**Angelic Name:** Vixpalg
**Governor:** Zurchol
**Sign:** Virgo
**Direction:** South-Southwest
**Sigil:**

**Location:** Southern Turkey, between the Euphrates River and Syria.

## Part 64 – LIN (22)

**Mundane Name:** Apulia
**Angelic Name (*Tabula Recensa*):** Osidaia
**Angelic Name (*Liber Scientia*):** Ozidaia
**Governor:** Arfaolg
**Sign:** Pisces

**Direction:** North-Northwest
**Sigil:**

**Location:** The Southeastern portion of the Italian peninsula.

## Part 65 – LIN (22)

**Mundane Name:** Marmarica
**Angelic Name (*Tabula Recensa*):** Paoaoan (Laxdizi)
**Angelic Name (*Liber Scientia*):** Paraoan (Laxdizi)
**Governor:** Olpaged
**Sign:** Aries
**Direction:** East
**Sigil:**

**Location:** A portion of the North African coast spanning the border of modern-day Egypt and Libya. According to Cousins, the Nile forms the eastern boundary, but this is likely incorrect. Historically, Egypt included the whole of the Nile valley on both sides of the river. Therefore, it is more correct to describe the eastern boundary of this region as the Nile river valley and delta. This difference is significant for current political operations because Egypt's modern-day capital, Cairo, spans the Nile, but in fact lies entirely within Aegyptus, Part 1, rather than Marmarica.

Sloane 3191 shows Paraoan listed as the Angelic name of this part, which is unusual because this word is not drawn from one of the characters traced onto the Great Table but rather formed from the letters that remain once all of the characters are accounted for. One of these letters does change on the *Tabula Recensa,* so the name becomes Paoaoan. Likewise, one of the sigils remains unallocated if Paoaoan is used here, which spells out the name Laxdizi. This last sigil is the one supplied above.

It is not clear why Dee departed from his scheme for the parts in this one case and looking over the diary entries surrounding the reception of the name sheds little light on his reasoning. This is likely a case where experimentation is required, and to that end I have included two versions of the talisman for LIN in this volume, one with Paoaoan and the other with Laxdizi.

## *Part 66 – LIN (22)*

**Mundane Name:** Concava Syria
**Angelic Name:** Calzirg
**Governor:** Arfaolg
**Sign:** Pisces
**Direction:** North-Northwest
**Sigil:**

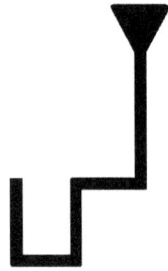

**Location:** Northern Syria.

## Part 67 – TOR (23)

**Mundane Name:** Gebal
**Angelic Name (*Tabula Recensa*):** Ronoomb
**Angelic Name (*Liber Scientia*):** Ronoamb
**Governor:** Zarnaah
**Sign:** Cancer
**Direction:** North
**Sigil:**

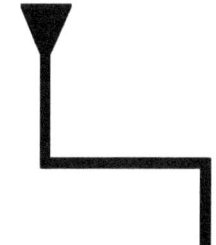

**Location:** Northern Lebanon.

## Part 68 – TOR (23)

**Mundane Name:** Elam
**Angelic Name:** Onizimp
**Governor:** Lavavot
**Sign:** Capricorn
**Direction:** South-Southeast
**Sigil:**

**Location:** Western Iran on the Persian Gulf Coast, bordering Iraq.

## Part 69 – TOR (23)

**Mundane Name:** Idunia
**Angelic Name:** Zaxanin
**Governor:** Zinggen
**Sign:** Aquarius
**Direction:** West-Southwest
**Sigil:**

**Location:** The continental United States, southern and eastern Canada. Includes the modern capitals of both countries, Washington D.C. and Ottawa.

## Part 70 – NIA (24)

**Mundane Name:** Media
**Angelic Name (*Tabula Recensa*):** Orancir
**Angelic Name (*Liber Scientia*):** Orcamir
**Governor:** Zarnaah
**Sign:** Cancer
**Direction:** North
**Sigil:**

**Location:** Northwestern Iran, including the modern capital, Tehran.

## Part 71 – NIA (24)

**Mundane Name:** Arriana
**Angelic Name (*Tabula Recensa*):** Chaslpo
**Angelic Name (*Liber Scientia*):** Chialps
**Governor:** Lavavot
**Sign:** Capricorn
**Direction:** South-Southeast
**Sigil:**

**Location:** Eastern Iran and southern Afghanistan.

## Part 72 – NIA (24)

**Mundane Name:** Chaldea
**Angelic Name:** Soageel
**Governor:** Zinggen
**Sign:** Aquarius
**Direction:** West-Southwest
**Sigil:**

**Location:** As I discussed with respect to the location of Chaldea, this part alludes to the capital city of the Chaldean region and can only be the ancient city of Babylon. Note that Part 80, called Babylon in *Liber Scientia*, alludes to the entire Babylonian region. Today the city of Babylon is an archaeological site located 76 miles from the Iraqi capital of Baghdad. Baghdad is therefore part of the greater region rather than the ancient city itself and lies within Part 80.

## Part 73 – VTI (25)

**Mundane Name:** Serici Populi
**Angelic Name:** Mirzind
**Governor:** Zarnaah
**Sign:** Cancer
**Direction:** North
**Sigil:**

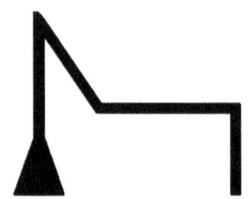

**Location:** China and the Far East.

## Part 74 – VTI (25)

**Mundane Name:** Persia
**Angelic Name:** Obuaors
**Governor:** Ziracah
**Sign:** Taurus
**Direction:** South
**Sigil:**

**Location:** Southwest Iran, the seat of the ancient Persian empire.

## Part 75 – VTI (25)

**Mundane Name:** Gongatha
**Angelic Name:** Ranglam
**Governor:** Arfaolg
**Sign:** Pisces
**Direction:** North-Northwest
**Sigil:**

**Location:** Africa south of the Congo River basin, all the way to Cape Horn. Includes the modern nations of South Africa, Namibia, Botswana, Zimbabwe, Mozambique, Malawi, Zambia, and Angola.

## Part 76 – DES (26)

**Mundane Name:** Gorsim
**Angelic Name:** Pophand

**Governor:** Arfaolg
**Sign:** Pisces
**Direction:** North-Northwest
**Sigil:**

**Location:** Southeast of the Caspian Sea in Turkmenistan.

## Part 77 – DES (26)

**Mundane Name:** Hispania
**Angelic Name:** Nigrana
**Governor:** Cadaamp
**Sign:** Scorpio
**Direction:** North-Northeast
**Sigil:**

**Location:** Modern-day Spain and Portugal, which were united under the Iberian Union in the late sixteenth century.

## Part 78 – DES (26)

**Mundane Name:** Pamphilia
**Angelic Name (*Tabula Recensa*):** Lazhiim

**Angelic Name (*Liber Scientia*):** Bazchim
**Governor:** Arfaolg
**Sign:** Pisces
**Direction:** North-Northwest
**Sigil:**

**Location:** Region along the southern Turkish coast.

## Part 79 – ZAA (27)

**Mundane Name:** Oacidi
**Angelic Name:** Saziami
**Governor:** Ziracah
**Sign:** Taurus
**Direction:** South
**Sigil:**

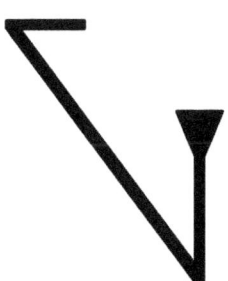

**Location:** Oasis region roughly corresponding to Sudan and South Sudan. The capital cities of both countries are located here.

## *Part 80 – ZAA (27)*

**Mundane Name:** Babylon
**Angelic Name:** Mathula
**Governor:** Zarnaah
**Sign:** Cancer
**Direction:** North
**Sigil:**

**Location:** Southern Iraq, between the Tigris and the Arabian Desert. This is the region referred to as Babylonia today, not the city of Babylon itself, and includes the modern capital of Iraq, Baghdad.

## *Part 81 – ZAA (27)*

**Mundane Name:** Median
**Angelic Name (*Tabula Recensa*):** Crpanib
**Angelic Name (*Liber Scientia*):** Orpanib
**Governor:** Gebabal
**Sign:** Leo
**Direction:** East-Southeast
**Sigil:**

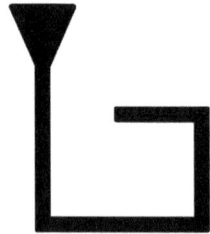

**Location:** As this part was described as "very far northward," it suggests that it lies to the north of the British Isles. I originally considered the Svalbard Archipelago for this part, as it is practically due north of Great Britain. However, as it was only discovered by Europeans in the early 1600s and was uninhabited at that time, it seems a poor choice. Better is Iceland, which lies far to the north and slightly to the west. The earlier version of my North America map combined Greenland and Iceland into a single part, but the people of those regions in Dee's time could not be more different. Iceland was settled by the Norse, but by the sixteenth century the Norse settlements in Greenland had failed. Instead, Greenland at that time was populated by the Thule people, the ancestors of the modern Inuit.

## Part 82 – BAG (28)

**Mundane Name:** Idumian
**Angelic Name (*Tabula Recensa*):** Pabnixp
**Angelic Name (*Liber Scientia*):** Labnixp
**Governor:** Lavavot
**Sign:** Capricorn
**Direction:** South-Southeast
**Sigil:**

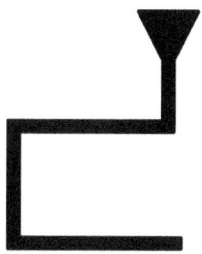

**Location:** Eastern Kazakhstan.

## Part 83 – BAG (28)

**Mundane Name:** Foelix Arabia
**Angelic Name (*Tabula Recensa*):** Pocisni

**Angelic Name (*Liber Scientia*):** Focisni
**Governor:** Zarzilg
**Sign:** Taurus
**Direction:** South
**Sigil:**

**Location:** Red Sea coastal region of the Arabia peninsula.

## Part 84 – BAG (28)

**Mundane Name:** Metagonitidim
**Angelic Name:** Oxlopar
**Governor:** Zurchol
**Sign:** Virgo
**Direction:** South-Southwest
**Sigil:**

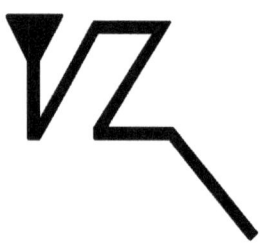

**Location:** Modern-day Tangiers and the surrounding area.

## Part 85 – RII (29)

**Mundane Name:** Assyria
**Angelic Name:** Vastrim

**Governor:** Hononol
**Sign:** Gemini
**Direction:** West
**Sigil:**

**Location:** Modern-day Iraq, between the Tigris River and the current border with Iran.

## Part 86 – RII (29)

**Mundane Name:** Affrica
**Angelic Name (*Tabula Recensa*):** Odraxti
**Angelic Name (*Liber Scientia*):** Odroxti
**Governor:** Zarnaah
**Sign:** Cancer
**Direction:** North
**Sigil:**

**Location:** According to *The Geography*, Affrica or Africa is the name for a small Mediterranean coastal region of North Africa in modern-day Libya. The name only later was attributed to the modern continent of Africa.

## Part 87 – RII (29)

**Mundane Name:** Bactriani
**Angelic Name (*Tabula Recensa*):** Gmtziam
**Angelic Name (*Liber Scientia*):** Gomziam
**Governor:** Arfaolg
**Sign:** Pisces
**Direction:** North-Northwest
**Sigil:**

**Location:** As discussed under Part 13, Bactriani alludes to the region governed by the ancient city of Bactra in northern Afghanistan, but not the city itself.

Bactra is called Balkh by modern archaeologists and today is mostly in ruins. It is, however, close to the current provincial capital of Mazar-i-Sharif which lies within its ancient sphere of influence, so this part can be used for operations specific to the city and Balkh province, which it currently governs.

## Part 88 – TEX (30)

**Mundane Name:** Afnan
**Angelic Name (*Tabula Recensa*):** Taaogba
**Angelic Name (*Liber Scientia*):** Taoagla
**Governor:** Arfaolg
**Sign:** Pisces

**Direction:** North-Northwest
**Sigil:**

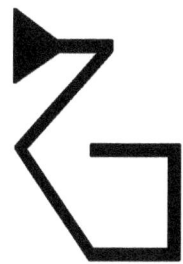

**Location:** The Congo River basin. Includes the capital of the Democratic Republic of the Congo, Kinshasa, and the entire Republic of the Congo.

## *Part 89 – TEX (30)*

**Mundane Name:** Phrygia
**Angelic Name:** Gemnimb
**Governor:** Zarnaah
**Sign:** Cancer
**Direction:** North
**Sigil:**

**Location:** A region in central Turkey. Includes the modern-day capital city of Ankara.

## Part 90 – TEX (30)

**Mundane Name:** Creta
**Angelic Name:** Advorpt
**Governor:** Hononol
**Sign:** Gemini
**Direction:** West
**Sigil:**

**Location:** The island of Crete.

## Part 91 – TEX (30)

**Mundane Name:** Mauritania
**Angelic Name (*Tabula Recensa*):** Doxmael
**Angelic Name (*Liber Scientia*):** Dozinal
**Governor:** Zurchol
**Sign:** Virgo
**Direction:** South-Southwest
**Sigil:**

**Location:** Morocco and the coastal regions of Algeria.

**Other Regions:** Significant areas that are not covered by the 91 Parts include Australia and New Zealand. Europeans first landed in Australia in 1606, only two years before John Dee's death. The expedition was Dutch, so it is not clear if Dee ever would have heard of the place. Europeans did not discover New Zealand until 1642, so it was completely unknown in England during Dee's lifetime. An edge of the coast of New Guinea can be seen on the Drake Map from the 1580's, which Dee would have been familiar with, so New Guinea should be grouped with the other islands of Indonesia and the Far East.

Cousins groups Australia and New Zealand with Antarctica, but especially as Australia reaches almost to the equator, that association strikes me as unsatisfactory. The easiest solution is to group them with the British Isles, as both countries are constitutional monarchies "ruled" by the British royal family. That certainly would have counted in Dee's time, even though today the royals have very little real political power in either country. According to this approach, it should be possible to group Canada in with the British Isles as well, although that country is also part of Idunia along with the continental United States.

**Maps:** I have assembled the following maps of the various continents based on the locations defined in this chapter. They provide a visual reference for the various parts and how they fit together.

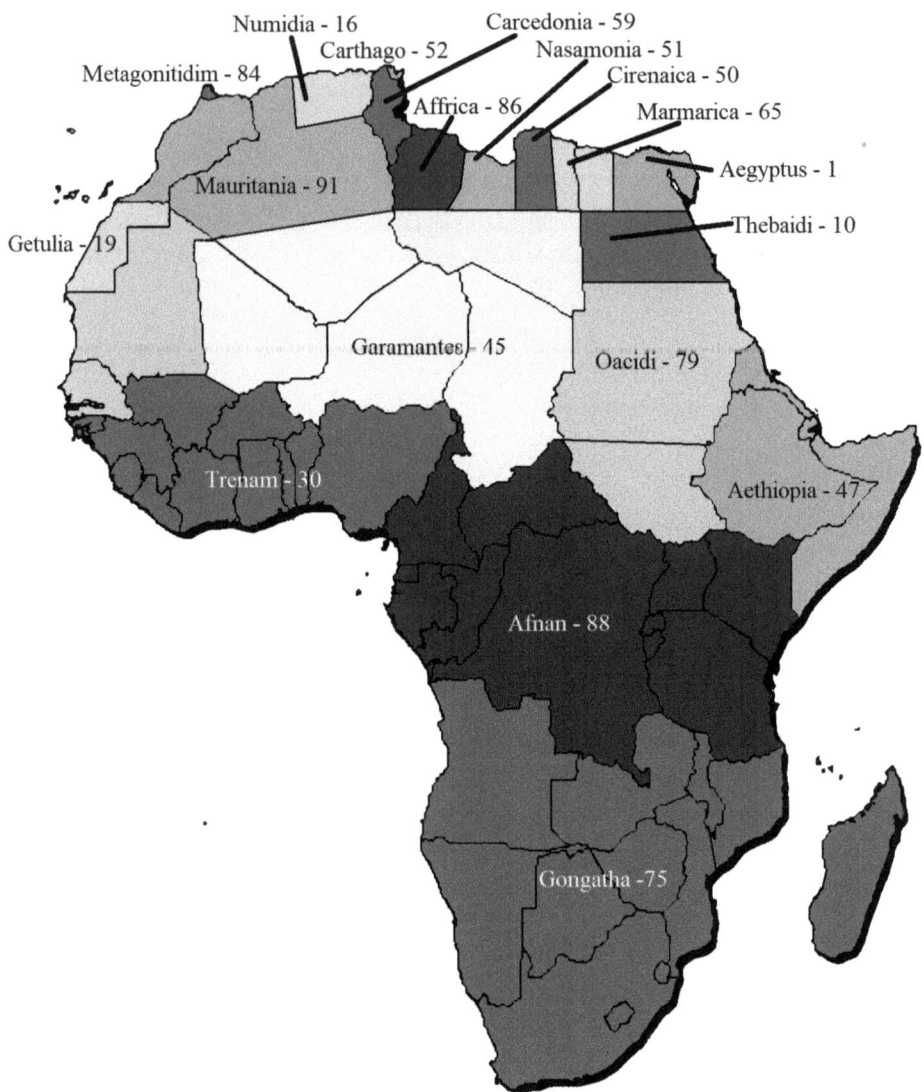

*Figure 4. Africa*

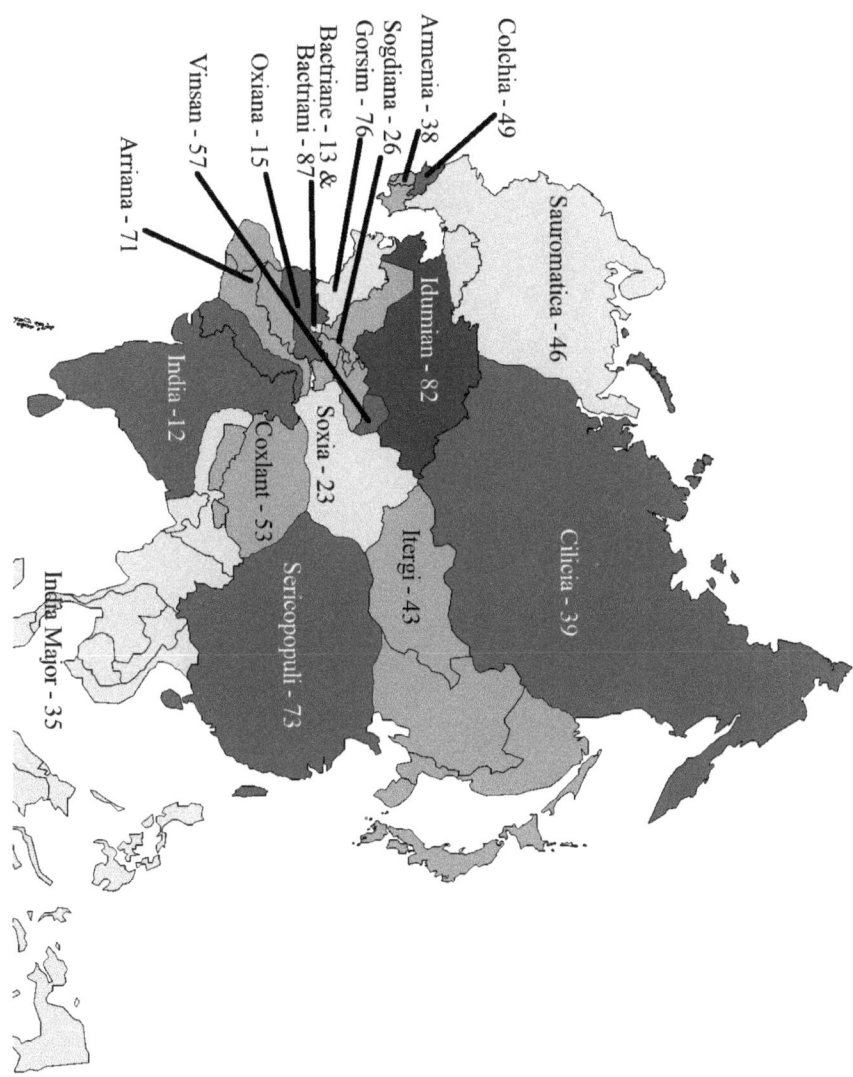

Figure 5. Asia

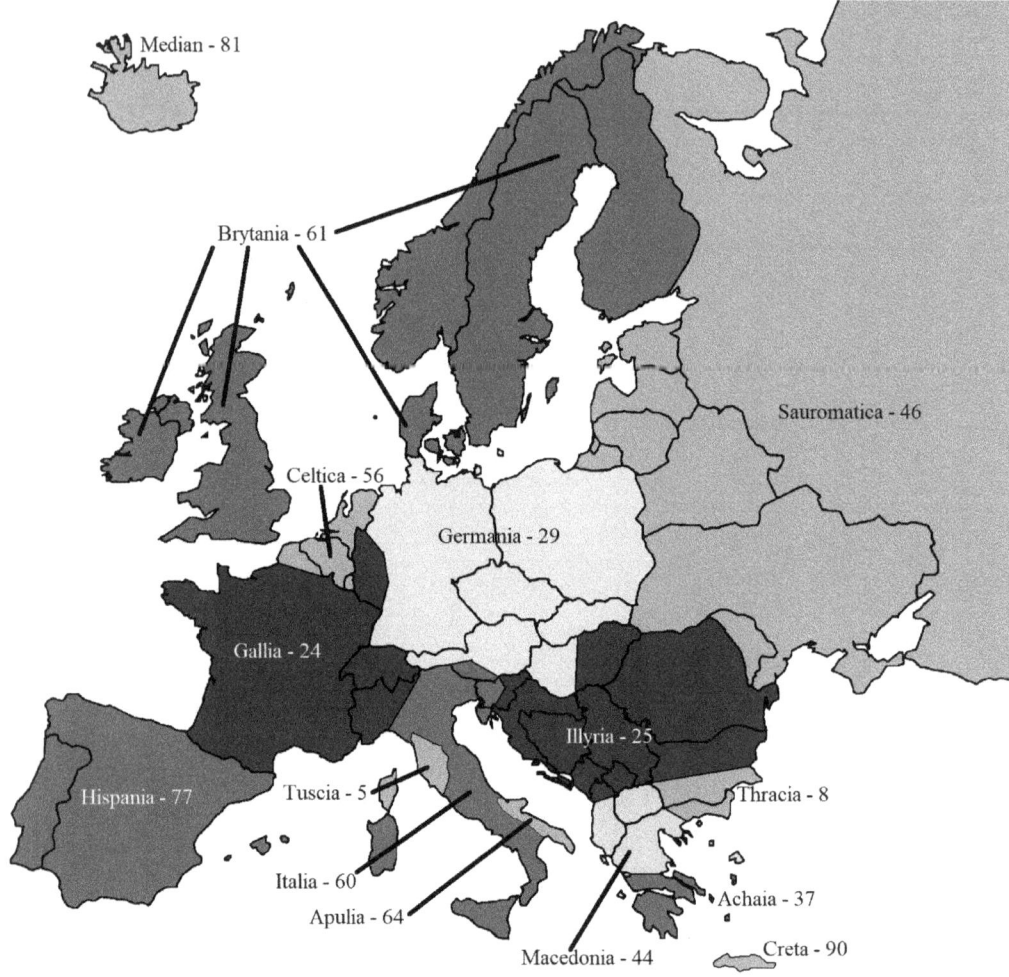

*Figure 6. Europe*

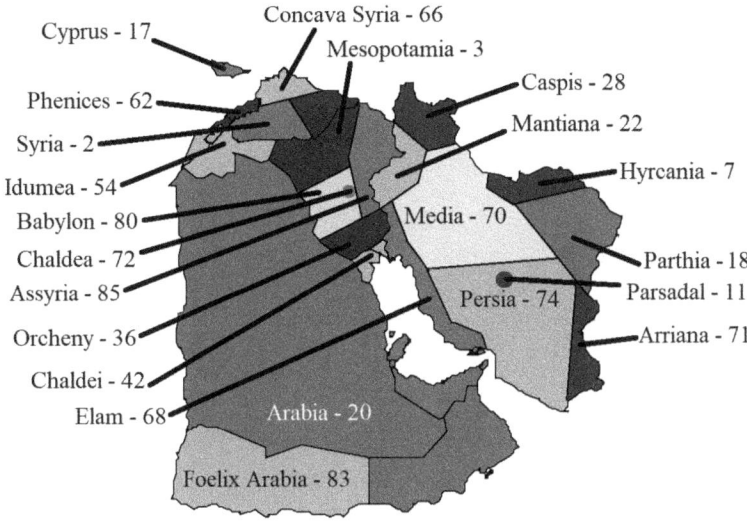

*Figure 7. Middle East*

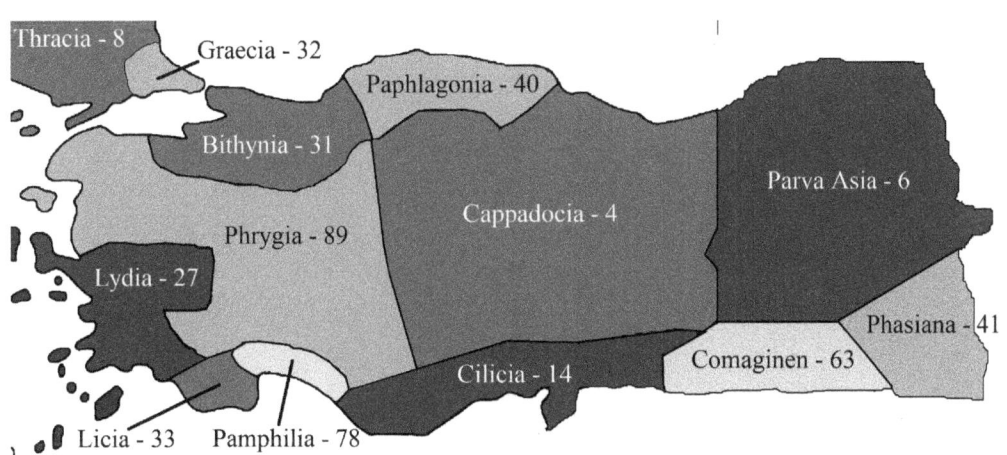

*Figure 8. Middle East - Turkey*

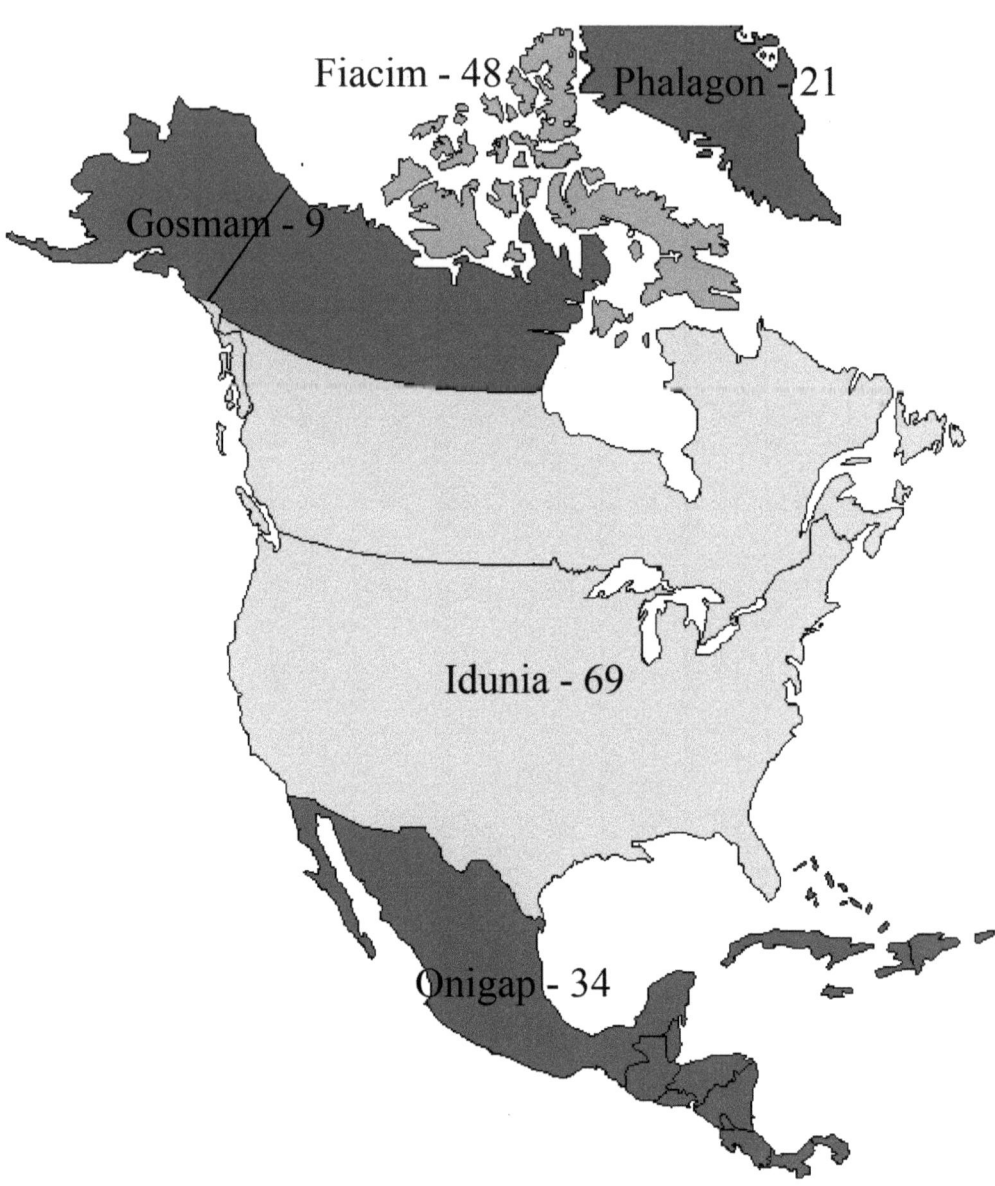

Figure 9. North America

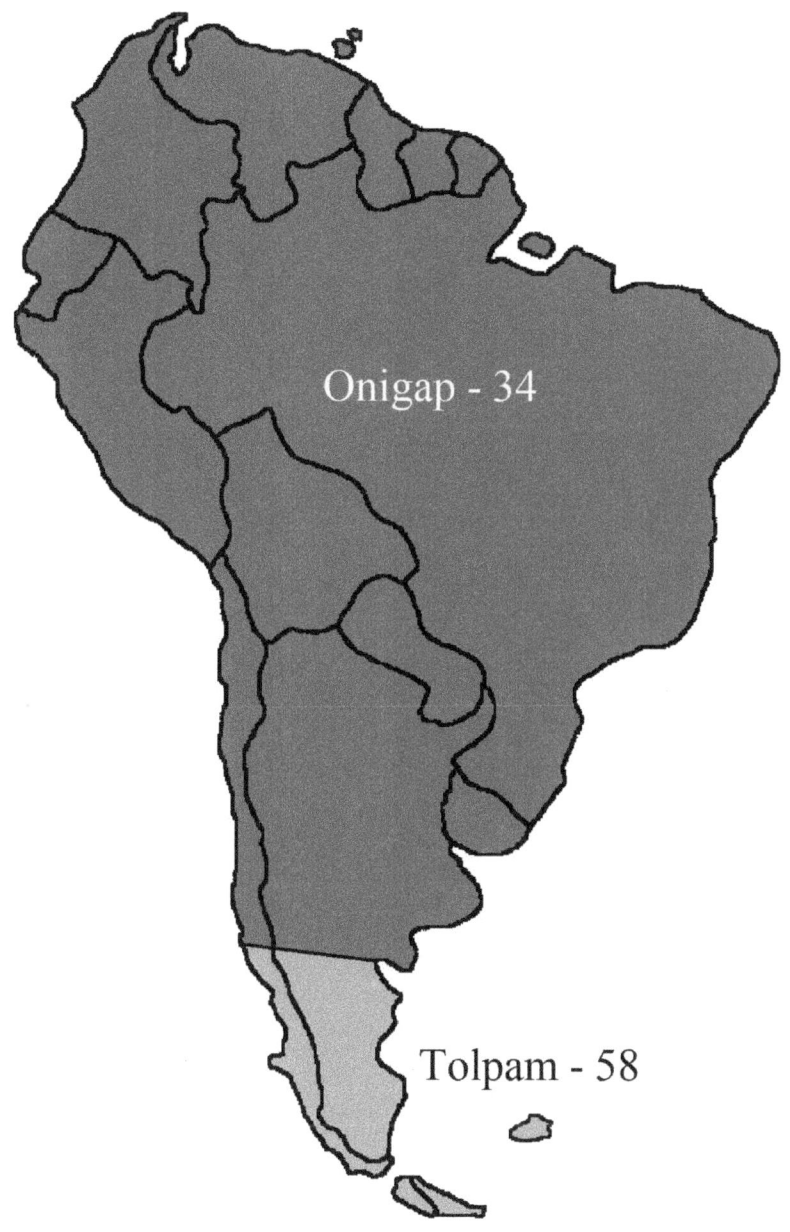

*Figure 10. South America*

**World Atlas:** The following section lists every country in the world at the time of this writing and the Part of the Earth that would be used to influence it. This is generally the location of the country's capital city. Parts that do not contain capitals can still influence issues specific to locations within their bounds, but it is the capitals that truly govern worldwide politics. The following list is in alphabetical order by country, to make looking up the corresponding parts easier. Also, a second list follows of parts that are related to specific cities that have their own parts and are still relevant on the world stage.

### Countries
Afghanistan - Ariana (71)
Albania – Macedonia (44)
Algeria - Numidia (16)
Andorra – Hispania (77)
Angola - Gongatha (75)
Anguilla – Onigap (34)
Antigua & Barbuda – Onigap (34)
Argentina - Onigap (34)
Armenia - Armenia (38)
Australia - Brytannia (61)
Austria – Illyria (25)
Azerbaijan – Armenia (38)
Bahamas - Onigap (34)
Bahrain – Arabia (20)
Bangladesh - India Major (35)
Barbados – Onigap (34)
Belarus - Sauromatica (46)
Belgium – Celtica (56)
Belize - Onigap (34)
Benin - Trenam (30)
Bermuda - Onigap (34)
Bhutan - Coxlant (53)
Bolivia - Onigap (34)
Bosnia & Herzegovina – Illyria (25)
Botswana - Gongatha (75)
Brazil - Onigap (34)
Brunei Darussalam – India Major (35)
Bulgaria – Illyria (25)
Burkina Faso - Trenam (30)

Myanmar/Burma - India Major (35)
Burundi - Afnan (88)
Cambodia - India Major (35)
Cameroon - Afnan (88)
Canada - Idunia (69)
Cape Verde - Mauritania (91)
Cayman Islands - Onigap (34)
Central African Republic - Afnan (88)
Chad – Garamantes (45)
Chile - Onigap (34)
China - Sericopopuli (73)
Colombia - Onigap (34)
Comoros – Gongatha (75)
Congo - Afnan (88)
Costa Rica - Onigap (34)
Croatia – Illyria (25)
Cuba - Onigap (34)
Cyprus - Cyprus (17)
Czech Republic - Germania (29)
Democratic Republic of the Congo - Afnan (88)
Denmark - Brytannia (61)
Djibouti - Aethiopia (47)
Dominican Republic - Onigap (34)
Dominica – Onigap (34)
Ecuador - Onigap (34)
Egypt - Aegyptus (1)
El Salvador - Onigap (34)
Equatorial Guinea - Afnan (88)
Eritrea - Aethiopia (47)
Estonia -Sauromatica (46)
Ethiopia - Aethiopia (47)
Fiji – India Major (35)
Finland - Brytannia (61)
France - Gallia (24)
French Guiana - Onigap (34)
Gabon - Afnan (88)
Gambia - Getulia (19)
Georgia - Colchia (49)
Germany - Germania (29)

Ghana - Trenam (30)
Great Britain - Brytannia (61)
Greece - Achaia (37)
Grenada - Onigap (34)
Guadeloupe – Onigap (34)
Guatemala - Onigap (34)
Guinea – Trenam (30)
Guinea-Bissau - Trenam (30)
Guyana - Onigap (34)
Haiti - Onigap (34)
Honduras - Onigap (34)
Hungary – Illyria (25), but note that the old Roman border for Germania (29) was the Danube River, which runs right through the center of the capital, Budapest. Hungary is grouped with Illyria here because the Hungarian Parliament sits on the eastern bank of the river, but Germania could also prove effective because the city occupies the western bank as well.
Iceland - Median (81)
India - India (12)
Indonesia - India Major (35)
Iran - Media (70)
Iraq - Mesopotamia (3)
Israel and the Occupied Territories – Idumea (54)
Italy – Italia (60)
Ivory Coast (Cote d'Ivoire) - Trenam (30)
Jamaica - Onigap (34)
Japan - Itergi (43)
Jordan – Idumea (54)
Kazakhstan - Idumian (82)
Kenya - Afnana (88)
Kosovo – Illyria (25)
Kuwait – Chaldei (42)
Kyrgyz Republic (Kyrgyzstan) – Sogdiana (26)
Laos - India Major (35)
Latvia - Sauromatica (46)
Lebanon – Phenices (62)
Lesotho - Gongatha (75)
Liberia - Trenam (30)
Libya - Affrica (86)

Liechtenstein - Germania (29)
Lithuania - Sauromatica (46)
Luxembourg - Celtica (56)
Republic of Macedonia - Macedonia (44)
Madagascar - Gongatha (75)
Malawi - Gongatha (75)
Malaysia - India Major (35)
Maldives – India (12)
Mali - Trenam (30)
Malta – Italia (60)
Martinique – Onigap (34)
Mauritania - Getulia (19)
Mauritius – Gongatha (75)
Mayotte – Gongatha (75)
Mexico - Onigap (34)
Moldova, Republic of – Sauromatica (46)
Monaco - Gallia (24)
Mongolia - Itergi (43)
Montenegro – Illyria (25)
Montserrat – Onigap (34)
Morocco - Mauritania (91)
Mozambique - Afnan (88)
Namibia - Gongatha (75)
Nepal - Coxlant (53)
Netherlands – Celtica (56)
New Zealand - Brytannia (61)
Nicaragua - Onigap (34)
Niger - Garamantes (45)
Nigeria - Trenam (30)
Korea, Democratic Republic of (North Korea) - Itergi (43)
Norway - Brytannia (61)
Oman – Arabia (20)
Pacific Islands – India Major (35)
Pakistan - India (12)
Panama - Onigap (34)
Papua New Guinea - India Major (35)
Paraguay - Onigap (34)
Peru - Onigap (34)
Philippines - India Major (35)

Poland - Germania (29)
Portugal - Hispania (77)
Puerto Rico - Onigap (34)
Qatar – Arabia (20)
Reunion – Gongatha (75)
Romania – Illyria (25)
Russian Federation - Sauromatica (46)
Rwanda - Afnan (88)
Saint Kitts and Nevis – Onigap (34)
Saint Lucia – Onigap (34)
Saint Vincent's & Grenadines – Onigap (34)
Samoa – India Major (35)
Sao Tome and Principe – Gongatha (75)
Saudi Arabia – Arabia (20)
Senegal - Getulia (19)
Serbia – Illyria (25)
Seychelles – Afnan (88)
Sierra Leone - Trenam (30)
Singapore – India Major (35)
Slovak Republic (Slovakia) - Germania (29)
Slovenia – Italia (60)
Solomon Islands – India Major (35)
Somalia - Aethiopia (47)
South Africa - Gongatha (75)
Korea, Republic of (South Korea) – Itergi (43)
South Sudan - Oacidi (79)
Spain - Hispania (77)
Sri Lanka - India (12)
Sudan - Oacidi (79)
Suriname - Onigap (34)
Swaziland - Gongatha (75)
Sweden - Brytannia (61)
Switzerland - Gallia (24)
Syria - Syria (2)
Tajikstan – Sogdiana (26)
Tanzania - Afnan (88)
Thailand - India Major (35)
Timor Leste – India Major (35)
Togo – Trenam (30)

Trinidad & Tobago - Onigap (34)
Tunisia - Carthago (52)
Turkey - Phyrygia (89)
Turkmenistan - Gorsim (76)
Turks & Caicos Islands – Onigap (34)
Uganda - Afnan (88)
Ukraine - Sauromatica (46)
United Arab Emirates – Arabia (20)
United States of America (USA) - Idunia (69)
Uruguay - Onigap (34)
Uzbekistan - Sogdiana (26)
Venezuela - Onigap (34)
Vietnam - India Major (35)
Virgin Islands (UK) - Onigap (34)
Virgin Islands (US) - Onigap (34)
Yemen - Foelix Arabia (83)
Zambia - Gongatha (75)
Zimbabwe - Gongatha (75)

**Non-Capital Cities**

The following is a list of major cities that are outside the capital region of their respective countries. If a city is not listed here, you can assume that the capital region in the list above includes it. When a Part of the Earth spans an entire country, all its cities are located in that part. The cities here are mostly located in the area around the Mediterranean Sea and especially the Middle East. Since the geography Dee used was based on that of Claudius Ptolemy, the divisions of the Roman Empire that existed in the second century are by far the most detailed and subdivided sections.

Herat (Afghanistan) – Oxiana (15)
Kunduz (Afghanistan) – Oxiana (15)
Mazar-i-Sharif (Afghanistan) – Bactriani (87)
Pul-e Khomri (Afghanistan) Oxiana (15)
Taloqan (Afghanistan) – Oxiana (15)

Oran (Algeria) - Mauritania (91)
Sidi Bel Abbes (Algeria) - Mauritania (91)
Tiaret (Algeria) - Mauritania (91)
Tlemcen (Algeria) - Mauritania (91)

Comodoro Rivadavia (Argentina) - Tolpam (58)
Ushuaia (Argentina) - Tolpam (58)
Río Grande (Argentina) - Tolpam (58)
Rio Gallegos (Argentina) - Tolpam (58)

Punta Arenas (Chile) - Tolpam (58)

Luxor (Egypt) – Thebaidi (10)

Heraklion (Greece) – Creta (90)
Thessaloniki (Greece) – Macedonia (44)

Pecs (Hungary) - Germania (29)
Gyor (Hungary) - Germania (29)

Abadam (Iran) - Elam (68)
Ahvaz (Iran) - Elam (68)
Ardabil (Iran) - Caspis (28)
Bander Abbas (Iran) - Persia (74)
Birjan (Iran) - Parthia (18)
Bojnord (Iran) - Hyrcania (7)
Bushehr (Iran) - Elam (68)
Dezful (Iran) - Elam (68)
Gorgan (Iran) - Hyrcania (7)
Ilam (Iran) - Elam (68)
Kerman (Iran) - Persia (74)
Kermanshah (Iran) - Mantiana (22)
Khorramabad (Iran) - Elam (68)
Khoy (Iran) - Caspis (28)
Mashhad (Iran) - Parthia (18)
Nishapuir (Iran) - Parthia (18)
Sabzevar (Iran) - Parthia (18)
Sanandaj (Iran) - Mantiana (22)
Sari (Iran) - Hyrcania (7)
Shiraz (Iran) - Persia (74)
Sirjan (Iran) - Persia (74)
Tabriz (Iran) - Mantiana (22)
Urmia (Iran) - Mantiana (22)

Zahedon (Iran) - Arriana (71)
Zanjan (Iran) - Caspis (28)

Al Hillah (Iraq) - Assyria (85)
Amarah (Iraq) - Orcheny (36)
Basra (Iraq) - Chaldei (42)
Erbil (Iraq) - Assyria (85)
Kirkuk (Iraq) - Assyria (85)
Kut (Iraq) - Assyria (85)
Mosul (Iraq) - Mesopotamia (3)
Nasiriyah (Iraq) - Orcheny (36)
Sulaymaniyah (Iraq) - Assyria (85)

Haifa (Israel) – Phenices (62)

Bari (Italy) – Apulia (64)
Florence (Italy) – Tuscia (5)

Aktobe (Kazakhstan) – Sauromatica (46)
Almaty (Kazakhstan) – Vinsan (57)
Oral (Kazakhstan) – Sauromatica (46)

Tobruk (Libya) - Marmerica (65)
Bayda (Libya) - Cirenaica (50)
Benghazi (Libya) - Cirenaica (50)
Sabha (Libya) - Garamantes (45)

Al-Hasakah (Syria) – Mesopotamia (3)
Aleppo (Syria) – Concava Syria (66)
Deir ez-Zor (Syria) – Mesopotamia (3)
Hama (Syria) – Concava Syria (66)
Homs (Syria) – Concava Syria (66)
Latakia (Syria) – Concava Syria (66)
Qamishli (Syria) – Mesopotamia (3)
Raqqa (Syria) – Mesopotamia (3)

Adana (Turkey) – Cilicia (14)
Adapazari (Turkey) – Bithynia (31)
Adıyaman (Turkey) – Comaganen (63)

Antalya (Turkey) – Pamphilia (78)
Antanka (Turkey) – Cilicia (14)
Aydın (Turkey) – Lydia (27)
Batman (Turkey) – Comaginen (63)
Bursa (Turkey) – Bithynia (31)
Çorlu (Turkey) – Thracia (8)
Çorum (Turkey) – Cappadocia (4)
Denizli (Turkey) – Lydia (27)
Diyarbakir (Turkey) – Comaganen (63)
Elazig (Turkey) – Cappadocia (4)
Erzurm (Turkey) - Parva Asia (6)
Gaziantep (Turkey) – Cilicia (14)
Gebze (Turkey) – Bithynia (31)
İskenderun (Turkey) – Cilicia (14)
Istanbul (Turkey) – Graecia (32)
Izmir (Turkey) – Lydia (27)
Izmit (Turkey) – Bithynia (31)
Kahramanmaraş (Turkey) – Cilicia (14)
Kayseri (Turkey) – Cappadocia (4)
Malatya (Turkey) – Cappadocia (4)
Mersin (Turkey) – Cilicia (14)
Osmaniye (Turkey) – Cilicia (14)
Samsun (Turkey) – Paphlagonia (40)
Sivas (Turkey) – Cappadocia (4)
Tarsus (Turkey) – Cilicia (14)
Trabzon (Turkey) – Cappadocia (4)
Urfa (Turkey) – Comaganen (63)
Van (Turkey) – Phasiana (41)

Tangier (Morocco) – Metagonitidim (28)

Anchorage, Alaska (USA) – Gosmam (9)

### **Non-Capital Regions**

This section was created for cases in which it makes more sense to delineate regions rather than individual cities in countries divided into multiple Parts of the Earth. For example, China is divided into four Parts of the Earth and has over a hundred cities with population greater than one million, making a full list quite exhaustive.

Heilongjiang Province (China) – Itergi (43)
Inner Mongolia Autonomous Region (China) – Itergi (43)
Jiayuguan Division, Gansu Province (China) – Soxia (23)
Jilin Province (China) – Itergi (43)
Jinchang Division, Gansu Province (China) – Soxia (23)
Jiuquan Division, Gansu Province (China) – Soxia (23)
Liaoning Province (China) – Itergi (43)
Qinghai Province (China) – Soxia (23)
Tibet Autonomous Region (China) – Coxlant (53)
Xinjian Autonomous Region (China) – Soxia (23)
Zhangye Division, Gansu Province (China) – Soxia (23)

India east of the Ganges River (India) – India Major (35)

Tombouctou Region (Mali) - Garamantes (45)
Kidal Region (Mali) - Garamantes (45)
Gao Region (Mali) - Garamantes (45)

Pakistan west of the Indus River (Pakisatan) - Arriana (71)

Tunisia outside the Tunis metropolitan area – Carcedonia (59)

# 5
# The Temple Arrangement

As THE TEMPLE ARRANGEMENT for working with the Thirty Aires is the same as that for Great Table operations, the material in this chapter has been covered in the first two books of the Mastering Enochian Magick Series in greater detail. It is summarized here so that this volume may be used as a stand-alone text.

Note that the Neo-Enochian Scrying the Aethyrs technique detailed in Chapter 13 does not make use of the Holy Table setup, as the energies of the Aires are *invoked* rather than *evoked* into the Table when using that method. That is, according to the technical terminology used by the Golden Dawn and Thelemic traditions, they are called into your own sphere of consciousness rather than externalized into the Table. The distinction is specific to those two traditions, as in standard English the two words share the definition of "to call up spirits."

**The Enochian Ring:** For the proper working of Enochian magick, the Magician must wear a ring made from pure gold inscribed with the specific arrangement of shapes and letters shown here.

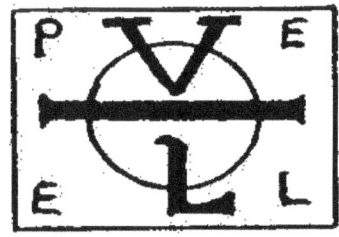

*Figure 11. Face of the Enochian Ring*

The Angels told Dee and Kelley that without it they would "accomplish nothing." Therefore, some sort of ring bearing this design should be worn during all Enochian operations, even if it must be constructed from a less expensive material than gold. I have gotten good results with rings made from brass.

The ring does not require any special consecration to work. However, as detailed in the *Five Books of Mystery* the design for the ring was presented to Dee and Kelley by the Archangel Michael. Therefore, Michael would be the appropriate Angel to conjure should you wish to perform such a consecration. This can be as simple as holding the ring between both hands and vibrating his name a number of times appropriate for solar operations, such as 36 (6 x 6, with 6 being the numeration of Tiphareth, the sphere of the Sun), or as complex as a ceremonial solar conjuration appropriate to your magical tradition.

**The Lamen:** Like the ring, the lamen should also be worn when performing Enochian rituals. It is made up of a grid of Angelic characters arranged as shown.

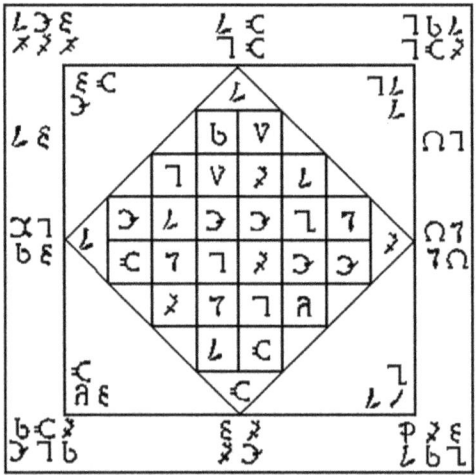

*Figure 12. Enochian Lamen*

The lamen was supposed to be drawn on parchment, which in those days referred to paper made from animal hide. The lamen I currently use is a brass plate with the Angelic characters engraved on one side and is worn around the neck on a cord or chain such that it covers the anahata chakra or heart center. It does not need to be visible. Dee received two designs for the lamen and was told that the first "false" version should be hidden in "some scarf." This instruction was not repeated for the second "true" version, but it could still apply.

**The Robe:** According to the spirit diaries, the robe worn when working with the Enochian system should be white, unadorned, and, if possible, made from linen. I use a simple white linen tau-shaped robe, which conforms exactly to the text, but was expensive to make and is rather scratchy. I have also used robes made from other natural fibers such as cotton, which are easy to procure and less expensive, with good results.

**The Holy Table:** The Holy Table is the centerpiece of an Enochian temple. The Angels specified that it should be approximately three feet square with legs of the same height and made from "sweet wood." Geoffrey James has suggested cedar,[13] which was sometimes referred to as "sweet" during the period in question. I also have heard that the term could sometimes refer to wood from a fruit tree, of which cherry is probably the easiest to find at a lumber store. On the top of the Table is painted a set of lineal figures and Angelic characters in yellow.

*Figure 13. Holy Table*

---

13 Geoffrey James, *Enochian Evocation* (Berkeley Heights, NJ: Heptangle, 1984), 181.

A good inexpensive way to build a Holy Table is to pick up a 3-foot square card table. They are still often built to the exact dimensions recommended to Dee and Kelley, three feet square with four three-foot legs. Finding one with a wooden surface is ideal, but if that proves too difficult or costly you can go ahead and draw the appropriate figures onto the top with acrylic paint or even permanent marker. This may not work quite as effectively as a Table corresponding to the original specifications, but it should be sufficient.

**The Sigillum Dei Aemeth:** The Sigillum Dei Aemeth ("True Seal of God") is a pantacle, or disk, that is placed in the center of the Holy Table. It should be nine inches in diameter and made from pure wax, though paraffin is an acceptable modern substitute. The top bears the design below, which may be easier to cast in some fashion than manually engrave into the wax due to its complexity.

*Figure 14. Top of the Sigillum Dei Aemeth.*
*The asterisk below the Y/14 square near the bottom*
*of the diagram indicates that some experts believe*
*the number in the square should be 15 rather than 14.*

The bottom, on the other hand, bears the design shown in this next figure, which is much simpler and not at all difficult to engrave by hand.

*Figure 15. Bottom of Sigullum Dei Aemeth.*

In addition to the primary Sigillum that occupies the center of the Holy Table, smaller copies of it, four and a half inches in diameter, should be placed under each of the Table's four legs. As my Table lacks permanent legs I omit this portion of the temple setup, but my suspicion is that if your construction skills are superior to mine, you will find that having them adds to the effectiveness of the overall setup.

**The Ensigns of Creation:** The Ensigns of Creation are seven talismans that are placed on the Holy Table surrounding the Sigillum Dei Aemeth. They were originally supposed to be made from purified tin, but later Dee and Kelley were told to paint them onto the table itself using blue for the lines and red for the characters and letters. The seven Ensigns should be arranged or drawn evenly around the Sigillum as shown here.

*Figure 16. Holy Table with Positions
of Sigillum Dei Aemeth and Ensigns*

The Ensigns are drawn or engraved as shown in the following figures and are attributed to the seven ancient planets.

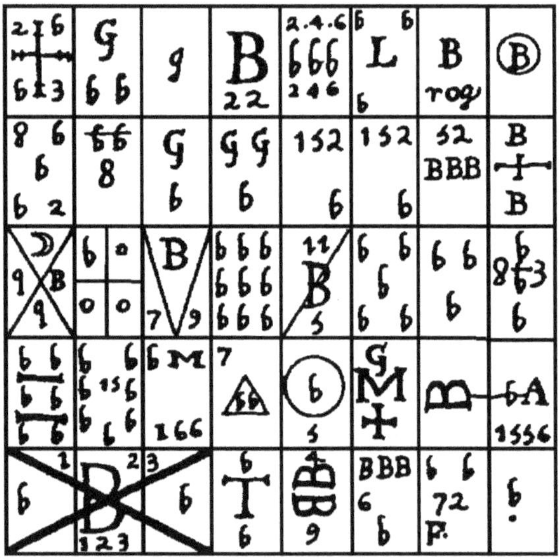

*Figure 17. Ensign of Venus*

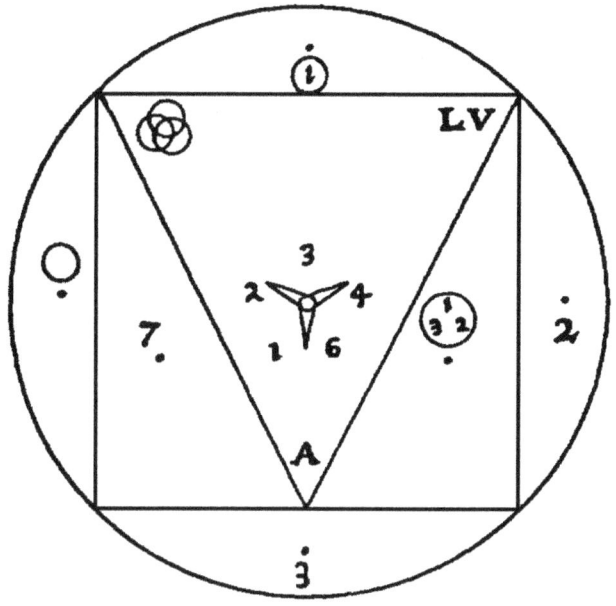

*Figure 18. Ensign of the Sun*

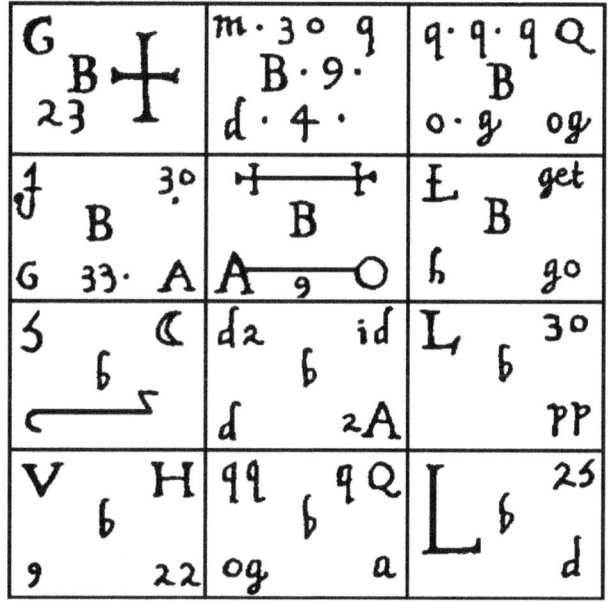

*Figure 19. Ensign of Mars*

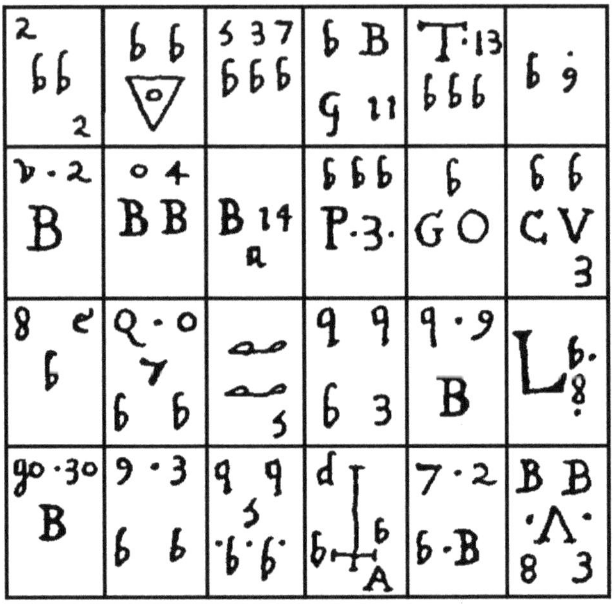

*Figure 20. Ensign of Jupiter*

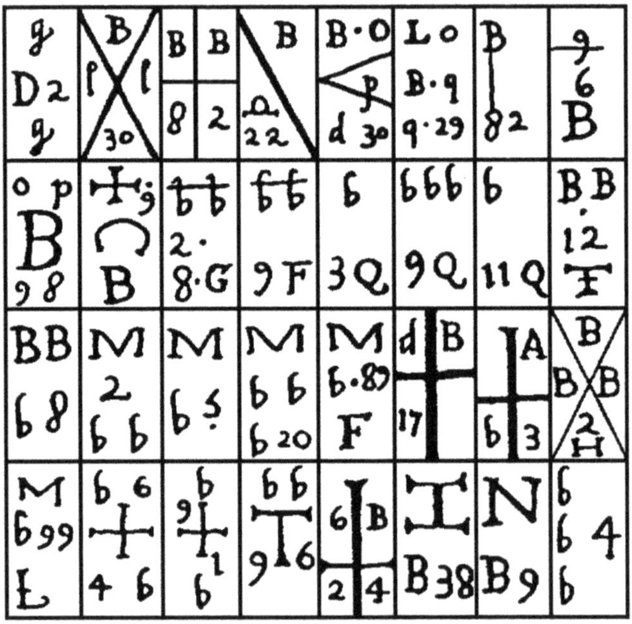

*Figure 21. Ensign of Mercury*

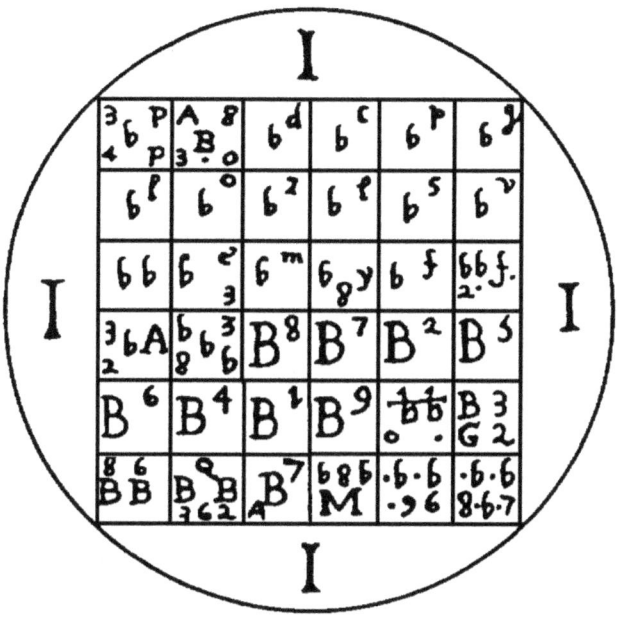

*Figure 22. Ensign of Saturn*

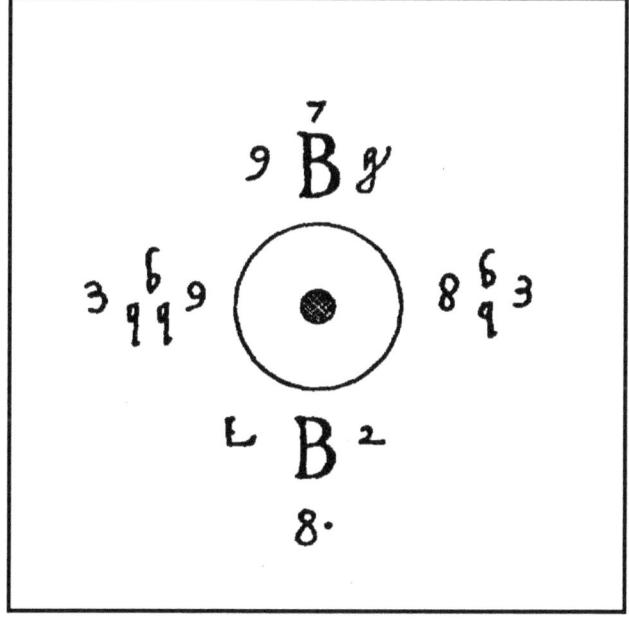

*Figure 23. Ensign of the Moon*

**The Shewstone:** Dee and Kelley used a Shewstone, or scrying crystal much like the fairy-tale "crystal ball," to communicate with the Enochian angels. The stone should be placed in the center of the Holy Table, on top of the Sigillum Dei Aemeth and above the cloth so that it can be seen.

**The Cloth**: The Sigillum, Ensigns, and Holy Table should be covered with a cloth of either red silk or "changeable red and green silk," presumably some sort of double-weave. Dee recommends both in different places in the diaries and as far as I can tell either will work. Silk, which Dee was directed to use, is best but natural fibers of whatever sort such as cotton will also work.

**The Carpet:** The floor under the Holy Table should likewise be covered with a red carpet also made from silk. It is possible to find oriental-style rugs made from red silk, and though they are expensive they are just about the best solution to the problem. You can also use a sheet of red fabric or a red blanket, but make sure that you can walk comfortably around the Holy Table without disturbing the carpet too much or tripping over it.

**The Book:** Dee was told to make a book containing all the prayers, invocations, and conjurations that he and Kelley received so that he could read the various texts in ritual. In this your task is already done for the Angels of the Thirty Aires—you are holding that book in your hands right now. The ritual template in the next chapter contains all the necessary page references to flip back and forth between the appropriate texts for any sort of operation supported in the system. The other two volumes in this series contain similar templates for the Angels of the Mystical Heptarchy and the Great Table.

**The Banners:** Twelve fabric banners are hung around the perimeter of the working space, forming a magical circle. The cloth of the banners should be silk, colored according to the four directions as seen in what is generally called the "golden talisman" vision.

> East –Red ("Fresh Red Cullor")
> South – White ("Lilly White")
> West – Green ("Dark greene Cullor like garlicke blades")
> North – Black ("Blacke as of bilbery Juyce")

Each of these banners bears one of the twelve names of God formed by reading across the central row of each Great Table quadrant, drawn in the Angelic script. The color for the wording on the banners is not specified, but I have found the Golden Dawn "flashing color" method to be particularly effective in their construction. This consists of cutting the letters of the name from cloth that is of the background's complementary color and then sewing them onto the background. Dee's diagram of the banners shows them hung like flags, but I have found that they work better hung vertically from dowels that are suspended on poles as shown here.

*Figure 24. Banner for ORO  
Displayed Vertically*

According to the Solomonic grimoire tradition, the most common diameter for a magical circle is nine feet. With a three-foot-square Holy Table, however, this winds up being a bit cramped and as a Thelemite I prefer an eleven-foot circle for the space delineated by the banners. If your working space does not permit a full circle setup, the banners can also be hung on the four walls of your temple, with three to each of the four directions. The red banners should be hung on the east wall, the white banners on the south wall, and so forth.

# 6
# Thirty Aires Ritual Template

As in *Mastering the Mystical Heptarchy* and *Mastering The Great Table*, this chapter breaks down the essential ritual structure for operations involving the Thirty Aires into their basic components. The template presented here is labeled in the same manner and includes some of the same elements, with steps derived from modern magical practices marked as optional so that they may be skipped by traditional Solomonic grimoire practitioners. The modern practices shown here are adapted from my own magical work, and I have found them to be highly effective when performed in the manner shown.

### Thirty Aires Ritual Template

**0. Preparation**

Set up the Enochian temple to the best of your ability as described in Chapter 5. Wear the Enochian ring, robe, and lamen. For conjurations, stand to the west of the Holy Table facing east. For Scrying the Aethyrs, the entire Holy Table setup should not be present and instead you should stand in the center of the circle formed by the twelve banners.

**1A. Opening the Temple – Ceremonial (Optional)**

A. Perform the banishing AOEVEAE pentagram ritual (Appendix A). Alternatively, you may open the temple with the Golden Dawn Lesser Banishing Ritual of the Pentagram (LBRP, Appendix A) or Aleister Crowley's Star Ruby.

B. If you intend your ritual to have a macrocosmic effect that extends beyond the psychological realm, perform the invoking

MADRIAX hexagram ritual (Appendix A). Alternatively, if you opened with the LBRP you should perform the Lesser Invoking Ritual of the Hexagram (LIRH, Appendix A), or if you opened with the Star Ruby you should perform the Star Sapphire. The combination of a banishing pentagram ritual and an invoking hexagram ritual forms an operant field, as is briefly explained in Chapter 7.

**1B. Opening the Temple - Devotional**

Perform the Prayer of Enoch (page 123). This prayer may be performed on its own to open the temple, or it may follow the ceremonial opening performed as step 1A.

**2. The Preliminary Invocation**

A. Perform the NAZ OLPIRT energy work exercise (Optional) (Appendix A).

B. Perform the original or revised Fundamental Obeisance (page 130).

**3. The Opening Keys**

A. For an evocation, intone the First Key in Angelic followed by English (page 136).

B. For an invocation, intone the Second Key in Angelic followed by English (page 138).

C. For a ritual including both evocatory and invocatory elements, perform the First Key (page 136) followed by the Second Key (page 138). If you are working with another individual like Dee and Kelley did, with one person acting as magician and the other as scryer, the magician should read the First Key followed by the scryer reading the Second Key.

D. For Scrying the Aethyrs, intone the Second Key in Angelic followed by English (page 138), as this method involves invocation only. This is marked as an optional step because Aleister Crowley's original method employed only the Aethyr Key (Optional).

## 4. Tuning the Space

A. Operations opening an entire Aire such as Scrying the Aethyrs do not correspond to any one sign, and therefore no tuning is required.

B. If you are opening a particular Part of the Earth, your ritual may be scheduled so that it is being performed on the appropriate zodiacal day and/or hour. This step is drawn from traditional grimoire practice, but it is nonetheless not required according to the original text as no timing methods for Aire operations are described in Dee's diaries (Optional).

C. If you are opening a particular Part of the Earth, perform the Greater Ritual of the Hexagram corresponding to the sign appropriate to your operation (page 199) (Optional).

## 5. The Aire Key

A. Recite the Angelic Key corresponding to the Aire that you will be opening, inserting the appropriate name and number. This step is performed for all operations involving the Thirty Aires, including Scrying the Aethyrs.

## 6. The Conjurations

A. No talismans or conjurations are necessarily used when Scrying the Aethyrs. Crowley's method does not make use of any of the standard temple equipment, though you should feel free to experiment with them.

B. For operations involving opening an entire Aire, place the talisman corresponding to the Aire on the floor to the west of the Holy Table.

C. For operations involving opening a particular Part of the Earth, move clockwise to the side of the Holy Table opposite the direction associated with the Part and place the talisman corresponding to the proper Aire on the floor there.

D. Stand on the talisman facing the Holy Table and recite the appropriate conjuration. You need only stand on the talisman while reciting the conjuration, but you will remain in this location until you give the License to Depart.

## 7. The Charge to the Spirit

   A. Deliver the Charge to the spirit or spirits that you have personally composed according the instructions given in Chapter 12.

## 8. Closing the Temple

   A. Perform the License to Depart (page 230).

   B. Move clockwise so that you are standing to the west of the Holy Table facing east, if you are facing any other direction.

   C. For rituals opened using the ceremonial method, conclude the MADRIAX (page 206) and AOEVEAE (page 204). Alternatively, if the ritual was opened with the Golden Dawn Lesser Rituals of the Pentagram and Hexagram, perform the Lesser Banishing Ritual of the Pentagram for a ritual that has only an external target or the Qabalistic Cross by itself for a ritual that is intended to affect the magician exclusively or both the magician and an external target. For the Star Ruby/Star Sapphire the same rules apply—close with either the Star Ruby or that ritual's form of the Qabalistic Cross depending upon the ritual's target.

   D. Declare the temple closed. The ritual is now complete.

# 7
# Opening the Temple

As shown in the ritual template the temple may be opened for workings with Thirty Aires using devotional prayers, ceremonial forms, or both. I prefer to use both and find my Enochian rituals at their most potent when incorporating the modern methods outlined in the ritual template. However, the prayers are quite effective on their own for those practitioners who prefer to work with the original material on its own terms.

**The Prayer of Enoch:** This prayer was given to Dee and Kelley by the angel Ave on July 7th of 1584 in Krakow.[14] It is the essential initial devotional prayer used to open the Enochian temple.

> Lord God the Fountain of true wisdom, thou that openest the secrets thy own self unto man, thou knowest mine imperfection and my inward darknesse: How can I (therefore) speak unto them that speak not after the voice of man; or worthily call on thy name, considering that my imagination is variable and fruitlesse, and unknown to myself? Shall the Sands seem to invite the Mountains: or can the small Rivers entertain the wonderful and unknown waves? Can the vessel of fear, fragility, or that is of a determined proportion, lift up himself, heave up his hands, or gather the Sun into his bosom?
>
> Lord it cannot be: Lord my imperfection is great: Lord I am lesse than sand: Lord, thy good Angels and Creatures excell me far: our proportion is not alike; our sense agreeth not: Notwithstanding I am

---

[14] Meric Casaubon, *True and Faithful Relation* (New York, NY: Magickal Childe, 1992), 196-197.

comforted; For that we have all one God, all one beginning from thee, that we respect thee a Creatour: Therefore will I call upon thy name, and in thee, I will become mighty. Thou shalt light me, and I will become a Seer; I will see thy Creatures, and will magnifie thee amongst them.

Those that come unto thee have the same gate, and through the same gate, descend, such as thou sendest. Behold, I offer my house, my labour, my heart and soul, If it will please thy Angels to dwell with me, and I with them ; to rejoyce with me, that I may rejoyce with them ; to minister unto me, that I may magnifie thy name. Then, lo the Tables (which I have provided, and according to thy will, prepared) I offer unto thee, and unto thy holy Angels, desiring them, in and through thy holy names: That as thou art their light, and comfortest them, so they, in thee will be my light and comfort.

Lord they prescribe not laws unto thee, so it is not meet that I prescribe laws unto them: What it pleaseth thee to offer, they receive; So what it pleaseth them to offer unto me, will I also receive. Behold I say (O Lord) If I shall call upon them in thy name, Be it unto me in mercy, as unto the servant of the Highest. Let them also manifest unto me, How, by what words, and at what time, I shall call them. O Lord, Is there any that measure the heavens, that is mortal? How, therefore, can the heavens enter into man's imagination? Thy creatures are the Glory of thy countenance: Hereby thou glorifiest all things, which Glory excelleth and (O Lord) is far above my understanding.

It is great wisdom, to speak and talke according to understanding with Kings: But to command Kings by a subjected commandment, is not wisdom, unlesse it come from thee. Behold Lord, How shall I therefore ascend into the heavens? The air will not carry me, but resisteth my folly, I fall down, for I am of the earth. Therefore, O thou very Light and true Comfort, that canst, and mayst, and dost command the heavens: Behold I offer these Tables unto thee, Command them as it pleaseth thee: and O you Ministers, and true lights of understanding, Governing this earthly frame, and the elements wherein we live, Do for me as for the servant of the Lord: and unto whom it hath pleased the Lord to talk of you.

Behold, Lord, thou hast appointed me 50 times; Thrice 50 times will I lift my hands unto thee. Be it unto me as it pleaseth thee, and thy holy Ministers. I require nothing but thee, and through thee, and for thy honour and glory: But I hope I shall be satisfied, and shall not die, (as thou hast promised) until thou gather the clouds together, and judge all things: when in a moment I shall be changed and dwell with thee forever. Amen.

From some of the feedback I have received about this prayer, some Thelemites working with my system have had problems with it. It does contain language that on the surface sounds self-deprecating and "old Aeon," and I invite anyone who has such issues to rewrite it and see if they can come up with something that works better. Also, in Aleister Crowley's Invocation of Horus, the Confession contains similar statements and many Thelemites have no problem with it. Most local bodies of Ordo Templi Orientis perform that ritual regularly on or around the Vernal Equinox every year.

Here is what I think is going on. One of the most potent magical methods I employ is what I call the Operant Field. The idea is to banish at the level of the individual personality and invoke into the resulting psychic "space" the powers of nature in order to shape and influence them through the activity of concentrated thought. This sort of superficially self-denigrating prayer has the effect of taking the focus off the mundane personality and placing it on aspiration to the divine. In the language of contemplative Christian mysticism, this prayer comprises the "banishing" portion of the Operant Field, but as a prayer rather than a ceremonial ritual.

**Ceremonial Forms:** For those who are unfamiliar with the first book in this series, a few notes regarding my use of the Golden Dawn pentagram and hexagram rituals are in order. The Lesser Ritual of the Pentagram and Lesser Ritual of the Hexagram are presented here according to my operant method, in which the LBRP is followed by the LIRH to open what I call an operant field. This is different than how these rituals are generally taught in the Golden Dawn tradition, where students are instructed to follow the LBRP with the LBRH, banishing at both the microcosmic and macrocosmic levels. I have found, however, that much more potent magical results can be achieved by banishing at the microcosmic level followed by invocation at the macrocosmic level, which blends the two realms together into a unified field.

This allows the combinations of banishing and invoking forms of the Lesser Rituals to be grouped according to the following general schema. I refer to these combinations as **Fields** of four basic types.

**Banishing Field (LBRP/LBRH):** This field in effect constitutes the "full shutdown" - it clears mental and spiritual forms from both the interior and exterior worlds. In can be used to completely cleanse a temple, banish spirits permanently, or neutralize a magical effect that is targeting the magician. What it also does, though, is shut down any ongoing spells that you have running unless they are bound to some anchor other than your personal consciousness. If, for example, you are casting a spell that you want to work over the next week, do not end the ritual with this combination unless you are convinced that you made a mistake and want to stop the spell from going into effect.

**Invoking Field (LIRP/LIRH):** This combination energizes all ongoing magical effects, and can be used to begin a ritual that you want to operate in both the interior and exterior worlds. A good example of this is a spell to get a better job. You want the spell to affect your psyche in such a way that you seem more confident and capable, but you also want it to shift probabilities in the material world so that the right opportunity will come your way.

**Centering Field (LIRP/LBRH):** This combination sets up a field in which the interior world is engaged while influences from the exterior world are neutralized. This field is ideal for exclusively psychological magical work of all sorts.

**Operant Field (LBRP/LIRH):** This field clears the interior world and then merges it with the exterior world, setting up a space in which thought more easily becomes material reality. All of the energy of a spell cast within this field is targeted on the macrocosm, and the resulting probability shifts show that magick done this way influences the outside world significantly better.

Of these four the operant field is the primary field that you should be using when working with practical Enochian magick, and as a result this is the field that is set up when you follow the instructions in the template.

You should always banish before you invoke, and thus the centering and invoking fields should be preceded by an initial LBRP. This makes their use somewhat more cumbersome, since the resulting sequences are LBRP/LIRP/LIRH and LBRP/LIRB/LBRH.

My original Enochian opening rituals, the AOEVEAE and MADRIAX, are also structured in this manner, based on my findings regarding the standard pentagram and hexagram rituals. Aleister Crowley's Star Ruby and Star Sapphire may also be substituted for the Lesser Pentagram and Lesser Hexagram rituals respectively, keeping in mind that the invoking form of the Star Sapphire should follow the banishing form of the Star Ruby for the same reasons as described above. The ritual forms for the Lesser Ritual of the Pentagram, the Lesser Ritual of the Hexagram, the AOEVEAE, and the MADRIAX can be found in Appendix A.

# 8
# Preliminary Invocations

WHEN WORKING WITH CEREMONIAL FORMS TO open the temple, the NAZ OLPIRT energy work ritual (Appendix A) should be performed before the corresponding preliminary invocation prayer. This ritual activates the microcosmic elements within the subtle body of the magician and energizes the central nervous system. If magick is viewed as a form of communication, then energy work is like turning up the power on your transmitter. You can transmit the same information without it, but with it the signal you send will be much stronger.

My usual recommendation to students is that the ritual opening up to this point be adopted as a daily practice. Most magical orders teach variations on this method; for example, in most of the Golden Dawn orders the standard daily practice generally includes the Lesser Banishing Ritual of the Pentagram followed by the Middle Pillar Exercise. Some add the Lesser Banishing Ritual of the Hexagram between the Lesser Ritual of the Pentagram and the Middle Pillar. My methods are similar to the latter, except that I generally replace the banishing form of the lesser hexagram ritual with the invoking form for operant workings.

The advantage of adopting the opening and preliminary invocation phases of ritual work as a daily practice is twofold. First of all, doing so will increase your skill with the preliminary invocation itself. The better you become at it, the better your rituals will work. Second of all, it allows you to approach more complex rituals in a modular fashion, as any ritual you perform will open with the same set of actions that you practice every day. This means that in order to memorize a new ritual you have a lot less to learn. While some portions of ceremonial rituals like the

Angelic Keys and Aire Conjurations are designed to be read, it is much more effective to have the openings, closings, and basic ritual structure memorized.

**The Fundamental Obeisance:** Like Great Table operations, operations involving the Thirty Aires employ John Dee's Fundamental Obeisance as a preliminary invocation. It calls upon the twelve names of God that rule over the four quadrants of the Great Table. The AOEVEAE and MADRIAX rituals can be combined with the Fundamental Obeisance as a highly effective daily practice regimen, as the Fundamental Obeisance calls upon the twelve names of God to transform the practitioner into a powerful and effective Enochian magician.

As discussed in more detail in *Mastering the Great Table*, the four quadrants of the Holy Table may be related to the four Qabalistic worlds and these in turn can be related to points on the human body. When reciting the Fundamental Obeisance it is a useful practice to vibrate each name slowly and fully while directing your attention to the corresponding point. This may be accompanied by the visualization of a bright sphere of appropriately colored light centered on the point. As the three names are vibrated, you imagine this sphere becoming brighter, larger, and more coherent. The following table shows these associations.

| Names | World | Point | Color |
| --- | --- | --- | --- |
| ORO IBAH AOZPI | Atziluth | Center of Forehead | Red |
| MPH ARSL GAIOL | Briah | Throat | White |
| OIP TEAA PDOCE | Yetzirah | Heart Center | Green |
| MOR DIAL HCTGA | Assiah | Feet | Black |

*Table 19. Names, Worlds, and Points*

You may direct and concentrate this light by touching the first three points for the first three sets of names respectively, and then standing with your arms at your sides for the final set.

John Dee's Fundamental Obeisance reads as follows, with the twelve names of God shifted to match the 1587 *Tabula Recensa* order:

O YHVH TzABAOTh, we invoke and implore most earnestly your Divine Power, Wisdom and Goodness, and most humbly and faithfully ask you to favor and assist us in all our works, words and cogitations, concerning, promoting or procuring your praise, honor and Glory. And by these your twelve mystical names. ORO, IBAH, AOZPI, MPH, ARSL, GAIOL, OIP, TEAA, PDOCE, MOR, DIAL, HCTGA, most ardently do we entreat and implore your Divine and Omnipotent Majesty: that all your faithful Angelic Spirits whose mystical names are expressed in this book and whose offices are briefly noted, in whatever part of the world they be and, in whatever time of our lives they are summoned by us by means of their peculiar powers or authority of your Holy Names (likewise contained in this book), that most swiftly they come to us visible, affable, and appear to us peacefully and remain with us visibly according to our wishes, and that they disappear at our request from us and from our sight. And through you and that reverence and obedience which they owe you in those twelve mystical names above mentioned, that they give satisfaction amicably to us also, at each and every moment in our lives, and in each and every deed or request to all, some or one of them, and to do this quickly, well, completely and perfectly to discharge, perfect and complete all this according to their virtues and power both general and individual and through the injunctions given them by you (O God) and their charged offices and ministry. AMEN.

**The Revised Fundamental Obeisance:** The following revised Fundamental Obeisance is what my magical working group and I use in our own ritual operations, modified to make it more generic in terms of theology. I have also added a reference to the Enochian name MAD (MAHD), which is given as the highest name of God by the Angel Madimi in one of the early portions of the *True and Faithful Relation*. The name MAD should be vibrated with your hands at your sides. The sphere of light should encompass your entire body, and the light itself should be visualized as brightness composed of all colors at once.

O Almighty and Omnipotent MAD, Lord and Creator of the universe, I, *[Your Magical Name]*, devoted worshipper of the Highest, most earnestly invoke and call upon your divine power, wisdom, and goodness. I humbly and faithfully seek your favor and assistance to me in all my deeds, words, and thoughts, and in the promotion, procuring, and mingling of your praise, honour, and glory. Through these, your twelve mystical Names: ORO, IBAH, AOZPI, MPH, ARSL, GAIOL, OIP, TEAA, PDOCE, MOR, DIAL, HCTGA, I conjure and pray most zealously to your divine and omnipotent majesty, that all your Angelic spirits might be called from any and all parts of the universe through the special domination and controlling power of your holy Names. Let them come most quickly to me. Let them appear visibly, friendly, and peacefully to me. Let them remain visible according to my will. Let them vanish from me and from my sight when I so request. Let them give reverence and obedience before you and your twelve mystical Names. I command that they happily satisfy me in all things by accomplishing each and every one of my petitions, if not by one means, then by another, goodly, virtuously, and perfectly, with an excellent and thorough completeness, according to their virtues and powers, both general and unique, and by your united ministry and office, O God, Amen. So mote it be.

This invocation acts as a counterpoint to the Prayer of Enoch, which precedes it in the Thirty Aires ritual sequence. The self-deprecating portions of the Prayer of Enoch serve to purify the intent of the practitioner and prepare him or her to receive the majesty of God. The Fundamental Obeisance, on the other hand, invokes that majesty by means of the particular divine names of power that correspond to the Great Table and by extension to the Thirty Aires.

# 9
# The Angelic Keys

THIS TABLE SHOWS THE TWENTY-ONE ANGELIC letters along with their names, English equivalents, and sounds. The Angelic Keys in this chapter include phonetic breakdowns, but this is the system by which those breakdowns were constructed and is also the system that I use to pronounce other Enochian names and words.

| Angelic | Name | English | Sound | Value (Hebrew) |
|---|---|---|---|---|
| A | Un | A | Short A | 1 (Aleph) |
| B | Pa | B | B | 2 (Beth) |
| C | Veh | C | K | 20 (Kaph) |
| D | Gal | D | D | 4 (Daleth) |
| E | Graph | E | Short E | 5 (Heh) |
| F | Or | F | F | 6 (Vav) |
| G | Ged | G | Hard G | 3 (Gimel) |
| H | Na | H | H | 5 (Heh) |
| I | Gon | I/Y | Long E or Y | 10 (Yod) |
| L | Ur | L | L | 30 (Lamed) |
| M | Tal | M | M | 40 (Mem) |
| N | Drux | N | N | 50 (Nun) |
| O | Med | O | Long O | 70 (Ayin) |
| P | Mals | P | P | 80 (Peh) |
| Q | Ger | Q | Q (KW) | 100 (Qoph) |
| R | Don | R | R | 200 (Resh) |
| S | Fam | S | S | 60 (Samekh) |
| T | Gisg | T | T | 9 (Teth) |

| Angelic | Name | English | Sound | Value (Hebrew) |
|---|---|---|---|---|
| V | Van | U/V | Short U or V | 6 (Vav) |
| X | Pal | X | X | 90 (Tzaddi) |
| Z | Ceph | Z | Z or Zod | 7 (Zayin) |

*Table 20: The Angelic Alphabet*

According to this scheme, Angelic vowel sounds do not combine whereas consonant sounds do. Whether or not this was how Dee intended his notes to be read is impossible to determine from the surviving diaries, but I have found that in practice it works well. For example, the word QAA which is part of my magical motto *Ananael Qaa* is pronounced **QUAH-ah** rather than **QUAH**, but the name **OMEBB** is pronounced **OH-meb** rather than **OH-meh-beb** or some similar rendering in which the two B's are kept as separate sounds. In addition, for the purposes of determining gematria values, **SH** may be calculated as 300 for Shin, **CH** may be calculated as 8 for Cheth, and **TH** may be calculated as 400 for Tau.

In the Golden Dawn pronunciation system Z is always pronounced as the syllable "Zod" but in fact what was communicated to Dee was that this is only done some of the time and that it changes the meaning of words. In effect, the use of "Zod" rather than the Z consonant sound marks the word as more strongly associated with God or the divine. As such, "Zod" should only be used in Great Table names that are referred to as names of God. So, for example, for the Parts of the Earth the Z sound would be used, but for the names of the zodiacal angels that rule over them "Zod" would be more appropriate.

While the Golden Dawn pronunciation system of inserting the vowel from the corresponding Hebrew letter between consonants is awkward, it is also true that sometimes vowel insertion is necessary. Generally, I insert vowel sounds according to the Golden Dawn method simply because it sounds better than inserting schwa sounds[15] between every difficult consonant set. This is done according to the vowel sound found in the name of the corresponding Hebrew consonant, as shown here.

---

15 The schwa is a shortened "uh" sound, as pronounced between consonants in the second syllable of the English word "rhythm."

| Hebrew Consonant | Hebrew Letter Name | Angelic Letter | Vowel Sound |
|---|---|---|---|
| B | Beth | B | E |
| G | Gimel | G | I |
| D | Daleth | D | A |
| H | Heh | H | E |
| V | Vav | V | A |
| Z | Zain | Z | A |
| Ch | Cheth | CH | E |
| T | Teth | T | E |
| Y | Yod | Y | O |
| K | Kaph | C | A |
| L | Lamed | L | A |
| M | Mem | M | E |
| N | Nun | N | U |
| S | Samekh | S | A |
| P | Peh | P | E |
| Tz | Tzaddi | X | A |
| Q | Qoph | Q | O |
| R | Resh | R | E |
| Sh | Shin | SH | I |
| Th | Tau | TH | A |

*Table 21: Golden Dawn Vowel Insertions*

This vowel insertion system has no basis in the original Dee material, so I use it sparingly. For example, I pronounce the word VORSG pretty much as written so that it sounds a lot like "VORSK" with the last letter a hard G rather than a K. However, according to the traditional Golden Dawn pronunciation it would be "VaOReSaJi," inserting the A from Vav, the E from Resh, the A from Samekh, and the I from Gimel, in addition to using a soft G that is not marked as such in Dee's pronunciation notes for the word. In fact, once you practice the unfamiliar "SG" sound for a bit you will find that you do not need any of the additional vowels in order to say it properly.

In some cases, though, vowel insertion is the best option. The first of the three names of God corresponding to the south on the *Tabula Recensa*,

MPH ARSL GAIOL, consists of three consonants and no vowel sounds. In the modern Golden Dawn Tradition, MPH is generally pronounced as "EM-peh," which does not conform to even the standard Golden Dawn rules. This pronunciation is not found in Aleister Crowley's *Liber Chanokh* but does appear in Israel Regardie's *The Golden Dawn*, so it most likely was adopted by the later Stella Matutina lineage at some point between around 1900 and 1934. While some sort of vowel sound has to be inserted into MPH and other words like it, I prefer to conform to the more standard Golden Dawn pronunciation of inserting the appropriate vowel sound after the consonant. MPH is thus pronounced "MEH-peh" inserting the short e vowel sounds from Mem and Peh. Since I only use this rule as necessary to allow pronunciation of the word, I would not add an extra short e from Heh after the H and pronounce the name "MEH-peh-heh" as the full Golden Dawn pronunciation method would dictate.

## The Opening Keys

**Silence – the True "First Key":** As I first mentioned in *Mastering the Mystical Heptarchy*, the true "First Key" is "not to be sounded," that is, it is silent. I implement this Key by performing a brief meditation that serves to quiet my wandering thoughts and separate my ritual thoughts from those of my normal life prior to the start any magical ritual, as well as by inserting a brief pause prior to reading the so-called First and/or Second Keys.

**The First Key:** While this "First Key" is in fact the second, I have not labeled it as such in order to maintain consistency with other writings on Enochian Magick. The First Key is used to activate the Enochian Temple when performing rituals involving evocation—that is, the calling of the Enochian angels into the Holy Table. As an Opening Key, it precedes the use of the Aire Key for operations involving the Thirty Aires.

## The First Angelic Key

OL SONF VORSG, GOHO IAD BALT LANSH CALZ VONPHO, SOBRA Z-OL ROR I TA NAZPSAD GRAA TA MALPRG. DS HOL-Q QAA NOTHOA ZIMZ OD COMMAH TA NOBLOH ZIEN: SOBA THIL GNONP PRGE ALDI DS VRBS OBOLEH GRSAM: CASARM

OHORELA CABA PIR DS ZONRENSG CAB ERM JADNAH: PI-
LAH FARZM ZURZA ADNA GONO IADPIL DS HOM TOH SOBA
IPAM LU IPAMIS DS LOHOLO VEP ZOMD POAMAL OD BOGPA
AAI TA PIAP PIAMOL OD VAOAN. ZACARE CA OD ZAMRAN
ODO CICLE QAA ZORGE, LAP ZIRDO NOCO MAD HOATH
JAIDA.

## Phonetic

OL SONF VORSG go-HO i-AD BALT LANSH KALZ VON-pho,
SO-bra zod-OL ROR I TA NAZ-psad GRA-a TA MAL-perg. DES
HOL-quo QUA-a not-HO-a ZIMZ, OD KO-mah TA NO-bloh
zi-EN: SO-ba THIL gi-NONP per-GE AL-di DES VURBS O-bu-leh
gir-SAM: ka-SARM o-ho-RE-la ka-BA PIR DES zon-RENSG KAB
ERM JAHD-na: PE-lah FARZM OD ZUR-za ad-NA GO-no i-AHD-
pil DES HOM TOH SO-ba i-PAM LU i-PAHM-is, DES LO-huh-lo
VEP ZOMD po-A-mal OD BOG-pa ah-uh-I TA pi-AP pi-A-mol OD
VA-o-an. za-ka-REH KA OD ZAM-ran: O-do kik-LEH QUA-a zor-
GEH, LAP ZIR-do NO-ko MAD ho-ATH ja-I-da.

## English

I reign over you, sayeth the God of Justice in power exalted above the
firmaments of wrath, in whose hands the Sun is as a sword, and the
Moon as a through-thrusting fire which measureth your garments in
the midst of my vestures, and trussed you together as the palms of my
hands: whose seats I garnished with the fire of gathering, and beauti-
fied your garments with admiration to whom I made a law to govern
the Holy Ones and delivered you a rod with the Ark of Knowledge.
Moreover you lifted up your voices and swore obedience and faith
to him that liveth and triumpheth whose beginning is not, nor end
cannot be which shineth as a flame in the midst of your palace and
reigneth among you as the balance of righteousness, and truth: move,
therefore, and show yourselves: open the mysteries of your creation:
be friendly unto me: for I am the servant of the same your God: the
true worshipper of the highest.

**The Second Key:** The Second Key is used to open the Enochian temple for rituals involving invocation—that is, the calling of the Enochian angels into your own sphere of consciousness. Invocation and evocation are not necessarily contradictory; I have performed rituals in which I invoked the form of one angel in order to call a second angel into the Holy Table that was under the authority of the first. In such rituals, both Keys are read beginning with the First. Otherwise, for a ritual such as Scrying the Aethyrs, the Second Key replaces the First.

## The Second Angelic Key

ADGT VPAAH ZONGOM FAAIP SALD VIIV L SOBAM IALPRG IZAZAZ PIADPH CASARMA ABRAMG TA TALHO PARACLEDA Q-TA LORS-L-Q TURBS OOGE BALTOH GIUI CHIS LUSD ORRI OD MICALP CHIS BIA OZONGON. LAP NOAN TROF CORS TAGE O-Q MANIN JAIDON. TORZU GOHEL ZACAR CA CNO-QUOD, ZAMRAN MICALZO OD OZAZM VRELP LAP ZIR IOIAD.

## Phonetic

AD-git VEH-puh-a ZONG-om fa-uh-IP SALD VI-iv LA so-BAM i-AL-perg i-zuh-ZAZ pi-AD-peh, kas-AR-ma ab-RAMG TA TAL-ho pa-ruh-KLEH-da QUO-ta LORS-el-quo TURBS O-uh-ge BAL-toh gi-u-I CHIS OR-ri OD mi-KALP CHIS bi-A O-zun-gon. LAP no-AN TROF KORS ta-GE O-quo ma-NIN JA-i-don tor-ZU GO-hel za-KAR KA KNO-quod, ZAM-ran mi-KAL-zo OD o-ZA-zam VRELP LAP ZIR i-O-i-ad.

## English

Can the wings of the winds understand your voices of wonder, O you the second of the first, whom the burning flames have framed within the depths of my jaws, whom I have prepared as cups for a wedding, or as the flowers in their beauty for the chamber of righteousness. Stronger are your feet than the barren stone: and mightier are your voices than the manifold winds. For, you are become a building such as is not but in the mind of the all-powerful. Arise, sayeth the first, move therefore unto his servants: show yourselves in power. And make me a strong seething: for I am of him that liveth forever.

## The Thirty Aire Keys

There is only one Aire Key with thirty variations that differ by a single word. This word is the name of the Aire that is being opened, and it is inserted into the first sentence of the Key. As listed in Chapter 3, the Aires are named as shown here, along with the corresponding number to insert into the English version of the Key:

| Number | Aire |
|---|---|
| First | LIL |
| Second | ARN |
| Third | ZOM |
| Fourth | PAZ |
| Fifth | LIT |
| Sixth | MAZ |
| Seventh | DEO |
| Eighth | ZID |
| Ninth | ZIP |
| Tenth | ZAX |
| Eleventh | ICH |
| Twelfth | LOE |
| Thirteenth | ZIM |
| Fourteenth | VTA |
| Fifteenth | OXO |
| Sixteenth | LEA |
| Seventeenth | TAN |
| Eighteenth | ZEN |
| Nineteenth | POP |
| Twentieth | CHR |
| Twenty-First | ASP |

| Number | Aire |
|---|---|
| Twenty-Second | LIN |
| Twenty-Third | TOR |
| Twenty-Fourth | NIA |
| Twenty-Fifth | VTI |
| Twenty-Sixth | DES |
| Twenty-Seventh | ZAA |
| Twenty-Eighth | BAG |
| Twenty-Ninth | RII |
| Thirtieth | TEX |

*Table 22: The Thirty Aires and their Numbers*

The Aire Key is the longest and most intricate of the various keys written in the Angelic language. It also seems to be notated for pronunciation in a slightly different manner than the other 18 keys in Sloane 3191, the surviving Dee manuscript of the Keys currently housed at the British Museum. This notation is clearer and more comprehensible, and from it can be deduced a few exceptions to my general pronunciation rules.

In three places, the letter C is glossed as S, which indicates a soft C. This notation is found in NONCA and twice in NONCF. Those words, then, should be pronounced NON-sa and NON-saf rather than according to the general rules. This implies that all other C's use the hard sound, rendering the pronunciation of CICLE as "SEE-kayl," which I took issue with in *Mastering the Mystical Heptarchy*, as explicitly wrong. Likewise, in four places G is deliberately glossed as DG, indicating a soft G. This notation is found in FARGT, TONUG, FAORGT, and QTING, meaning that they should be pronounced as FAR-jit, to-NUJ, fah-OR-jit, and quo-TINJ rather than according to the standard rules. This implies that all other G's use the hard sound. Finally, in IAIDA, IAODOF, and MADRIIAX I's are glossed as Y's, indicating pronunciations of YA-i-da, YA-o-daf, and MA-dri-yax in this Key.

One other issue that I encountered is the issue of the handwriting itself. Elizabethan script is slightly different than modern English, and few efforts had been made at that point to standardize spelling. As a result, in the handwriting of the "fair copy" from Sloane 3191 the letters U and

V are commonly transposed. In *Elizabethan Magic*, Robert Turner simply transcribed the letters as they appear. However, going through the English it is clear to me that u and v are likewise interchangeable; words can be found there that look as if they read "vnderstanding," "gouern," "heuens," "vnderneath," and so forth. For this reason, I have glossed the U's and V's as they make the most sense to me in terms of the flow of the language, not necessarily as they explicitly appear in the manuscript. Keep in mind that both U and V are represented by the same letter in the Angelic language, just as is the case with I, Y, and J.

## The Aire Angelic Keys (19-48)

MADRIAX DS PRAF *[Aire Name]*, CHIS MICAOLZ SAANIR CAOSGO, BALZIRAS IAIDA: NONCA GOHULIM, MICMA ADOIAN MAD, IAOD BLIORB, SABA OOAONA CHIS LICIFTIAS PERIPSOL: DS ABRAASSA NONCF NETAAIB CAOSGI, OD TILB ADPHAHT DAMPLOZ TOOAT NONCF GMICALZOMA LRASD TOFGLO MARB YARRY IDOIGO OD TORZULP IAODAF, GOHOL, CAOSGA TABAORD SAANIR OD CHRISTEOS YRPOIL TIOBL BUSDIR TILB NOALN PAID ORSBA OD DODRMNI ZYLNA: ELZAPTILB, PARMGI PERIPSAX: OD TA QURLST BOOAPIS: LNIBM OVCHO SYMP OD CHRISTEOS AGTOLTORN MIRC, Q TIOBL LEL: TON PAOMBD DILZMO ASPIAN: OD CHRISTEOS AGLTORTORN PARACH ASYMP: CORDZIZ DODPAL OD FIFALZ LS MNAD: OD FARGT BAMS OMAOAS: CONISBRA, OD AVAVOX TONUG: ORSCAT BL NOASMI TABGES LEVITHMONG: UNCHI OMPTILB ORS. BAGLE? MOOOAH OL CORDZIZ. LCAPIMAO IXOMAXIP, OD CACOCASB GOSAA: BAGLEN PII TIANTA ABABALOND, OD FAORGT TELOCVOVIM: MADRIIAX, TORZU, OADRIAX OROCHA, ABOAPRI: TABAORI PRIAZ ARTABAS: ADRPAN CORSTA DOBIX: YOLCAM PRIAZI ARCOAZIOR: OD QUASB QTING: RIPIR PAAOXT SAGACOR. UML OD PRDZAR, CACRG AOIVEAE CORMPT: TORZU, ZACAR, OD ZAMRAN ASPT SIBSI BUTMONA, DS SURZAS TIA BALTAN: ODO CICLE QAA: OD OZAZMA PLAPLI IADNAMAD.

## Phonetic

MA-dri-ax DES PRAF *[Aire Name]*, CHIS mi-ca-OLZ sa-ah-NIR ca-OS-go, bal-ZI-ras YA-ida: NON-sa go-hu-LIM, MIC-ma ah-do-i-AN MAD, i-ah-OHD bli-ORB, SA-ba oh-oh-AH-oh-na CHIS lu-CIF-ti-as PEH-rip-sol: DES ah-RA-ah-sa NON-saf ne-ta-ah-IB ca-OS-gi, OD TILB AD-phaht DAM-ploz toh-oh-AT NON-saf gmi-cal-ZO-ma LRASD TOF-glo MARB YAR-ri i-do-I-go OD TOR-zulp YA-o-daf. Go-HOL, ca-OS-ga ta-ba-ORD sa-ah-NIR OD CHRIS-te-os yr-po-IL, ti-OBL BUS-dir TILB no-ALN pa-ID ORS-ba OD DO-drem-ni ZYL-na: el-zap-TILB, PARM-gi PE-rip-sax: OD TA QURLST bo-o-AH-pis: la-NIMB OV-cho SYMP OD CHRIS-te-os ag-TOL-torn MIRC, QUO ti-OBL LEL: TON pa-OMBD DILZ-mo AS-pi-an: OD CHRIS-te-os ag-la-TOR-torn pa-RACH A-symp: cord-ZIZ DOD-pal OD fi-FALZ LAS meh-NAD: OD FAR-jit BAMS o-MA-o-as: co-NIS-bra, OD ah-va-VOX TO-nuj: ORS-cat BEL no-AS-mi TAB-ges le-VITH-mong: UN-chi OMP-tilb ORS. ba-GLE? mo-o-o-AH OL cord-ZIZ. la-ca-pi-MA-oh ix-o-MAX-ip, OD CA-co-ca-sab go-SAH-ah: BA-glen pi-I ti-AN-ta a-BA-ba-lond, OD fah-OR-jit te-loc-vo-VIM: MA-dri-yax, TOR-zu, o-AD-ri-ax o-RO-cha, ah-bo-AH-pri: ta-ba-O-ri pri-AZ ar-co-AH-zi-or: OD QUA-sab quo-TINJ: ri-PIR pa-ah-OXT sa-ga-COR. U-mel OD perd-ZAR, CA-carg ah-o-i-VEH-ah-eh CORMPT: tor-ZU, za-CAR, OD ZAM-ran ASPT SIB-si but-MO-na, DES SUR-zas ti-AH BAL-tan: O-doh CIC-leh QUA-ah: OD o-ZAZ-ma PLA-pli i-AD-na-mad/

## English

O you heavens which dwell in the *[Aire Number]* Aire, are mighty in the parts of the Earth, and execute the judgment of the highest: to you it is said, behold the face of your God, the beginning of comfort: whose eyes are the brightness of the heavens: which provided you for the government of the Earth, and her unspeakable variety furnishing you with a power understanding to dispose all things according to the providence of him that sitteth on the holy throne, and rose up in the beginning, saying, the Earth, let her be governed by her parts, and let there be division in her, that the glory of him may be always drunken and vexed in itself: Her course, let it roam with the heavens: and as a handmaid let her serve them: One season let it confound another, and let there be no creature upon or within her, the same: All her members let them differ in their qualities: And let there be no one creature equal with another: The reasonable creatures of the earth and men, let them vex and weed out one another: And the dwelling places let them forget their names: The work of man and his pomp, let them be defaced: his buildings, let them become caves for the beasts of the field: Confound her understanding with darkness. For why? It repenteth me I made man. One while let her be known, and another while a stranger: Because she is the bed of a harlot and the dwelling place of him that is fallen: O you heavens, arise, the lower heavens underneath you, let them serve you: Govern those that govern: Cast down such as fall: Bring forth with those that increase: And destroy the rotten: No place let it remain in one number: Add and diminish until the stars be numbered: Arise, move and appear before the covenant of his mouth, which he hath sworn unto us, in his Justice: Open the Mysteries of your Creation: And make us partakers of undefiled knowledge.

## English (Crowley)

For the Scrying the Aethyrs operations that produced *The Vision and the Voice*, Aleister Crowley used his own re-translation of the Aire Key based on the understanding of it that he claimed to possess as the reincarnation of Edward Kelley. The English of this version goes as follows:

O Ye Heavens which dwell in the *[Aire Number]* Aire, ye are mighty in the parts of the Earth, and execute therein the Judgment of the Highest! Unto you it is said: Behold the Face of your God, the beginning of Comfort, whose eyes are the brightness of the Heavens, which provided you for the Government of the Earth, and her unspeakable variety, furnishing you with the power of understanding to dispose of all things according to the Foresight of Him that Sitteth on the Holy Throne, and rose up in the Beginning, saying: The Earth, let her be governed by her parts, and let there be Division in her, that the glory of her may be always ecstasy and imitation of orgasm. Her course, let it run with the Heavens; and as an handmaid let her serve them. One season, let it confound another, and let there be no creature upon or within her the same. All her members, let them differ in their qualities, and let there be no one Creature equal with another. The reasonable Creatures of the Earth, and Men, let them vex and weed out one another; and their dwelling-places, let them forget their Names. The work of man and his pomp, let them be defaced. His building, let it be a Cave for the Beast of the Field! Confound her understanding with darkness! For why? It repenteth me concerning the Virgin and the Man. One while let her be known, and another while a stranger: because she is the bed of an Harlot, and the dwelling place of him that is fallen.

O ye Heavens arise! The lower heavens beneath you, let them serve you! Govern those that govern! Cast down such as fall. Bring forth with those that increase, and destroy the rotten. No place let it remain in one number. Add an diminish until the stars be numbered. Arise! Move! and appear before the Covenant of His mouth, which He hath sworn unto us in His Justice. Open the Mysteries of your Creation, and make us partakers of THE UNDEFILED KNOWLEDGE.

Crowley also made use of the Golden Dawn pronunciation for the Angelic during his operations, which I will not reproduce here. This version of the Key may be found in several places, including *The Vision and the Voice* itself and *Liber Chanock*, which can be found online.

# 10

# Tuning the Space

"Tuning" is my term for the process of aligning the temple environment with the specific working at hand. The temple opening itself is generic and is not attributed to any one force or characteristic. Likewise, the preliminary invocation serves to identify the magician with the divine in such a way that he or she gains authority over the conjured entities. Even the Angelic Key corresponding to the Aire is still somewhat generic, as each Aire contains multiple Parts of the Earth. Tuning the space to a single force or property will facilitate the manifestation of your objective, whatever that may be.

**Zodiacal Hours:** The traditional grimoire method of tuning the working space according to planetary hours can easily be adapted to signs of the zodiac by incorporating the notion of Sect as described in Chapter 2. Since every astrological sign is also attributed to either the **Diurnal** or **Nocturnal** sect, and planetary hours are grouped into day and night hours, the correspondences are straightforward. The following table, repeated from Chapter 2, shows the twelve signs along with their traditional planetary rulers and sects.

| Sign | Ruler | Day | Sect |
|---|---|---|---|
| Aries | Mars | Tuesday | Diurnal |
| Taurus | Venus | Friday | Nocturnal |
| Gemini | Mercury | Wednesday | Diurnal |
| Cancer | Moon | Monday | Nocturnal |
| Leo | Sun | Sunday | Diurnal |
| Virgo | Mercury | Wednesday | Nocturnal |

| Sign | Ruler | Day | Sect |
|---|---|---|---|
| Libra | Venus | Friday | Diurnal |
| Scorpio | Mars | Tuesday | Nocturnal |
| Sagittarius | Jupiter | Thursday | Diurnal |
| Capricorn | Saturn | Saturday | Nocturnal |
| Aquarius | Saturn | Saturday | Diurnal |
| Pisces | Jupiter | Thursday | Nocturnal |

*Table 23: Signs, Day Rulers, and Sects*

Recall that the Sun and Moon rule one sign each. The Sun rules the day and the diurnal sign Leo, while the Moon rules the night and the nocturnal sign Cancer. Each of the other planets then rules one diurnal and one nocturnal sign, which provides some additional insight into how the rulers were allocated in ancient times and how they relate to the essential nature of the signs.

To determine the length of day and night hours for any day of the year, take the number of minutes from sunrise to sunset and divide by twelve to get the length of each day hour, and then divide the number of minutes from sunset to the following sunrise and divide by twelve to get the length of each night hour. Days begin at sunrise rather than midnight. Then assign the day that rules the planet to the first day hour, and assign each subsequent hour to the next planet in sequence according to the Chaldean Order:

**Saturn → Jupiter → Mars → Sun → Venus → Mercury → Moon**

So on a Sunday, the first hour would be attributed to the Sun, the second to Venus, and so forth.

To obtain the appropriate planetary hours for each sign, allocate Leo to all Sun hours and Cancer to all Moon hours, with day hours preferred for Leo and night hours preferred for Cancer. Then combine the planetary ruler and sect shown above to obtain the others. The hours of Aries are the day hours of Mars, the hours of Taurus are the night hours of Venus, the hours of Gemini are the day hours of Mercury, and so forth.

**Ceremonial Forms:** According to Aleister Crowley's *Liber O vel Manus et Sagittae*, the Greater Ritual of the Hexagram is used to tune the working space for both planets and signs of the zodiac. Some Golden Dawn groups teach that the Greater Ritual of the Pentagram should be used instead, but as both the planets and signs occupy macrocosmic space I believe that the hexagram ritual is more appropriate. As is generally the case, I encourage experimentation, and if you were taught to use the pentagram ritual and have found that it works better for you than the hexagram ritual, by all means keep using it. As I use the hexagram ritual in my own work, that is what I will be covering in this book.

The hexagram that you trace for each of the signs is the hexagram of the sign's ruling planet, derived from the diagram below. You start at the point attributed to the planet and trace clockwise to invoke and counter-clockwise to banish. Once you complete the first triangle, you trace the second from the opposite point in the same direction. As the Sun occupies the center of the figure, its hexagram is an amalgam of the other six, which are traced starting with Saturn and ending with the Moon, following the Chaldean Order.

*Figure 25: Planetary Hexagram*

The color in which the hexagram is traced for each sign can be found in Crowley's *Liber 777*. As the signs are attributed to paths rather than spheres on the Tree of Life, the natural color for a sign is found on the King Scale rather than the Queen Scale. The hexagram traced is that of the sign's planetary ruler as shown on the hexagram above.

These are all shown in the following table:

| Sign | Ruler | Color | Complement |
|---|---|---|---|
| Aries | Mars | Scarlet | Emerald Green |
| Taurus | Venus | Reddish Orange | Greenish Blue |
| Gemini | Mercury | Orange | Blue |
| Cancer | Luna | Amber | Indigo |
| Leo | Sol | Greenish Yellow | Violet |
| Virgo | Mercury | Yellowish Green | Crimson |
| Libra | Venus | Emerald Green | Scarlet |
| Scorpio | Mars | Greenish Blue | Reddish Orange |
| Sagittarius | Jupiter | Blue | Orange |
| Capricorn | Saturn | Indigo | Amber |
| Aquarius | Saturn | Violet | Greenish Yellow |
| Pisces | Jupiter | Crimson | Yellowish Green |

*Table 24: Signs, Rulers, and Colors*

The godnames used for the signs are the permutations or banners of Tetragrammaton These are twelve names constructed from the letters Yod, Heh, Vav, and Heh-final. The original scheme is found in Agrippa and is reproduced in *Liber 777*. It is constructed as follows:

| Sign | Name | Pronunciation |
|---|---|---|
| Aries | YHVH | Yah-WEH |
| Taurus | YHHV | Yah-HOO |
| Gemini | YVHH | Yoo-HEH |
| Cancer | HVHY | Hoo-HEY |
| Leo | HVYH | Hoo-YAH |
| Virgo | HHVY (HHYV) | Heh-VEE (Heh-YOO) |
| Libra | VHYH | Weh-YAH |
| Scorpio | VHHY | Weh-HEY |
| Sagittarius | VYHH | Way-HEH |

| Sign | Name | Pronunciation |
|---|---|---|
| Capricorn | HYHV | Hey-HOO |
| Aquarius | HYVH | Hey-WEH |
| Pisces | HHYV (HHVY) | Heh-YOO (Heh-VEE) |

*Table 25: Banners of Tetragrammaton, Agrippa / Liber 777 (Rectified)*

The pronunciations are approximate, since YHVH has no vowel markers and it is not clear how any of these names are properly pronounced. Still, a couple of basic rules can be applied.

In Hebrew, the last syllable of a word is almost always emphasized. Furthermore, Yod and Vav can serve as both consonants and vowels depending upon what works best for the pronunciation, and V as a consonant can represent both V and W. As usual, I will add that if you have already worked with these names and have pronunciations that give you good results, go with those. I also recommend that if you have trouble maintaining your concentration due to their similarity to English words ("Yahoo," "Heavy," and so forth), you should experiment to find a pronunciation that allows you to focus on the ritual better.

Some practitioners, rather than worrying about pronunciation, spell out the permutations letter by letter. So, for example, YHVH would be vibrated as "YOD HEH VAV HEH," and YHHV would be vibrated as "YOD HEH HEH VAV." Sometimes the Lesser Ritual of the Pentagram is taught with YHVH in the east spelled out in this manner, and to anyone who learned it that way it might seem logical to do it here as well. However, I do not personally recommend this practice—either here or in the Lesser Ritual of the Pentagram. Each of the permutations of Tetragrammaton is a word of power and I fail to see how spelling it out could accomplish anything but weakening its effectiveness.

In *Shem ha-Mephoresh: The Divine Name of Extension*,[16] Aaron Leitch points out that except for two of the names above, the whole set follows a

---

16 Aaron Leitch, *Shem ha-Mephoresh: The Divine Name of Extension* (Retrieved 1-30-2018 from http://www.hermeticgoldendawn.org/leitch-shemhamephoresh.html). Note that at the time I retrieved the article, there was an error in Leitch's list of permutations—he changed the name for Pisces to match the revised schema, but not the one for Virgo.

regular pattern. The names with parentheses after them are the two that do not fit, and the names and pronunciations shown in parentheses reflect the rectified values.

1. Starting with Aries, the first letters of the first three signs start with Yod, the next three with Heh, the next three with Vav, and the last three with Heh.

2. Moving back one sign and starting with Pisces, the second letters of the first three signs start with Heh, the next three with Vav, the next three with Heh, and the last three with Yod.

3. Moving back one more sign and starting with Aquarius, the third letters of the first three signs start with Vav, the next three with Heh, the next three with Yod, and the last three with Heh. In *Liber 777*, this pattern does not hold for Pisces and Virgo which are swapped.

4. Finally, the last letter of each name is the letter of YHVH that has not been used yet.

The names as found in *Liber 777* can easily be rectified by switching the names for Pisces and Virgo (which is how the parenthesized versions are derived) and it strikes me that this could easily represent a copying error that was made centuries ago and perpetuated. As always, I highly recommend experimentation with both versions so that you can find out which one works best for you.

The Greater Ritual of the Hexagram may begin and end with the Keyword Analysis ("I N R I, Yod Nun Resh Yod," etc.) depending upon whether or not your opening forms include the Lesser Ritual of the Hexagram. Since that ritual includes the Keyword Analysis, you need not repeat it again for the Greater ritual. On the other hand, if you opened with the Lesser Ritual of the Pentagram on its own (and thus are working microcosmically) you should include it so that it precedes the tracing of any hexagrams.

The keyword ARARITA is a notariqon or acronym of a Hebrew phrase that may be translated as "One is His Beginning, One is His Individuality, His Permutation is One." In operant field terms, the essential meaning of the word may be thought of as the unity of the microcosm and macrocosm.

This is why it is most appropriate for use with the figure of the hexagram, which represents the macrocosmic realm.

When performing the Greater Ritual of the Hexagram, you vibrate ARARITA while tracing the hexagram in the color associated with the sign. You then trace the symbol of the sign in the center of the hexagram in the color's complement while vibrating the corresponding permutation of Tetragrammaton. You start in the east and move clockwise, tracing the same hexagram to each of the four quarters and then return to face the east.

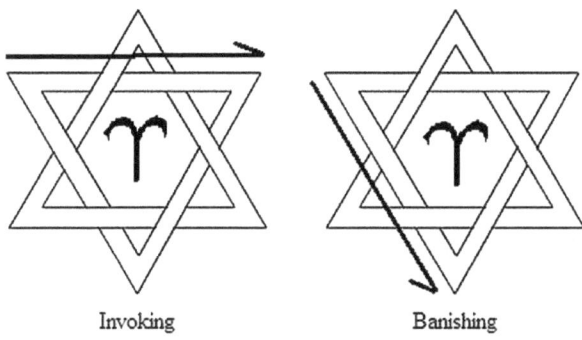

*Figure 26. Aries – Hexagram of Mars in Scarlet with ARARITA, Symbol of Aries in Emerald Green with YHVH (Yah-WEH).*

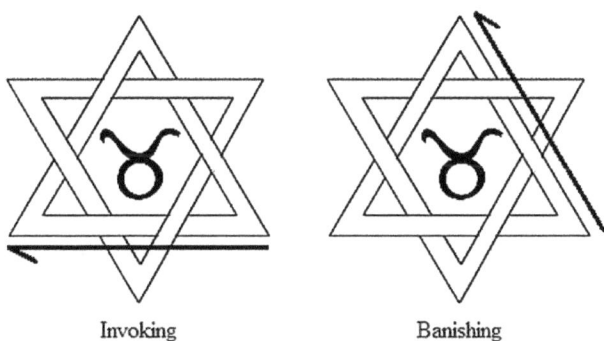

*Figure 27. Taurus – Hexagram of Venus in Reddish Orange with ARARITA, Symbol of Taurus in Greenish Blue with YHHV (Yah-HOO).*

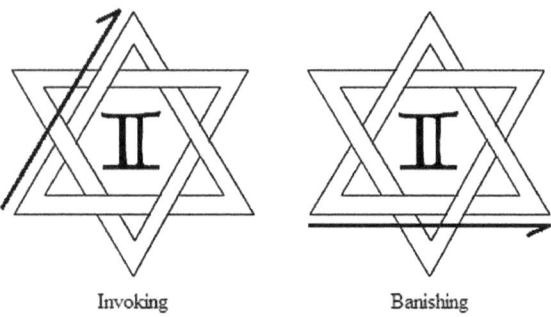

*Figure 28. Gemini – Hexagram of Mercury in Orange with ARARITA, Symbol of Gemini in Blue with YVHH (Yoo-HEH).*

*Figure 29. Cancer – Hexagram of Luna in Amber with ARARITA, Symbol of Cancer in Indigo with HVHY (Hoo-HEY).*

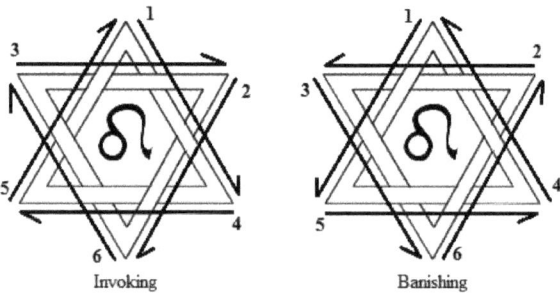

*Figure 30. Leo – Hexagram of Sol in Greenish Yellow with ARARITA, Symbol of Leo in Violet with HVYH (Hoo-YAH).*

*Figure 31. Virgo – Hexagram of Mercury in Yellowish Green with ARARITA, Symbol of Virgo in Crimson with HHVY (Heh-VEE) or HHYV (Heh-YOO).*

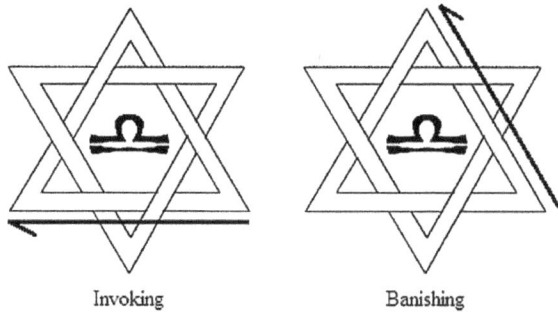

*Figure 32. Libra – Hexagram of Venus in Emerald Green with ARARITA, Symbol of Libra in Scarlet with VHYH (Weh-YAH)*

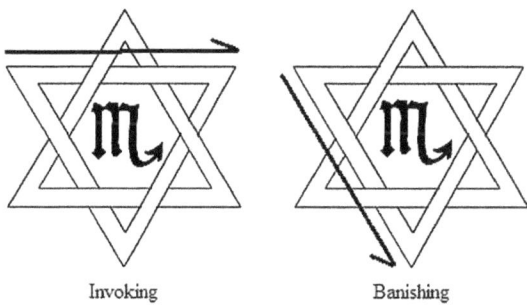

*Figure 33. Scorpio – Hexagram of Mars in Greenish Blue with ARARITA, Symbol of Scorpio in Reddish Orange with VHHY (Weh-HEY).*

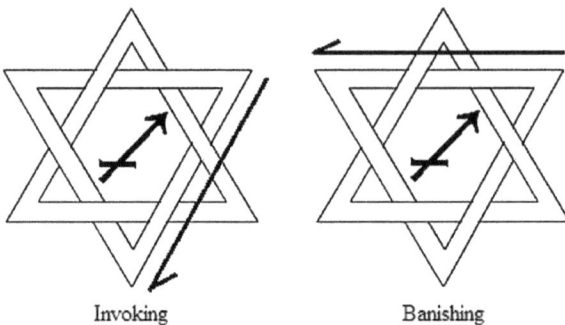

*Figure 34. Sagittarius – Hexagram of Jupiter in Blue with ARARITA, Symbol of Sagittarius in Orange with VYHH (Way-HEH).*

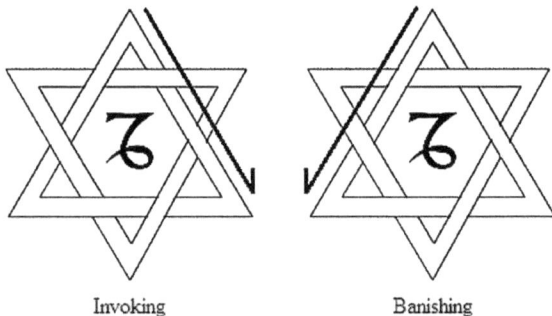

*Figure 35. Capricorn – Hexagram of Saturn in Indigo with ARARITA, Symbol of Capricorn in Amber with HYHV (Hey-HOO).*

For Capricorn, the term Indigo in *Liber 777* refers to purple that is more blue than red. Also, there are several different versions of the Capricorn symbol found in different astrological traditions. Any of them will work, as long as the symbol is firmly linked with the sign in your mind.

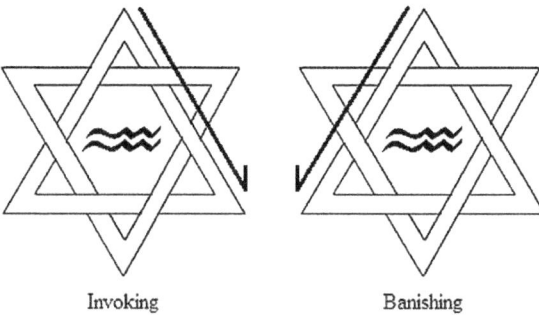

*Figure 36. Aquarius – Hexagram of Saturn in Violet with ARARITA, Symbol of Aquarius in Greenish Yellow with HYVH (Hey-WEH).*

For Aquarius, the term Violet in *Liber 777* refers to purple that is more red than blue.

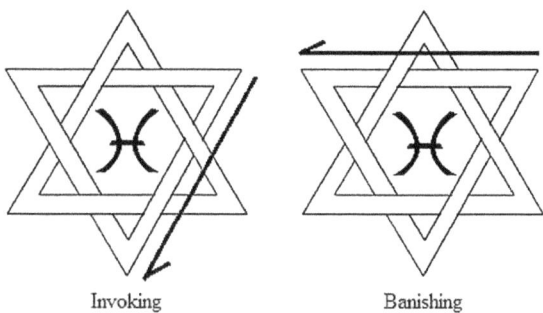

*Figure 37. Pisces – Hexagram of Jupiter in Crimson with ARARITA, Symbol of Pisces in Yellowish Green with HHYV (Heh-YOO) or HHVY (Heh-VEE).*

While I include the banishing hexagrams here as well as those used for invoking, I rarely if ever will banish a sign. I use the invoking forms for tuning the space, and usually close with either the Lesser Banishing Ritual of the Pentagram or Qabalistic Cross on its own, depending upon the type of operation. Some groups teach that you must specifically banish every force you invoke when closing your ritual, but I have found that, if anything, doing so limits the effectiveness of the rite.

**Incense:** Scents may be used to facilitate the tuning of your ritual space. Not only do scents stimulate certain states of consciousness, according to Western esoteric folklore the spirits prefer to manifest in a space filled with elements attuned to their basic natures.

The Dee diaries do not mention the use of any particular incense, but the incenses associated with the signs of the zodiac will work well for this purpose. They are attributed as follows:

| Sign | Incense |
| --- | --- |
| Aries | Dragon's Blood |
| Taurus | Storax |
| Gemini | Wormwood |
| Cancer | Onycha |
| Leo | Olibanum |
| Virgo | Narcissus |
| Libra | Galbanum |
| Scorpio | Siamese Benzoin, Opoponax |
| Sagittarius | Lign-aloes |
| Capricorn | Musk, Civet, Assafoetida, Scrammony, Indigo, Sulphur. |
| Aquarius | Galbanum |
| Pisces | Ambergris |

*Table 26: Incense*

In some cases, substitution may be necessary due to the availability of certain materials. Real ambergris, for example, has not been available since the end of the whaling industry. However, faux-ambergris incense is available from many suppliers and is sufficient for tuning purposes.

The incense should be lit following the preliminary invocation. It may be extinguished following the license to depart, or it may be allowed to burn out on its own. I generally do the latter, as it is easier, and I have found little difference in practice between the two methods.

# 11
# Thirty Aires Conjurations

As far as we know, John Dee never wrote up any conjurations for the Thirty Aires. It is possible that he did, and the text has not survived, or that any magical work he performed employed the *Heptarchia Mystica*, the only portion of the material that he ever assembled into a usable grimoire. Therefore, for work with the Thirty Aires I have written my own simple conjuration which works quite well.

**Thirty Aires Conjuration:** As with the Angelic Key for the Aires, I use a single conjuration for all the Aires and Parts and insert the necessary names as appropriate. As this conjuration is one of mine rather than Dee's, it is short and to the point.

The most important point to keep in mind with these is that in practice, you do not need to directly conjure the zodiacal governor. You open the Aire by the name of the governor, and once you do that the governor is present. That may be one reason that the Golden Dawn adepts never worked out that the name they called "the governor" was the Angelic name of the Part rather than a spiritual entity. The governors are also intelligent enough that even if you address them by the name of the Part, they still understand that you are directing your charge to them.

Note that when Scrying the Aethyrs as described in Chapter 13, no conjuration is employed. However, if you want to scry a Part of the Earth, the conjuration here will open that Part, and what you experience should partake of its nature.

I, *[Your Magical Name]*, a true worshipper of the highest, hereby open *[Part of the Earth]* by the name *[Zodiacal Governor]* and by the power, glory, and majesty of the almighty, living, and true God.

By the name *[Zodiacal Governor]*, open the mysteries of *[Part of the Earth]* unto me, that I may access the manifold powers and properties that reside within its bounds.

By the name *[Zodiacal Governor]*, ruler of *[Part of the Earth]* let this now and here be so. AMEN.

Once you have delivered the conjuration, you then repeatedly vibrate the name of the part until you can sense its presence unfolding before you. Recognizing this takes a little practice, just like sensing the arrival of Enochian entities, but it usually occurs within a minute or so, often less.

**Thirty Aires Talismans:** A single talisman is used for each Aire rather than each part, for a total of thirty Aire talismans. The first twenty-nine are attributed to three parts each, and the thirtieth is attributed to four.

Each Part of the Earth has a direction associated with it, as shown in Chapter 4. This is the direction that you should face when delivering the conjuration and you should deliver it across the Holy Table. So, for example, if you are opening a part attributed to the south you would stand to the north of the altar facing south. The talisman should be placed on the floor to the north of the Holy Table so that you can stand upon it as you conjure the Zodiacal Governor and open the part.

The designs that I use for these talismans, based on those created by Geoffrey James, are shown here. They are constructed using the 1587 *Tabula Recensa* names as they are the talisman designs that I use in my own work, but versions using the spellings from *Liber Scientia* should be easy enough to construct. In many cases they will be the same, and if they differ, the only thing that needs to be changed is the spelling of the name or names on the outer ring.

*Figure 38. TEX (30) Talisman*

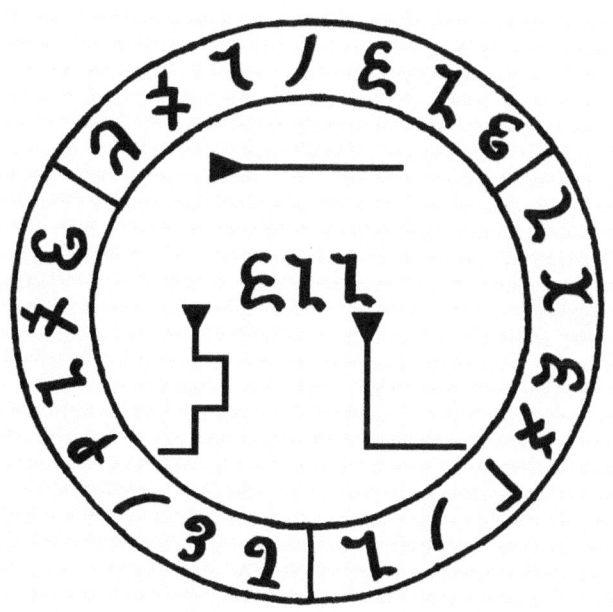

*Figure 39. RII (29) Talisman*

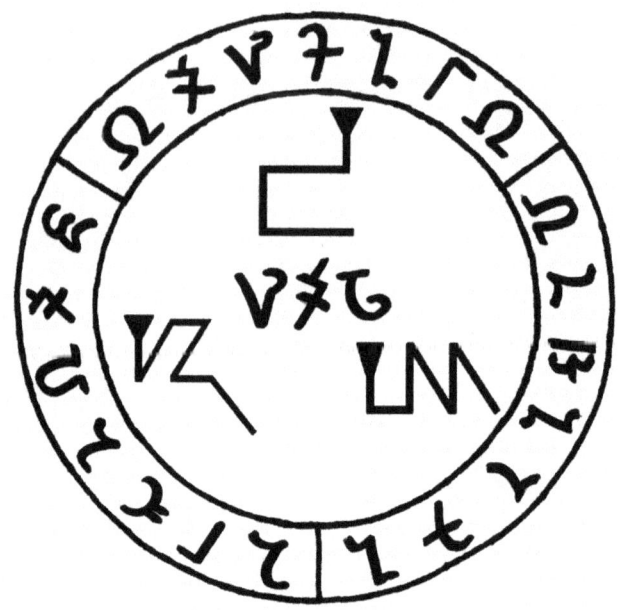

*Figure 40. BAG (28) Talisman*

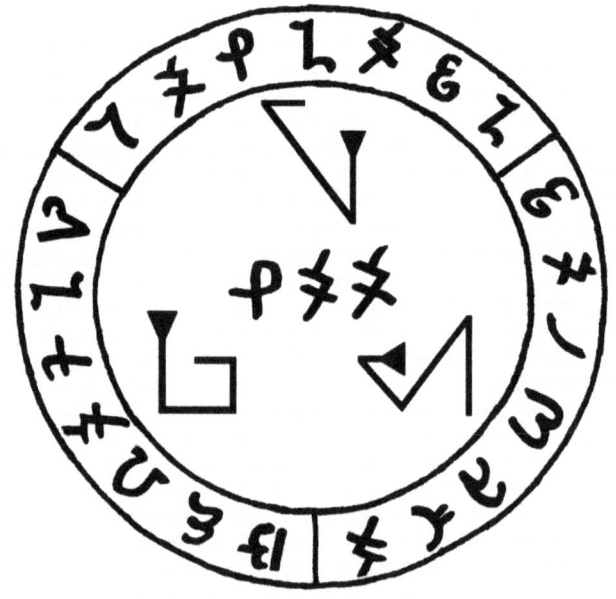

*Figure 41. ZAA (27) Talisman*

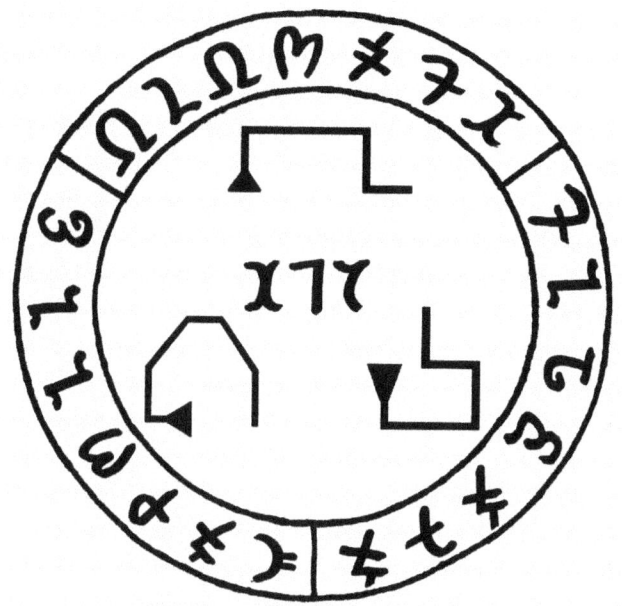

*Figure 42. DES (26) Talisman*

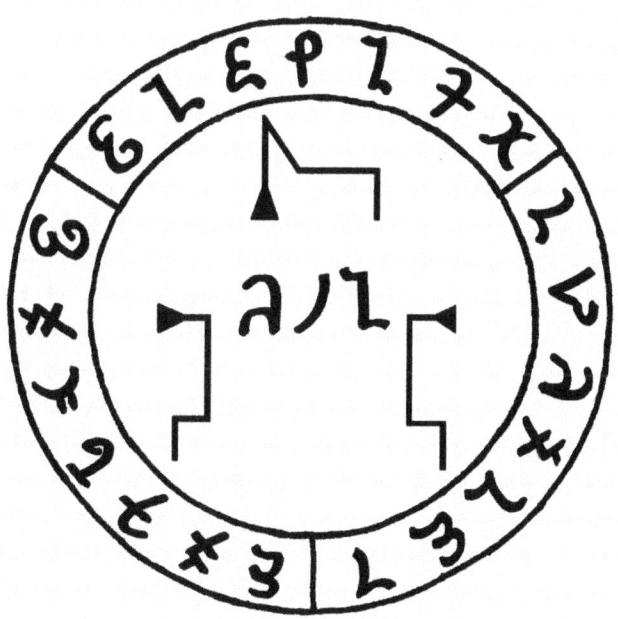

*Figure 43. VTI (25) Talisman*

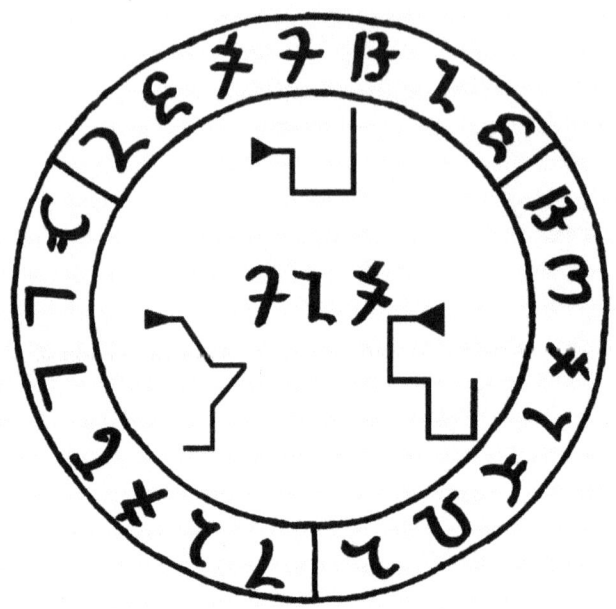

*Figure 44. NIA (24) Talisman*

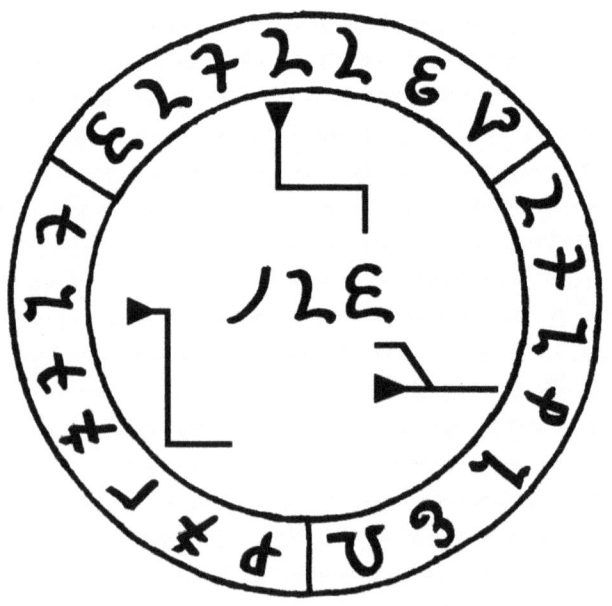

*Figure 45. TOR(23) Talisman*

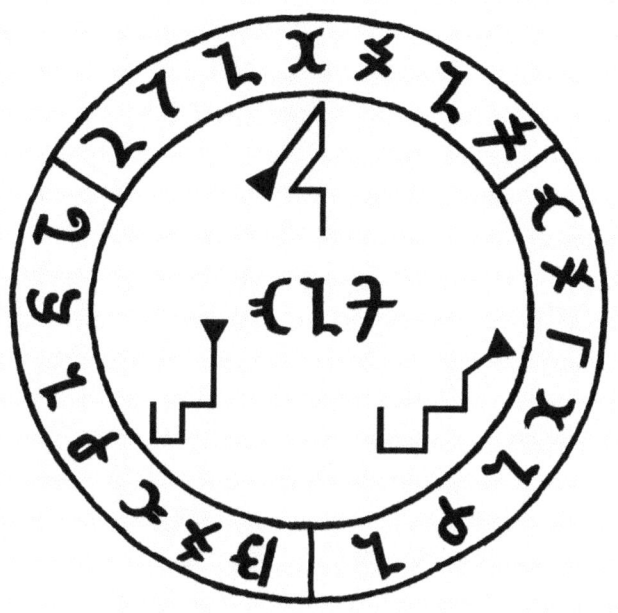

*Figure 46A. LIN (22) Talisman (Laxdizi)*

*Figure 46B. LIN (22) Talisman (Paoaoan)*

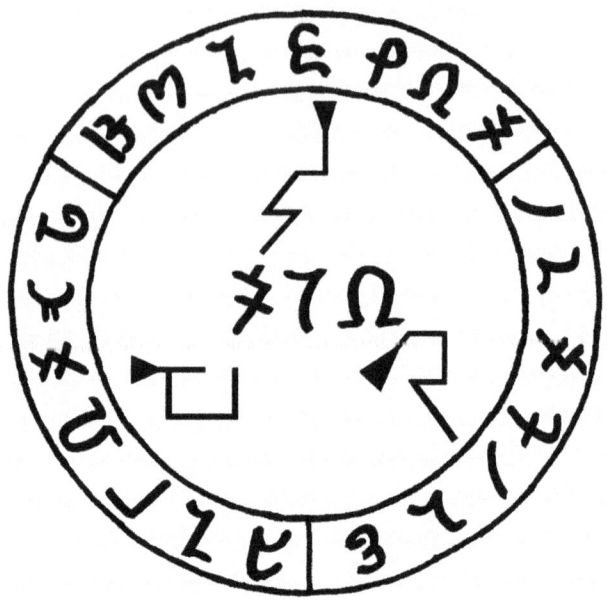

*Figure 47. ASP (21) Talisman*

*Figure 48. CHR (20) Talisman*

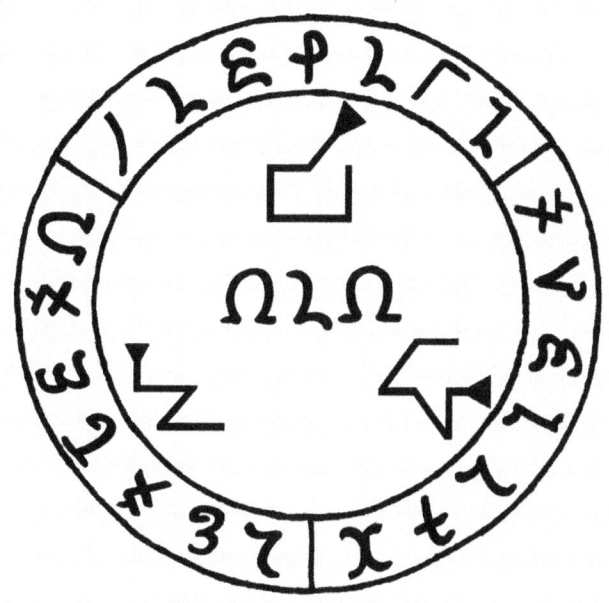

*Figure 49. POP (19) Talisman*

*Figure 50. ZEN (18) Talisman*

*Figure 51. TAN (17) Talisman*

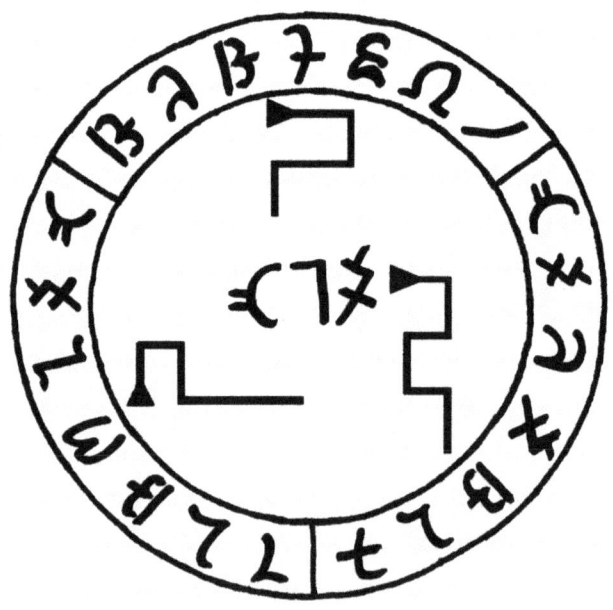

*Figure 52. LEA (16) Talisman*

*Figure 53. OXO (15) Talisman*

*Figure 54. VTA (14) Talisman*

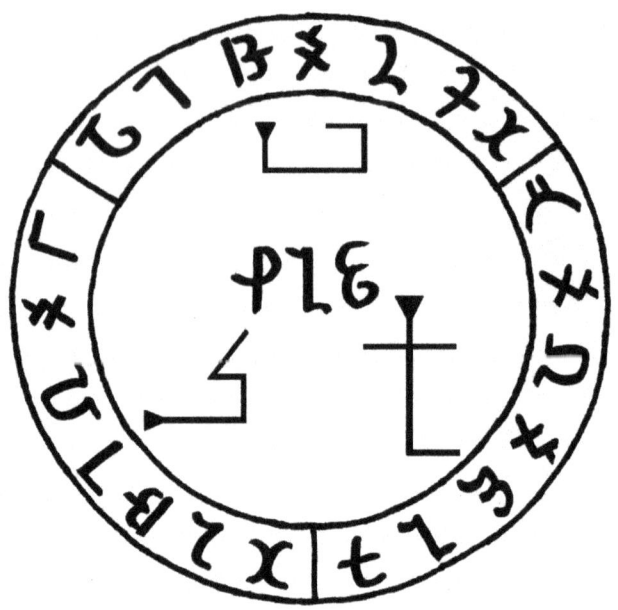

*Figure 55. ZIM (13) Talisman*

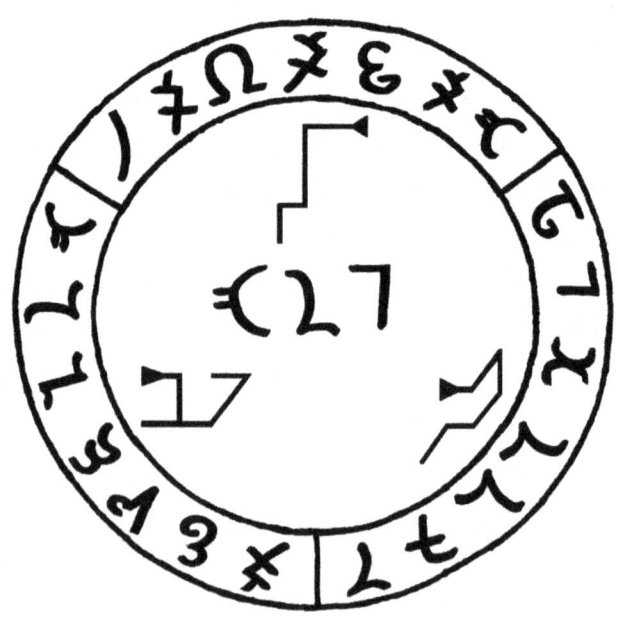

*Figure 56. LOE (12) Talisman*

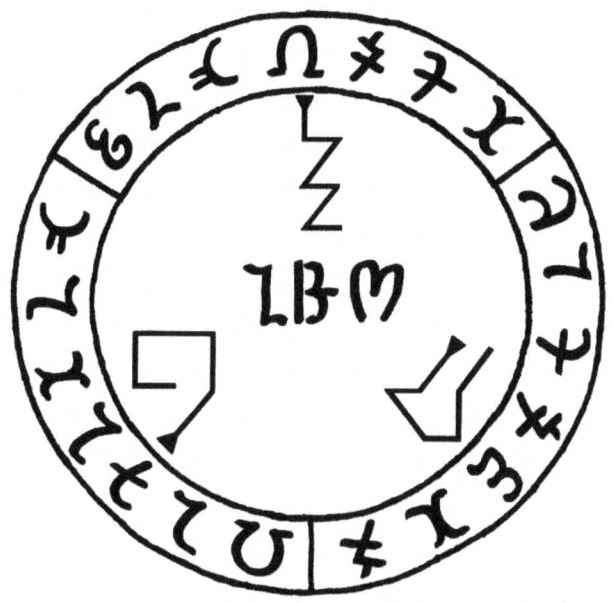

*Figure 57. ICH (11) Talisman*

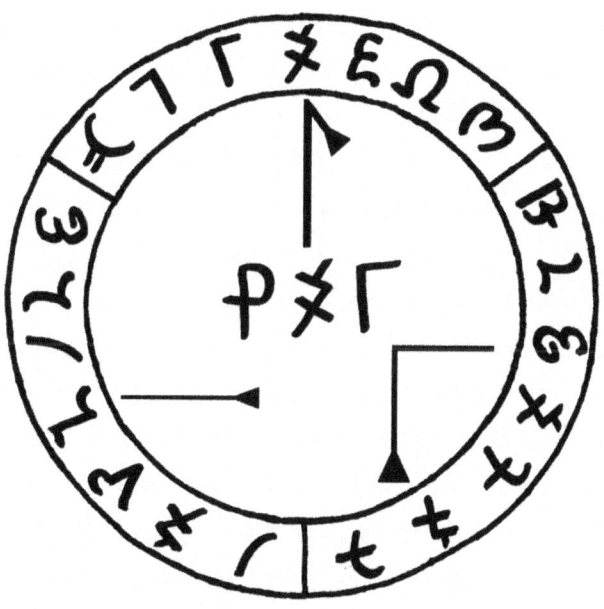

*Figure 58. ZAX (10) Talisman*

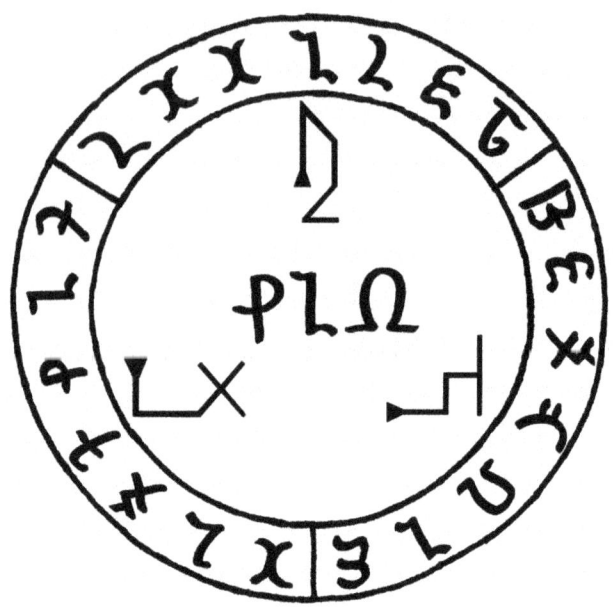

*Figure 59. ZIP (9) Talisman*

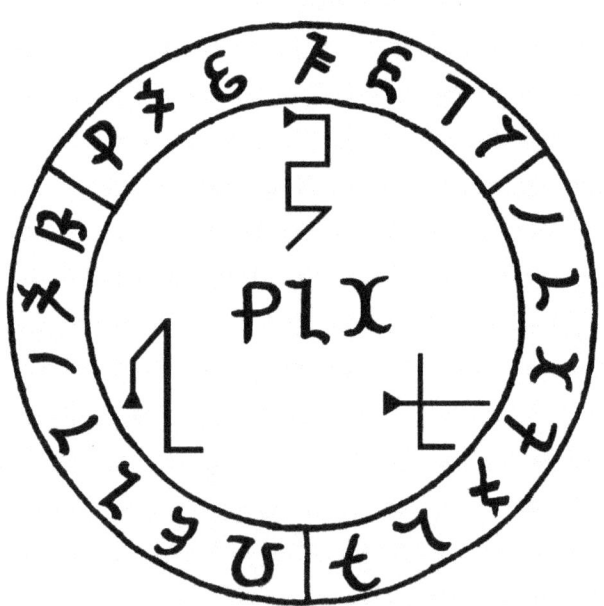

*Figure 60. ZID (8) Talisman*

*Figure 61. DEO (7) Talisman*

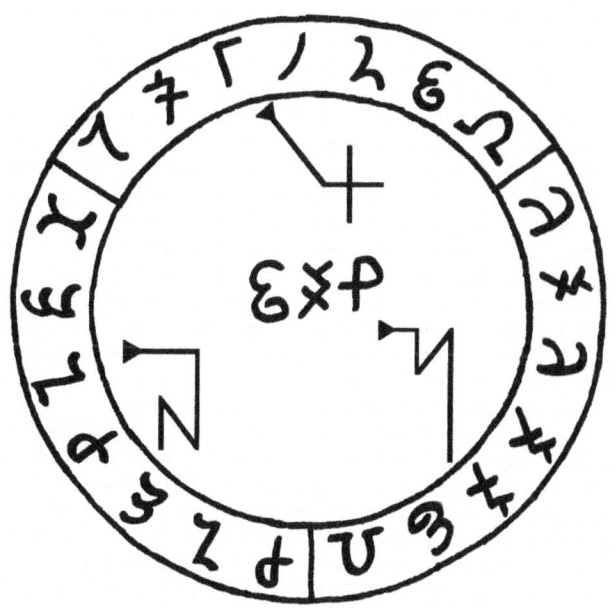

*Figure 62. MAZ (6) Talisman*

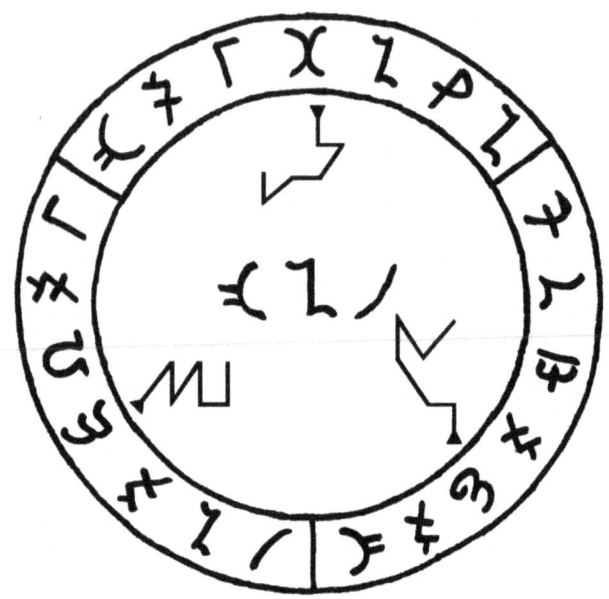

*Figure 63. LIT (5) Talisman*

*Figure 64. PAZ (4) Talisman*

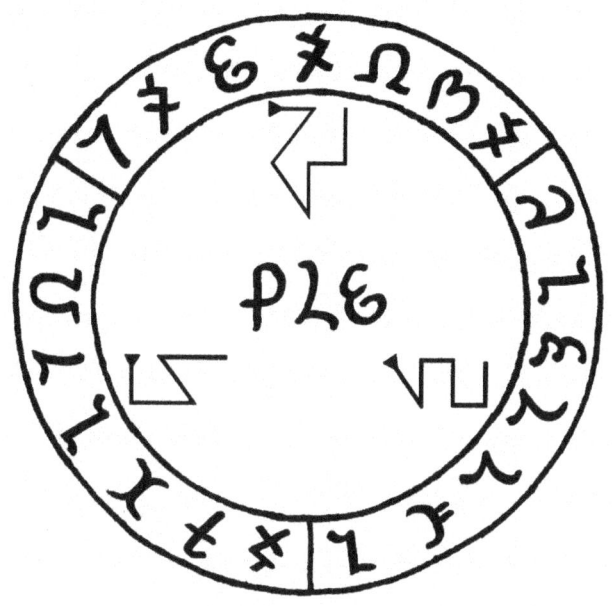

*Figure 65. ZOM (3) Talisman*

*Figure 66. ARN (2) Talisman*

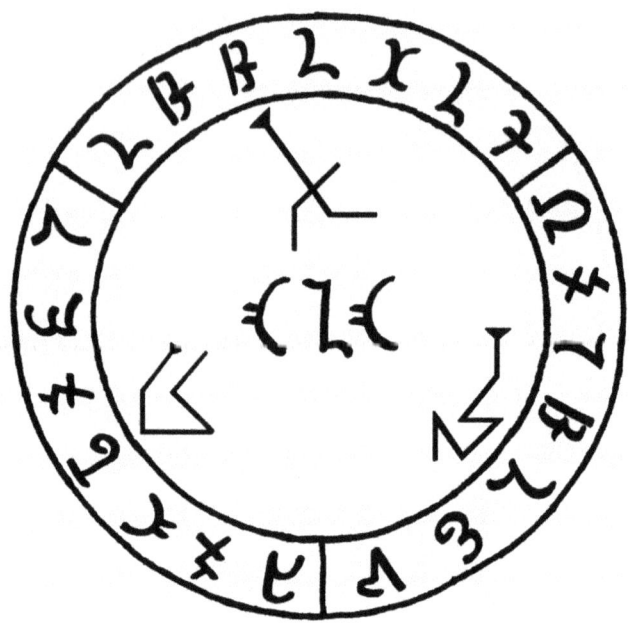

*Figure 67. LIL (1) Talisman*

# 12
# The Charge

LIKE THE HEPTARCHIAL AND WATCHTOWER KINGS, the zodiacal Governors are powerful and highly intelligent entities. As such, they may be called upon to perform a wide variety of actions, and generally can be trusted to inform you if you are asking them to perform a task that lies outside their sphere of influence. In such cases, I have had little difficulty obtaining from them the name of the proper entity to call upon. In the original system, their specific function was to facilitate political changes of whatever sort the operator desired, but they also can be called upon to perform practical tasks associated with the nature of the sign to which they are attributed.

**Political Operations:** Political magick often gets short shrift from modern magical practitioners. Spells abound for wealth, love, and revenge, but anything related to political issues seems to be for the most part ignored. As the original system of the Thirty Aires and Parts of the Earth was intended to affect political change, an overview of this sort of work is appropriate in the context of the sort of charges issued to the entities that inhabit them.

Political issues can have a great deal of influence over our material lives, much more so than people often like to admit. Such issues fall well within the scope of magick done with the intent of directly influencing our material and mundane lives, just as our personal wealth and relationships do. In the case of John Dee, he hoped to create what was just a pipe dream during his lifetime, but which later would become a major player in the history of the Western world—a British Empire.

In some respects, during the Renaissance it was a far easier prospect to influence the government of nations than it is today. To influence a country ruled by a single monarch, all that was necessary was to influence the thoughts of a single individual and perhaps a small cadre of advisors. Modern democratic governments are far more complex, but at the same time I have found them to still be susceptible to the entities of the Thirty Aires—at least up to a point.

One of the most straightforward ways to influence a modern government is to use the entities of the Thirty Aires to influence elections. This is quite possible, since the electorate taken as a whole is a highly chaotic system ripe for magical influence. As I mentioned in the previous books in this series, it's not unreasonable to expect a skilled and experienced magician to be able to produce a 100 to 1 probability shift, and a system with many feedback loops and degrees of freedom can amplify this effect much further.

If you look at the relative numbers posted on election analysis websites such as fivethirtyeight.com, you can see that if you run a large series of election simulations, the result is that even unlikely candidates usually have at least a one percent chance of winning. In that context, it seems reasonable to think that a magician might very well be able to pick and choose his or her candidates and get to work. The probabilities involved are well within range.

However, there are a couple of caveats related to that assertion. For all magicians rarely discuss political magick, I happen to know from personal experience that there are a number of them out there besides myself who routinely perform them. So, in order to succeed, the entities you summon will need to mediate the effects of other spell-casters in addition to the adjusting the dynamics of the electorate. Depending on whom you happen to be casting against, this could be more or less difficult.

It should be noted that you are not usually casting against "public opinion" in general. Just supporting and believing in a candidate is not a magical operation, and generally speaking it does not produce a probability shift on its own. However, even though statistically speaking there are not many spell-casters out there, there are enough to make it difficult for any one particular magician's objective to manifest. The strongest group of casters usually "wins," so to speak, regardless of the nature of their objective.

The second caveat is that for magick to work most effectively, personal coherence must be maintained. This precludes several possible strategic approaches to influencing elections. If you cast a spell for a candidate, but then turn around and vote for someone else, you will undermine your ritual. All of the mundane steps you take should be in the direction of the magical outcome you seek, rather than moving against it.

This is also true if you have no intention of actually voting. I will freely admit that this strikes me as a pretty bizarre mindset—that you would go through all the time and energy to cast a spell, but then not bother with something as simple as a vote—but perhaps because many magicians are contrarians at heart, it is more common than you might think.

I am strongly of the opinion that Americans should always vote, and that giving up and doing nothing is not a particularly magical approach to dealing with the political system. This does not mean that you should vote for "the lesser of two evils" over and over, as I think you should always vote for the candidate you want, whether or not he or she is a member of one of the two major political parties.

Personally, I always vote, but I vote third party a lot—and I will also point out to anyone who will listen that if a substantial percentage of the people who do not currently vote because they dislike the two-party system would go to the polls and vote for a third party, that third party would become viable pretty quickly. Maybe the parties would consolidate back into two major factions after that, but I find it hard to believe that when two parties merge, either one entirely dominates the other in the resulting coalition.

Also, in relation to the coherence idea, this method works far better when applied to a candidate that you actively support, rather than one you consider "the lesser of two evils." From personal experience, every failure I have encountered with the methods here has come when I was primarily trying to cast *against* a candidate I disliked, rather than *for* one that I found personally inspiring. It is difficult to sufficiently "enflame yourself in prayer" on behalf of someone for whom your support is only lukewarm.

The third and final caveat is that influencing elections alone is usually not enough. The political system itself tends to have a corrupting, or at the very least a discouraging, effect upon those who wind up winning elections, and while I think it is silly to claim the two major political parties in the United States are the same, it is also true that there are some serious issues out there that neither of them wants to do much about. With the way our system is currently set up, money equals speech—or, to put it another way, money is what talks.

Therefore, the would-be political magician does not only face the challenge of electing candidates who share his or her values, but also those who will stick to their beliefs in the face of constant lobbying and propaganda produced by the wealthiest corporations and individuals specifically designed to maintain their social and economic status, if necessary, at the expense of everyone else. Elections are a start and should not be neglected, but if you want to effect real change you need to work at the level of individual policies, proposals, and laws.

This latter approach, when combined with the former, is far more effective in practical terms, but it also is far more difficult to manage. Before a proposal can become a law, it has to pass through various stages, any of which could derail it. It has to be discussed and amended at the committee level, and it usually has to match the agenda of the majority party to come up for a vote at all—in both houses of congress. And even if a bill survives all that, it is still subject to veto by the President and possible constitutional review by the Supreme Court.

As I am American and most of my magical work in this area has involved the American political system, I cannot say for sure how much of this is applicable to parliamentary systems such as those found in Europe and member states of the British Commonwealth. I imagine that it might be easier in some sense, as parties publish their agendas and are looking to gain a certain overall percentage of the vote in order to govern or become part of a governing coalition. But I freely admit that opinion could be the result of naivety on my part or at the very least unfamiliarity with the intricacies of such systems.

In practical terms, national political issues are ruled by the Governor (that is, the Angelic King in Golden Dawn parlance) of the Part of the Earth in which the capital city of the nation in question is located. Otherwise, regional issues and/or elections are ruled by the Governor of the Part to which they correspond. This is less of an issue in the New World than the Old, as the majority of parts are defined according to the work of Roman geographer Claudius Ptolemy. As a result, there are far more parts within the bounds of the old Roman Empire than anywhere else.

The Kings and Seniors, as described in *Mastering the Great Table*, can also be effective in the context of this sort of work. The Seniors are attributed to "knowledge and judgment in human affairs," and while no specific attributions are given for the Kings, they partake of a similar nature and are quite powerful entities. You can call upon the Governor to open the Part, and then conjure the Kings and/or Seniors into the table and deliver the rest of your charge to them. In effect, this uses the system of Parts primarily for targeting the operation, while the Kings and/or Seniors do the rest of the work.

This is often an area in which you will find yourself casting against fewer other magicians, simply because the effort involved in keeping up on individual proposals and issues is non-trivial. Just as with lottery spells when jackpots climb into the hundreds of millions, more magicians tend to perform operations around big elections, such as the American presidential race. Few of them will put together a spell to make sure that, say, proposal two, subsection three, tenet one will make it out of committee and onto the floor, or be appended to some major piece of "must pass" legislation. Depending upon how esoteric your issue is, you might be the only one. Incidentally, this is also the case with low-profile elections such as municipal offices—but in some cases, having the right person in one of those positions can make a real difference.

When formulating a political charge, you should always first remember the basics: the **Injunction** is what you want the conjured entities to do, and the **Limitation** is what you don't want them to do. The political system is abstract enough that usually you will not be facing any sort of personal calamity if you fail to specify that no injury or damage comes to you or your property. But sometimes a particular proposal can pass in a way that has undesirable consequences, such as being used to "sweeten" a larger bill that has far more sinister implications. Your limitation should take into account any such eventualities that seem reasonably likely.

**Practical Operations:** From the title of this section I am not meaning to imply that political operations are not practical ones. They most certainly are, as they represent an attempt to influence events in the material world in ways that can be quite profound. However, they are different and abstract enough that they merit their own section. My use of "practical" here alludes to the traditional powers of the signs of the zodiac, as outlined in *Liber 777*.

These powers are defined as shown here:

| Sign | Power |
| --- | --- |
| Aries | Power of Consecrating Things |
| Taurus | The Secret of Physical Strength |
| Gemini | Power of being in two or more places at the same time, and of Prophecy |
| Cancer | Power of Casting Enchantments |
| Leo | Power of Training Wild Beasts |
| Virgo | Invisibility, Parthenogenesis, Initiation |
| Libra | Works of Justice and Equilibrium |
| Scorpio | Necromancy |
| Sagittarius | Transmutations, Vision of Universal Peacock (Alchemical) |
| Capricorn | The Witches' Sabbath so-called, the Evil Eye |
| Aquarius | Astrology |
| Pisces | Bewitchments, Casting Illusions |

*Table 27: Traditional Zodiacal Powers*

This list provides a wide variety of powers available to the zodiacal governors of the Aires. Not all of them are entirely literal, as is the case with the powers attributed to spirits in general. No matter how impressive a power may seem, whenever magick comes up against the physical world, probability shifts need to be taken into account.

Invisibility, attributed to Virgo, is a classic example. It is quite possible—and not even that difficult—to use this power to walk through a crowd of people without being noticed. As this is essentially a mind-to-mind effect, physical considerations do not even enter the picture. However, rendering yourself invisible to a security camera is an entirely different matter. The probability shifts required to bend light around your body or not leave magnetic traces on a tape are staggeringly high.

Personal operations such as this require some care in defining your Injunctions and Limitations. Using the invisibility example again, say that you want to create a talisman that will prevent police from noticing your car so that you will not get speeding tickets. This is a completely reasonable use of this power, but you should not just instruct the governor to make your car invisible. It could very well work; an invisibility spell on your car will make the police are far less likely to take notice of it.

However, you would want to set a limitation that the invisibility should only apply to police officers and not to other drivers, since otherwise your car will not be noticed in general and you could quickly find yourself in an accident. You also would probably want to clarify it to only apply to on-duty police officers who might ticket you, because otherwise an officer on his or her way home might not see you. Getting into an accident with a police officer, on duty or not, rarely works out well for any driver.

**Mystical Operations:** In addition to Aleister Crowley's mystical operation of Scrying the Aethyrs, detailed in the next chapter, *Liber 777* attributes all twelve signs of the zodiac to the Qabalistic sphere of Chockmah or Wisdom, sphere 2. The mystical vision associated with this sphere is "The Vision of God Face-to-Face." According to Thelemic cosmology, it is at Chockmah where the unity of God in Kether (the Crown, sphere 1) divides into the various "currents" that partake of the nature of particular signs.

Thelemic Aeonics includes the concept of the progression of the Earth's axis and treats the sign in which this axis falls during a particular period as the dominant sign for that epoch. The Earth's axis takes about two thousand years to navigate through a sign. According to Crowley's interpretation, as the Earth's axis was in Pisces beginning in the centuries leading up to the Christian era, Christianity partakes of the Piscean nature. This nature emphasizes the attainment of virtue through sacrifice, and this concept can also be found in other religious systems that developed during the same era such as Islam and Mahayana Buddhism.

The Thelemic current, which Crowley claims began in 1904 with the reception of *The Book of the Law*, partakes of the Aquarian nature, which emphasizes the sovereignty of the individual. Therefore, instead of a formula based on sacrifice, its formula is based on the nature process of life and growth that is inherent to the fundamental nature of all living things. In spiritual terms, instead of a progression in which the self must catastrophically "die" from the perspective of its current state of consciousness to be "reborn" in a new and more developed form, the Thelemic formula instead emphasizes gradual growth of the self from its current state into the next following the natural path of expansion and maturation.

To invoke a state of consciousness corresponding to one of the twelve zodiacal currents, you would use the godname JAH rather than the permutation of Tetragrammaton in the Greater Ritual of the Hexagram and trace both the hexagram and symbol of the sign in gray. This is the only case in which the hexagram and symbol are traced in the same color, as gray, the Queen Scale and therefore the natural color of Chockmah, is its own complement. The hexagram itself should still correspond to the planetary ruler of the sign that you are invoking. Also, such an operation should be opened using the Second Key rather than the First, as mystical visions of this kind are fundamentally invocatory in nature.

# 13
# Scrying the Aethyrs

"SCRYING THE AETHYRS" is the colloquial term for a mystical practice pioneered by Aleister Crowley. Unlike most of the other techniques I cover in this series, it is a purely neo-Enochian practice that has no foundation in the Dee diaries. However, it is quite popular among my fellow Thelemites, and Crowley's *The Vision and the Voice*, in which he recorded his experiences, seems to me to represent legitimate contact with the entities of the Enochian system. "Aethyr" is the term generally used by neo-Enochian magicians when referring to the Thirty Aires.

Crowley's method does not precisely line up with "scrying" as it is usually performed when working grimoire-style magick. Instead, it more closely resembles the Golden Dawn practice of "Scrying in the Spirit Vision," in which rather than gazing into a mirror or crystal, the magician attempts to perceive conjured entities employing only his or her magical imagination. Crowley did employ a topaz crystal in his operations, but rather than gazing into it he closed his eyes and pressed it to his forehead.

A few words here are necessary regarding the nature of the magical imagination. It is important to understand that the term "magical imagination" should not imply that any experience involving this faculty is "made up" or "imaginary" in the conventional sense. With inexperienced magicians this can be the case, which is why spirits encountered in this manner should be tested. But as your experiences grow and you become more skilled in your practices, you should find a distinction between the magical and conventional imaginary faculties.

Entities encountered via the magical imagination may be tested in the same manner as entities conjured during grimoire operations. They may be asked for a number that will later be checked against some sort of gematric value reference such as *Sephir Sephiroth*, included in the Weiser edition of *Liber 777*[17], or *Godwin's Cabalistic Encyclopedia*[18]. This is one of the simplest testing methods. Crowley also details a slightly more involved gematric technique that he personally employed during his Aethyr operations.

Early in the series, Crowley encountered an entity from which he demanded the Word of the Aeon, which he considered to be "Abrahadabra." The entity answered with the word "Makashanah," so he at first assumed that the entity must be false in some fashion. But later, when analyzing his account, he made a crucial realization. When transliterated into Hebrew, ABRAHADABRA sums to 418 thus:

A = 1
B = 2
R = 200
A = 1
H = 5
A = 1
D = 4
A = 1
B = 2
R = 200
A = 1

He found that likewise, MAKAShANH sums to the same value thus:

M = 40
A = 1
K = 20
A = 1
Sh = 300
A = 1
N = 50
H = 5

---

17  Aleister Crowley, *777 and Other Qabalistic Writings of Aleister Crowley* (York Beach ME: Weiser Books, 1986).
18  David Godwin, *Godwin's Cabalistic Encyclopedia* (St. Paul MN: Llewellyn, 1989).

Therefore, in a sense the entity had communicated the word to Crowley in a much more convincing fashion than if it had simply replied with a word that was known to him and which could easily have been a product of his own thoughts.

The Aethyrs should be scried from the bottom up, starting with TEX, and not from the top down. This is Crowley's order and in the context of the Dee diaries it makes the most sense when working in a series. As far as I know Benjamin Rowe is the only published Enochian author who advocates a top-down approach, and even he admits that he does so because the system of the Tree of Life he learned was the inverted form developed by Frater Achad. Crowley thought very little of Achad's "reformed tree" and few modern groups teach it. Rowe just happened to study with one of them.

According to what Crowley experienced in *The Vision and the Voice*, the Thirty Aires cover the same mystical "territory" as the Tree of Life, but the Aires and spheres do not line up exactly. Crowley described the relationship as one in which the Aire that you are scrying and every Aire beneath it acts as Malkuth (the Kingdom, sphere 10) to the rest of a Tree represented by the Aires above. Therefore, scyring LIL places "Kether in Malkuth" and represents the culmination of magical realization.

The other point where the Tree of Life and the Aires line up is in the Tenth Aire, ZAX, which Crowley attributes to the Abyss between Chesed (Mercy, sphere 4) and Binah (Understanding, sphere 3). According to his account, it was in this Aire that he encountered Choronzon, a malevolent entity embodying the principle of dispersion and confusion. In the diaries, Dee spells the name "Coronzon," and the angels refer to the name as that of "that mighty devil." Crowley developed the concept considerably further, identifying Choronzon with the dispersing properties of the Abyss itself.

Crowley's technique was extremely simple. After an opening procedure, for which I would personally use the LBRP/LIRH operant field, he recited the Angelic Key for the Aire, pressed his crystal to his forehead, and began to scry. As he experienced the Aire, he relayed his experiences to his associate Victor Neuburg, who acted as scribe. In only one case was the procedure made more elaborate—the scrying of the 10<sup>th</sup> Aire.

For that operation, Crowley had Neuburg sit within a properly made circle and swear an oath that he would not leave it under any circumstances. This proved fortuitous, as during the scrying of ZAX Crowley was possessed by Choronzon and charged at Neuburg. The scribe was able to ward him off by threatening to impose upon him some sort of curse from the grimoires—which, as it turned out, Neuburg did not even know from memory. Over a century later it is difficult to say how much of that whole drama was prompted by the seriousness of the initial preparations. But at the same time, modern grimoire magicians have noted that spirit possession is a real phenomenon for which Crowley's Golden Dawn training likely would not have prepared him.

None of this necessarily implies that if you scry the 10$^{th}$ Aire, you will be possessed by Choronzon as Crowley was. In fact, your experiences may not line up with his at all. Most of the time there seems to be at least some passing similarities between Crowley's accounts and those of other magicians, but the context can be radically different. As I keep recommending to my readers, never stop experimenting. You may not get good results with one technique, but from the standpoint of self-knowledge, failure can still provide you with valuable insights.

There is one more point with respect to Crowley's workings that I need to address. It's completely ridiculous, but I keep running into people online who apparently believe it. As I touched on in *Mastering the Great Table*, Donald Tyson has proposed the concept of an "Enochian Apocalypse" directly tied to Crowley's Scrying the Aethyrs.[19] Tyson starts by pointing out similarities between the imagery found in the Angelic Keys and certain passages from the Book of Revelation—all of which he describes accurately, as he is generally a competent researcher. But from there, he takes his argument in an utterly bizarre direction, asserting that working the Enochian system will basically lead to the end of the world as we know it.

> In my opinion the apocalypse prepared by the Enochian angels must be primarily an internal, spiritual event, and only in a secondary way an external, physical catastrophe. The gates of the Watchtowers that

---

19 Donald Tyson, *The Enochian Apocalpyse* (Gnosis Magazine: Summer 1996), retrieved Feb 2016 from http://www.bibliotecapleyades.net/bb/bluebook418.htm.

stand guard at the four corners of our dimension of reality are mental constructions. When they are opened, they will admit the demons of Coronzon not into the physical world, but into our subconscious minds.

Tyson's argument rests upon the idea that "an apocalypse" fundamentally refers to some sort of catastrophe. But that's not what the word originally meant. "Apocalypse" is a synonym for "revelation," which is why the final book of the New Testament is named as it is. If the latter definition were what Tyson was talking about, that working with the Enochian system has the potential to lead the individual magician to a revelation—that is, a greater level of mystical realization—I would basically agree with him. I believe that this is in fact the point of the undeniably apocalyptic language of the Keys. Unfortunately, he keeps going.

Spirits are mental, not material. They dwell in the depths of mind and communicate with us through our dreams, unconscious impulses, and more rarely in waking visions. They affect our feelings and our thoughts beneath the level of our conscious awareness. Sometimes they are able to control our actions, either partially, as in the case of irrational and obsessive behavior patterns, or completely, as in the case of full possession. Through us, and only through us, are they able to influence physical things.

This is incorrect in my experience. Spirits do not have much of a physical presence, but they do seem to be able to affect the probability of outcomes in situations where no human agency is present—for example, causing particular lottery numbers to come up in drawings. But as the next few paragraphs reveal, this small misunderstanding is the least of Tyson's problems.

The Enochian communications teach not only that humanity itself must initiate the apocalypse through the magical formula delivered to Dee and Kelley, but that humans must be the physical agents that bring about the plagues, wars, and famines described with such chilling eloquence in the vision of St. John. It is we who will let the demons of Coronzon into our minds by means of a specific ritual working. They will not find a welcome place there all at once, but will worm their way into our subconscious and make their homes there slowly over time. In the minds of individuals that resist this invasion they will find it difficult to gain a foothold, but in the more pliable minds of those who welcome their influence they will establish themselves readily.

This statement rests on the assumption that the vision of St. John describes a specific series of physical events. But there are a lot of ways to interpret that text. You could just as easily make the case that it describes a specific, individual magical working in allegorical terms. The literal interpretation of the apocalypse put forth by modern evangelicals did not even exist in Dee's time—that comes from Millerism, which only dates to the early nineteenth century. Miller's methods have been taken up by some modern evangelists but have produced little more than a long series of failed apocalypse predictions.

Once the demons have taken up residence, we will be powerless to prevent them from turning our thoughts and actions toward chaotic and destructive ends. These apocalyptic spirits will set person against person and nation against nation, gradually increasing the madness and chaos in human society until at last the full horror of Revelation has been realized upon the stage of the world. The corruption of human thoughts and feelings may require generations to bring to full fruition. Only after the wasting and burning of souls is well advanced will the full horror of the apocalypse achieve its final fulfillment in the material realm.

Here is where Tyson undeniably reveals that he has no idea how magick actually works. If we grant that (1) spirits are primarily mental, and (2) that "opening the gates" of the Enochian universe admits harmful spirits into my mind, it does not follow that (3) said spirits have now been admitted into *everyone's* mind. By Tyson's logic I might be able to render myself insane, even though as I have noted throughout this series, stories of Enochian entities inducing insanity are wildly exaggerated. Nonetheless, aside from any actions I might personally take when in that state, how would said harmful spirits affect anyone else?

Let us suppose for the sake of argument that the signal for the initiation of this psychic invasion occurred in 1904 when Crowley received the Book of the Law, as he himself believed. Crowley's Enochian evocations of 1909 then pried the doors of the Watchtowers open a crack enough to allow a foul wind to blow through the common mind of the human race. This would explain the senseless slaughter of the First World War and the unspeakable horror of the Nazi Holocaust during the Second World War. It would explain the decline of organized religions and why the soulless cult of science has gained supremacy. It would explain the moral and ethical bankruptcy of modern times and the increase in senseless violence.

In fact, Crowley *didn't* believe that the reception of *The Book of the Law* represented a "psychic invasion." He believed that it marked the turning of the Aeon, which Saint John foresaw as a calamity only because he was viewing the New Aeon from the perspective of the old. Tyson should make an effort to understand Thelema before he tries to characterize it or explain what Crowley believed. But once more, this misunderstanding is the least of Tyson's problems here.

Let me be clear. *Aleister Crowley's Scrying of the Aethyrs did not initiate either of the two world wars and did not lead to the Holocaust.* I honestly can barely comprehend the mindset of anyone who would genuinely accept either assertion.

Now to be fair, I do not even know if Tyson does himself. He published the article I am quoting in 1996 and repeated the same claims in *Tetragrammaton*. But after that, his next book was *Enochian Magic for Beginners*! If you truly believe that practicing a particular school of magic will *literally end the world*, why would you ever publish a primer for beginning students? The apocalypse theory itself may be bizarre but publishing what you honestly consider to be a guide on how to end the world is just plain stupid. I suspect that Tyson may simply have been playing this up the whole time to enhance the "scary reputation" of the Enochian system and sell more books. But if that is the case, what does that say about those who are still falling for it today, more than twenty years later?

At any rate, according to the history of the real world, the First World War was the inevitable result of military maneuvers and alliances by the powers of Europe dating back to the late nineteenth century. That was long before Crowley had ever heard of *The Book of the Law*, let alone performed his Enochian work. The "senseless slaughter" of that war stemmed from a strategic blunder by the Germans that stalled their army's advance and forced both sides into trench warfare. The Second World War was a direct consequence of the harsh terms of the Treaty of Versailles, which destroyed the German economy. The Nazi party originally came to power in no small part because of Hitler's pledge to defy the terms of that treaty and end the massive payments to France that it compelled.

With regard to Tyson's statements about the "senseless violence" of the modern age, I will grant that as this article was published in 1996, it was probably written at least a year or two before that. Violent crime peaked in the United States peaked around 1991, but as of this writing in 2018 has for the most part been declining ever since. 1991 is around the time I began my own work with Enochian magick, so does that mean I personally am responsible for this decline? Of course not, but that is the sort of logic Tyson is employing here. As far as I can tell, his problems with the modern world are his own, and have nothing to do with malevolent Enochian spirits or anyone else's magical workings.

We may not have long to wait before the individual known in the vision of St. John as the Antichrist, the one foretold in Crowley's Book of the Law to follow after the Beast, will succeed in completing the Apocalypse Working. Then the gates of the Watchtowers will truly gape wide, and the children of Coronzon will sweep into our minds as crowned conquerors. If this chilling scenario ever comes to pass, the wars of the twentieth century will seem bucolic to those who survive the slaughter.

Just to be clear one more time, the "one to follow" mentioned in *The Book of the Law* is never referred to as "the Antichrist" in any Thelemic text. Crowley believed that the phrase was an allusion to Charles Stansfield Jones, Frater Achad, who Crowley recognized as his "magical son" before their eventual falling-out. Again, Tyson shows his ignorance and misunderstanding of Thelema and Crowley's writings. But his idea that one individual person Scrying the Aethyrs will trigger a "slaughter" that will dwarf the deaths attributed to the two-world wars of the twentieth century is flat-out delusional. Tyson should stick to writing about H. P. Lovecraft and the Necronomicon and leave the Enochian system alone.

I hope to live to see the day that Tyson's wild and ridiculous theories about the Enochian apocalypse are put to rest. But so far, while it they are not accepted by most Enochian magicians, there are still a few out there who seem to believe in them. In my opinion, you should not allow such individuals to influence your attitude towards magical practice, since I see no way that a dialogue with them will accomplish anything but leading you astray or scaring you out of doing the work.

And doing the work is the entire point. As I see it, if you avoid practicing because you fear an "Enochian apocalypse" or any other sort of harmful outcome, you have most likely already done greater harm to yourself than you could possibly set in motion by performing any magical operation.

# 14

# Closing the Temple

As with the Heptarchial and Watchtower entities, Dee does not include any sort of License to Depart for the entities of the Thirty Aires. Over the years I have employed my own for that purpose, as it seems most appropriate to have one when working the grimoire-style magick with which Dee and Kelley would have been familiar. The references to "True Will" are explicitly Thelemic and are shown in italics because a Christian magician may want to omit them, though Saint Augustine's comment that one should "love, and do what thou wilt"[20] implies to me that this concept is not necessarily incompatible with Christian magick.

> You Angels of Light, I, *[Your Magical Name]*, by the power of the True, Almighty, and Living God, I hereby bid you to depart and accomplish your appointed tasks, *in the service of my True Will and* to the Glory and Honour of our aforementioned True God to whom you owe loyalty and obedience. I, *[Your Magical Name]*, hereby free the forces constrained, focused, and directed during this operation, that they may go forth and work their various powers upon the manifest universe, for thus is all True Magick and Perfect Power born. By the power *of my True Will* here embodied by the Magical Name *[Your Magical Name]*, AMEN.

So mote it be.

At this point, you will want to shroud any talisman that you created to anchor the power of the ritual with a piece of black cloth. Most modern magicians recommend silk, but I find that a cotton cloth works just as

---

20 Augustine of Hippo, *In Epistolam Loannis ad Parthos*.

well for this purpose. Then, the actions that follow depend upon how you opened the temple.

If you are working with the AOEVEAE and MADRIAX rituals, conclude them and proceed to declaring the temple closed, as they are designed to encapsulate larger rites with less repetition than the standard modern ritual forms. In the temple opening you will have performed these rituals up to the point at which you perform the rite proper, and now you will be finishing them up with the concluding gestures.

If you are working with the Lesser Rituals of the Pentagram and Hexagram or Star Ruby and Star Sapphire, you should repeat the banishing pentagram ritual if your charge involves some sort of macrocosmic influence—that is, a change you are attempting to make in the external world. The reason for this is that if you are sending your magical intent out into the world you want to perform a microcosmic banishing to essentially "let it go" so that the conjured entity can perform the appointed task.

On the other hand, if you are attempting to make a change within yourself, you should repeat the Qabalistic Cross only, using the version from the pentagram ritual that you used to open the temple. For the Star Ruby, follow this by repeating the initial action of the rite, drawing in the breath, placing your finger to at your lips, and then sweeping it behind you as you declare "*Apo Pantos Kakodaimonos!*" Since a microcosmic banishing affects your physical body and personal sphere of consciousness, you do not want to perform a microcosmic banishing before closing the rite if you want your intent to integrate itself into your life.

Finally, declare the temple closed. You may punctuate this with a knock or another sound such as a bell chime. The rite is at an end.

# 15

# Conclusion

THIS CHAPTER CONCLUDES MY OVERVIEW of the work of the Thirty Aires, and this volume concludes my Mastering Enochian Magick series. The Heptarchy, Watchtowers, and Aires cover the three sections of the Enochian work, and this series should provide you with ample material and instructions for performing just about any sort of Enochian operation according to the original attributions of Dee and Kelley's system.

As I mentioned in the introduction, simply reading all three of my Enochian books will in no way make you a master of Enochian magick. These are instructions only, for work that you as a magician must undertake if you want to achieve mastery of this remarkable system of magick that represented the very state of the art of magical working at the end of the English Renaissance and for many centuries thereafter.

It may very well be that this criticism arose precisely because when all is said and done, these books give the armchair magician little to do. The best method for exploring any system of magick is to learn the instructions, do the work, and record your results. Work with the spirits and build up relationships with them, so rather than trying to answer some question about the system through involved and complex analysis, you can go right to the source and just ask.

That is what these books are for, and why I wrote them the way that I did. Now, with methods for working with all three sections of the system outlined and in place, you should be ready to start conjuring spirits and performing magical operations. Always experiment, keep up the work, and share any new techniques you may come across for producing superior results. Secrecy has held the development of magical technology back for centuries, and it is about time for that whole perspective to be revised for the modern world.

And as mystics and magicians, the fate of the world really is in our hands. Our predecessors like Dee and Kelley were instrumental in the European Renaissance that gave birth to our modern Western world. The so-called "enlightenment" followed, ushering in an era of science and reason at the expense of the spiritual. Finally, modern magicians like Aleister Crowley and those who came after him worked to integrate the scientific and the mystical—"The Method of Science, the Aim of Religion."

Our technology is more advanced and powerful than ever before, but that power to create also gives us the power to destroy. Circumstances for most people have improved dramatically over the course of the last century or so, but there is still a lot of work to be done. That is where we come in. As magicians, we must engage the faculties of our imagination to envision a better world, and employ the powers, forces, and spirits with which we work to make that new reality come to pass. Happy conjuring!

Scott Michael Stenwick<br>
Minneapolis, Minnesota

# Appendix A
## Basic Ritual Forms

**The Lesser Ritual of the Pentagram:** This ritual can be found in just about any introductory book on ritual magick, particularly those covering the Golden Dawn and Thelemic traditions. While I am including the text of the ritual and some brief notations here for the sake of completeness, if you are a beginning magician you should do some additional research regarding how to do the visualizations, vibrations, breathing, and so forth correctly.[21] It should be committed to memory rather than read out of this book or any other.

1. Stand facing east. With the thumb of your right hand touch your forehead and intone ATEH (ah-TAY). Then trace down the center of your body to your genital area and intone MALKUTH (mal-KOOT), trace back up to the center of your chest then over to your right shoulder and intone VE GEBURAH (VAY geh-boo-RAH), then trace across to your left shoulder and intone VE GEDULAH (VAY geh-doo-LAH). Finally, clasp your hands over the center of your chest and intone LE OLAHM, AMEN (LAY oh-LAHM, ah-MEN).

---

21 One of the most popular introductory books of all time on Golden Dawn magick is Donald Michael Kraig's <u>Modern Magick</u> (St. Paul, MN: Llewellyn, 2010), originally published in 1988 and now in its third edition. Kraig is a good writer and covers a lot of material. However, his method of teaching certain ritual such as the Lesser Hexagram differs substantially from mine. He teaches that you should open every ritual with both the LBRP and LBRH—the banishing field—which in my experience can substantially limit your magical power.

This first section is called the Qabalistic Cross and can be performed on its own as a basic centering exercise. As you trace, visualize a cross of glowing white brilliance forming over your body, representing the Qabalistic Tree of Life and linking the spheres of Kether, Tiphareth, Yesod, and Malkuth on the middle pillar along with Geburah and Chesed at the right and left shoulders.

2. In the east, trace the appropriate Pentagram of Earth and vibrate YHVH (yah-WAY). The pentagram should be visualized as formed from living fire. Some authors recommend blue flames, but I personally prefer orange like in a regular fireplace.

*Figure 67. Banishing Pentagram of Earth*

*Figure 68. Invoking Pentagram of Earth*

3. Turn to the south. Trace the appropriate Pentagram of Earth and vibrate ADNI (ah-doh-NYE).

4. Turn to the west. Trace the appropriate Pentagram of Earth and vibrate AHIH (eh-hi-YAY).

5. Turn to the north. Trace the appropriate Pentagram of Earth and vibrate AGLA (ah-guh-LAH).

Note that as the color is different (blue or orange), this "Lesser Pentagram" is *drawn* like the Pentagram of Earth, but it does not represent the same thing. You are not "banishing the element of Earth" when you perform this ritual, but rather banishing *all microcosmic influences* from your sphere of awareness. These influences span all four elements.

6. Return to face the east. Extend your arms in the form of a cross and intone:

Before me RAPHAEL (rah-fay-EL),
Behind me GABRIEL (gah-bree-EL),
On my right hand MICHAEL (mee-kye-EL),
On my left hand URIEL[22] (oo-ree-EL).
For about me flames the pentagram,
And in the column stands the six-rayed star.

As you vibrate the name of each Archangel, visualize the appropriate figure standing in the corresponding direction. Raphael in the east wears a yellow robe and holds a caduceus wand, Gabriel in the west wears a blue robe and holds a chalice, Michael in the south wears a red robe and holds a flaming sword, and Uriel in the north wears a black robe and holds a scythe.

For the final two lines, you first visualize a pentagram forming over your body and then on the last line visualize yourself standing within a vertical hexagonal pillar of light inscribed with a hexagram. For the pentagram visualization, imagine yourself as Leonardo Da Vinci's *Vitruvian Man* with an upright pentagram inscribing the circle in the drawing. For the hexagram visualization, imagine your entire body within a round column of light extending from floor to ceiling and beyond. The hexagram then inscribes the cross-section of the pillar at a right angle relative to the vertical plane of the pentagram.

7. Repeat step 1, the Qabalistic Cross.

**The Lesser Ritual of the Hexagram** Like the Lesser Ritual of the Pentagram, this ritual can be found in most introductory books on Golden Dawn and Thelemic magick. As with the Lesser Ritual of the Pentagram

---

[22] Uriel and Auriel are alternate English spellings for the same angel name. "Uriel" is closer to how it sounds, but "Auriel" is a direct transliteration from the Hebrew as the name is written with an Aleph in front of the Vav. Dee wrote "Uriel," which is another reason that I use that spelling here rather than the more common "Auriel."

you will want to commit it to memory. Also, before using this ritual you will want to do some additional research above and beyond the instructions given here if you are unfamiliar with it. The main pitfall to watch out for is authors who teach that you should open or close rituals using only the banishing form. I have observed that in many cases this method can undermine your ability to work effective practical magick.

1. Stand facing east following the performance of the Lesser Ritual of the Pentagram. Intone the following:

   INRI – Yod Nun Resh Yod.
   Virgo, Isis, mighty mother,
   Scorpio, Apophis, destroyer,
   Sol, Osiris, slain and risen,
   Isis, Apophis, Osiris,
   IAO.

   This section is called the Keyword Analysis.

2. Give the Sign of Osiris Slain, extending both arms in the form of a cross. Say:

   Osiris slain![23]

   Then give the Sign of the Mourning of Isis. With open hands, bend both elbows at 90 degree angles, raising the right forearm to point up and dropping the left forearm to point down. The right palm should be up and facing forward and the left should be down and facing backwards. Turn slightly to your left and look down. Say:

   The Mourning of Isis!

   Then give the Sign of Apophis and Typhon, raising both arms straight above your head and holding them apart at an angle of about sixty degrees. The wrists should be straight, the hands open, and the palms toward each other. Say:

   Apophis and Typhon!

---

[23] The traditional Golden Dawn teaching regarding the first four statements in this section is to add "The Sign of" to the beginning of each. In practice I find this to be choppy and awkward, so when using this ritual I perform it as shown here.

Then give the Sign of Osiris Risen. Cross your arms on your chest, left over right, like an Egyptian mummy. The hands should be open with your right palm on your left shoulder and your left palm on your right shoulder. Say:

Osiris risen!

Repeat the Sign of Osiris Slain and say:

L – V – X – LUX.

Repeat the Sign of Osiris Risen and say:

The light of the Cross.

This section is called the Signs of LVX.

3. Trace the appropriate Hexagram of Fire in the east as you vibrate ARARITA. The two upward triangles should be visualized in red.

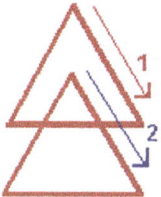

*Figure 69: Invoking Hexagram of Fire*

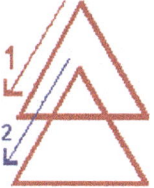

*Figure 70. Banishing Hexagram of Fire*

4. Turn to the south. Trace the appropriate Hexagram of Earth in the south as you vibrate ARARITA. The upward triangle should be visualized in red and the downward triangle should be visualized in blue.

*Figure 71. Invoking Hexagram of Earth*

*Figure 72. Banishing Hexagram of Earth*

5. Turn to the west. Trace the appropriate Hexagram of Air in the west as you vibrate ARARITA. The upward triangle should be visualized in red and the downward triangle should be visualized in blue.

*Figure 73. Invoking Hexagram of Air*

*Figure 74. Banishing Hexagram of Air*

6. Turn to the north. Trace the appropriate Hexagram of Water in the north as you vibrate ARARITA. The upward triangle should be visualized in red and the downward triangle should be visualized in blue.

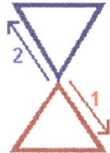

*Figure 75. Invoking Hexagram of Water*

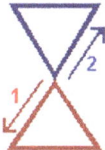

*Figure 76. Banishing Hexagram of Water*

7. Return to the east. Repeat the Keyword Analysis and the Signs of LVX.

**The Star Ruby and Star Sapphire:** Rather than the Golden Dawn ritual forms, Thelemic magicians may prefer to use the Star Ruby, Aleister Crowley's "improved version" of the Lesser Ritual of the Pentagram, and the Star Sapphire, which corresponds to the Lesser Ritual of the Hexagram. These rituals are not included here but can be found in Crowley's works[24] and in popular treatments such as Lon Milo Duquette's *The Magick of Aleister Crowley*.[25] As the Star Ruby is a banishing ritual and the Star Sapphire is an invoking ritual, together they form an operant field just like the LBRP/LIRH combination.

---

24 Aleister Crowley, *The Book of Lies* (York Beach, ME: Weiser Books, 1986) and *Magick: Book Four* (York Beach, ME: Weiser Books, 1998).
25 Lon Milo DuQuette, *The Magick of Aleister Crowley* (San Francisco, CA: Weiser Books, 2003).

**AOEVEAE ("Stars") Pentagram Ritual:** To replace the Golden Dawn Lesser Ritual of the Pentagram, I have developed an Enochian pentagram ritual that I call the AOEVEAE (a-o-i-ve-ah-EH – "stars" in Angelic). A number of writers have come up with Enochian pentagram rituals of this sort and they all share certain similarities. It is pretty clear that the most logical names to use when tracing the pentagrams are the threefold names of God from Dee and Kelley's Great Table (ORO IBAH AOZPI, MPH ARSL GAIOL, OIP TEAA PDOCE, and MOR DIAL HCTGA) and the most logical equivalents to the Archangels are the Kings of the four directions (BATAIVAH, RAAGIOSL, EDLPRNAA, and ICZHIHAL).

When attributing the names to the directions I use the directional arrangement from the 1587 *Tabula Recensa*.[26] The text shown here may be adapted to fit the traditional Golden Dawn arrangement of the Great Table by swapping the names associated with the west and south, so that you vibrate OIP TEAA PDOCE in the south and MPH ARSL GAIOL in the west, and swap the directions attributed to RAAGIOSL and EDLPRNAA when calling the Kings.

Start the ritual by standing in the center of your temple facing east, or to the west of the altar facing east if the Holy Table is present. Wear the Enochian PELE ring. If you wish to use a magical weapon, a dagger is probably the most appropriate for the banishing form, while a wand is best for the invoking form, but keep in mind that this is a modern practice and Dee and Kelley used neither. The ritual text follows:

1. With your finger or magical weapon, trace from your left hip to your right shoulder while vibrating NANTA (NAHN-ta – Earth), from your right shoulder to left shoulder while vibrating HCOMA (he-KO-ma – Water), from your left shoulder to right hip while vibrating EXARP (EX-arp – Air), from your right hip to your forehead while vibrating BITOM (BI-tom – Fire), and finally from your forehead back to your left hip while vibrating EHNB (EH-nub – Spirit). Then clasp your hands over your heart and vibrate JAIDA (ja-I-da – "The Highest"). Visualize the pentagram traced over your body in bright electric lavender.

---

26 DuQuette, *Enochian Vision Magick* (San Francisco, CA: Weiser Books, 2008), 135-137.

2. In the east, trace the Banishing Pentagram of Earth while vibrating ORO IBAH AOZPI. The pentagrams should be visualized as formed from burning flames and as vividly as possible.

*Figure 77. Banishing Pentagram of Earth*

3. Turn to the north. In the north, trace the Banishing Pentagram of Earth while vibrating MOR DIAL HCTGA (MOR DI-al hek-TGA).

4. Turn to the west. In the west, trace the Banishing Pentagram of Earth while vibrating OIP TEAA PDOCE (o-IP TE-ah-ah PDO-ke).

5. Turn to the south. In the south, trace the Banishing Pentagram of Earth while vibrating MPH ARSL GAIOL (MEH-peh AR-sal ga-i-OL).

6. Turn back to face the east. Extend your arms to form a cross and vibrate:

    RAAS I BATAIVAH ("In the East is BATAIVAH" – ba-ta-i-VAH),
    SOBOLN I EDLPRNAA ("In the West is EDLPRNAA" – ed-el-per-na-AH),
    BABAGE I RAAGIOSL ("In the South is RAAGIOSL" – ra-AH-gi-oh-sal),
    LUCAL I ICZHIHAL ("In the North is ICZHIHAL" – ik-zod-hi-HAL).

7. Make one full spin counter-clockwise while vibrating MICMA AO COMSELH AOIVEAE ("Behold the Circle of Stars" – MIK-ma AH-o KOM-seh-lah a-o-i-ve-a-EH), then clasp your hands over your heart while vibrating OD OL, MALPRG, NOTHOA ("And I, a Through-Thrusting Fire, in the Midst." – OD OL, MAL-perg, NOT-ho-ah).

    If you are using this ritual in conjunction with the MADRIAX hexagram ritual which follows, it should be inserted here.

8. With your finger or magical weapon, trace from your right hip to your left shoulder while vibrating EHNB, from your left shoulder to your right shoulder while vibrating BITOM, from your right shoulder to left hip while vibrating EXARP, from your left hip to your forehead while vibrating HCOMA, and finally from your forehead back to your right hip while vibrating NANTA. Then clasp your hands over your heart and vibrate IAIDA. Visualize the pentagram traced over your body in dark, deep purple.

This is the banishing form of the ritual. The invoking form is the same except that the pentagrams should be traced as the Invoking Pentagram of Earth.

*Figure 78. Invoking Pentagram of Earth*

In the invoking form, the directional names remain the same. However, they should be traced to the quarters in clockwise rather than counter-clockwise order. Also, the final spin should be counter-clockwise to align with your initial clockwise rotation.

**MADRIAX ("O Ye Heavens") Hexagram Ritual:** To replace the Golden Dawn Lesser Ritual of the Hexagram, I have developed an Enochian hexagram ritual that I call the MADRIAX ("o ye heavens" in Angelic).

In this revised ritual the four elements are attributed to the four quadrants of the Great Table based on the colors from Kelley's original vision of the Watchtowers[27] and the elemental attributions taken from the later "round house" vision[28]. The names vibrated are those of the Kings from the *Heptarchia Mystica*:

---

27 Meric Causaubon, ed. *A True and Faithful Relation of What Passed for Many Years Between Dr. John Dee and Some Spirits* (New York, NY: Magickal Childe, 1992), 168.
28 Ibid, 355-361.

Fire = East = BABALEL (Mars)
Air = South = BNASPOL (Mercury)
Water = West = BYNEPOR (Jupiter)
Earth = North = BALIGON (Venus)

If you wish to modify this ritual so as to conform to the zodiacal scheme used in the Golden Dawn Lesser Ritual of the Hexagram you should change these attributions as follows:

Fire = East = BABALEL (Mars)
Earth = South = BALIGON (Venus)
Air = West = BNASPOL (Mercury)
Water = North = BYNEPOR (Jupiter)

The use of planetary names with the elemental unicursal hexagram represents the union of the planetary and elemental realms, the microcosm and macrocosm. The "above" and "below" points of the ritual are then attributed to BNAPSEN (Saturn) and BLUMAZA (Luna). The figures traced for these points are the usual planetary hexagrams, not the unicursal. When working with the Holy Table the figures form a column running from the heavens to the earth with the hexagram on the Holy Table itself at its midpoint.

The final figure used in this ritual is attributed to BOBOGEL (the Sun). It is combined with the invoking unicursal hexagram of Earth to symbolize the invocation and grounding of the solar force. The ritual text is as follows:

1. With your finger or a tool such as a wand trace the Invoking Unicursal Hexagram of Earth over yourself while vibrating BOBOGEL (BO-bo-gel). This tracing is done is the following manner: forehead -> left hip -> right shoulder -> genitals -> left shoulder -> right hip -> forehead. This hexagram is visualized in yellow-gold as opposed to the green that is normally used for elemental earth, and it is always traced in the invoking form, even for the banishing form of the ritual.

*Figure 79. Invoking Unicursal Hexagram of Earth*

2. In the east, trace the invoking unicursal hexagram of Fire in red as you vibrate BABALEL (BA-ba-lel).

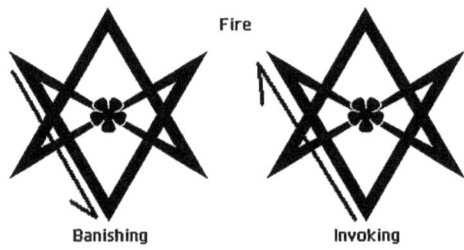

*Figure 80. Unicursal Hexagram of Fire*

3. In the south, trace the invoking unicursal hexagram of Air in white as you vibrate BNASPOL (BNAS-pol).

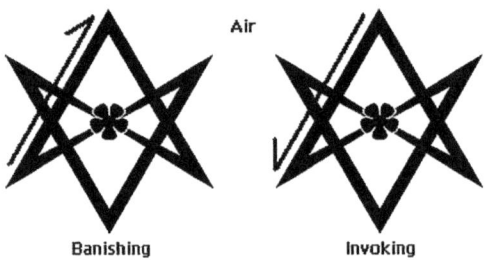

*Figure 81. Unicursal Hexagram of Air*

4. In the west, trace the invoking unicursal hexagram of Water in green as you vibrate BYNEPOR (BY-neh-por).

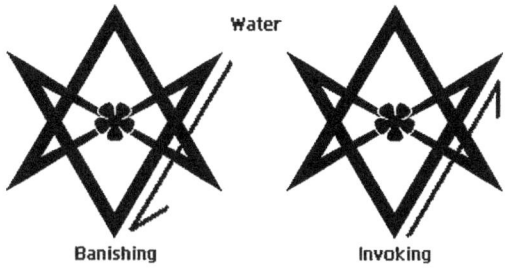

*Figure 82. Unicursal Hexagram of Water*

5. In the north, trace the invoking unicursal hexagram of Earth in black as you vibrate BALIGON (BA-li-gon).

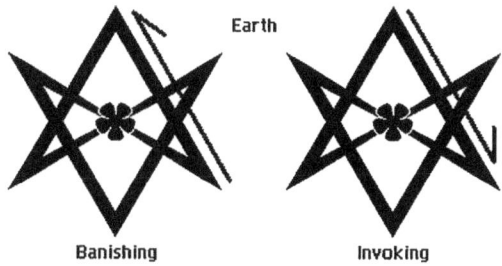

*Figure 83. Unicursal Hexagram of Earth*

6. Above you, trace the hexagram of Saturn in bright lavender as you vibrate BNAPSEN (BNAP-sen).

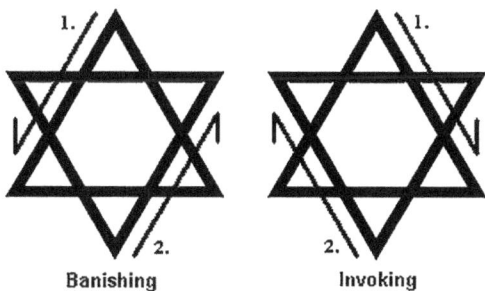

*Figure 84. Hexagram of Saturn*

7. Below you, trace the hexagram of the Moon in deep violet as you vibrate BLUMAZA (blu-MA-zah).

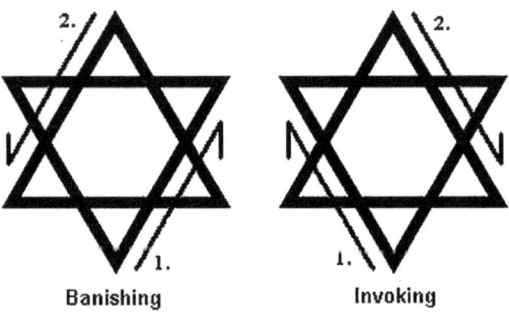

Figure 85. Hexagram of the Moon

8. Extend your arms and make one full clockwise rotation (or circumambulation of the temple if you are using the Holy Table) as you vibrate TA CALZ I OROCHA (TA CAL-zod I o-RO-ka – "as above the firmament so beneath you", probably the best Enochian rendering of "as above, so below"). Then clasp your hands over your heart for a moment and hold the full visualization of the rite in your mind.

9. For the invoking form of this ritual, hold your hands in front of you with the palms facing outwards and then separate them as though opening a heavy curtain as you vibrate MADRIAX CARMARA, YOLCAM LONSHI (MA-dri-ax kar-MA-ra, YOL-cam LON-shi – "O ye heavens of Carmara, bring forth power"). Carmara is the eighth Heparchial King who rules over the other seven.

10. The ritual work for which you opened the field goes here.

11. At the conclusion of the ritual work, hold your hands in front of you and to either side with palms facing inwards, and then bring them together as though closing a heavy curtain as you vibrate MADRIAX CARMARA, ADRPAN LONSHI (MA-dri-ax kar-MA-ra, AH-dra-pan LON-shi – "O ye heavens of Carmara, cast down power").

This is the invoking form of the ritual. For the banishing form, you would turn to each direction going in a counter-clockwise order (East ->

North -> West -> South -> East), trace banishing hexagrams as shown (aside from the opening Earth hexagram which should always be traced in the invoking form), and make the final rotation/circumambulation counter-clockwise.

This ritual works with the AOIVEAE to open and close magical fields just like the Lesser Ritual of the PentagramRitual of the Hexagram combinations. However, they are designed slightly differently from the other similar rituals found in the tradition in order to streamline magical operations. The main innovation I wanted to incorporate was to encapsulate my workings within both rituals rather than repeating either of them to close down a rite. As a result, the basic structure works like this.

A. AOIVEAE steps 1 to 7.
B. MADRIAX steps 1-9.
C. MADRIAX step 10 is the Enochian ritual itself.
D. MADRIAX step 11.
E. AOIVEAE step 8.

So according to this structure (A) and (B) are the opening, (C) is the ritual work itself, and (D) and (E) constitute the closing.

**NAZ OLPIRT ("Pillars of Light") Energy Work Exercise:** One of the areas that modern magicians sometimes neglect is the energetic state of the subtle body, or body of light. I have found that practices such as Hatha Yoga and Qigong make a great deal of difference in terms of the amount of magical force you can bring to bear upon a situation and thus your ability to create change successfully. In the Golden Dawn tradition, a common practice is the Middle Pillar Exercise, which associates various names of God with specific points on the subtle body and as a result empowers those areas with the energies of the associated godforms. In the Thelemic tradition, a similar practice is the Elevenfold Seal, found in Aleister Crowley's Liber V vel Reguli. This is a similar exercise based upon relating the Enochian elements to the elemental natures of the seven chakras of Eastern mysticism.

Start off by standing in a normal, relaxed pose. Keep your spine straight and imagine your head suspended by a thread from above. Breathe slowly and easily through the nose into your diaphragm. Place your tongue so that it is touching the roof of your mouth and keep it there except when vibrating the words of the ritual. Make sure you hold the tongue in that position when breathing in. The gestures are made with the hand or finger rather than any sort of magical weapon.

1. Make a clockwise circle above your head and intone MADRIAX ("the Heavens") three times. Visualize a sea of luminous brilliance above you, beyond and encompassing all colors.

2. Touch the center of your forehead (ajna chakra) and intone IAD (i-AHD – "God") three times. Visualize energy akin to pure, clear light forming at this point, sending its rays outward to the four cardinal directions. Do not completely drop the visualization of luminous brilliance above you. You are adding to your visualization, not replacing it. This instruction holds true for all the following steps.

3. Touch your throat (vishuddha chakra) and intone EHNB ("Spirit") three times. Visualize a sphere of bright lavender light forming at this point.

4. Touch the center of your chest (anahata chakra) and intone EXARP ("Air") three times. Visualize a sphere of vibrant white energy forming at this point.

5. Touch your solar plexus (samsara chakra) and intone BITOM ("Fire") three times. Visualize a sphere of glowing red energy forming at this point.

6. Touch the lower abdomen just below the navel (svadasthana chakra) and intone HCOMA ("Water") three times. Visualize a sphere of green energy forming at this point.

7. Touch the perineum (muladhara chakra) and intone NANTA ("Earth") three times. Visualize a sphere of solid black energy forming at this point.

8. Drop both hands to your sides and intone CAOSGO (ka-OS-go – "the Earth") three times. Visualize the completion of a circuit that begins above you in the heavens, descends below you into the deep earth down the front of your body and then ascends upwards to the heavens along the back of your body.

9. As you visualize the circulating energy, start with your hands at about the level of your perineum, palms turned upwards, and then raise them to the level of the top of your head as you inhale. Then turn the palms downward and drop them back to the level of the perineum as you exhale.

10. To conclude the exercise, make the Sign of Osiris Risen, crossing your arms over your chest, and intone TA CALZ I OROCHA ("As above the firmament so beneath you") as you visualize any excess energy you have focused at each of the points of your body descending below your feet into the vast darkness of the deep earth, breaking the circuit. Feel a wave of relaxation sweep over you from your head down to your feet, sweeping any remaining tension into the deep earth along with the grounded energy.

**The Revised Opening by Watchtower:** This ritual assumes a temple setup consisting of the Holy Table, Sigillum Dei Aemeth, Ensigns of Creation, Banners, and so forth. It should be noted that while the previous ritual forms are cast across the Holy Table, in the Opening by Watchtower the Officiant or some other participant should instead stand at the appropriate quarter and face outwards when tracing the pentagrams and performing the corresponding vibrations. This ritual uses the standard Golden Dawn tools, which may be placed on the Holy Table without impairing its function.

## I. *The Four Elements*

*Officiant begins at the west of the Holy Table facing east. He or she takes the Banishing Dagger, inhales deeply, and presses the dagger to the lips. As the breath is expelled, the dagger is swept down and back until it points downward and behind the Officiant at about a 45-degree angle.*

**Officiant: ADRPAN VOVINA OD CORS TA DOBIX!** (adr-PAN vo-VEE-nah OD KORS TA doh-BEEX)

*The Banishing Dagger is then returned to the altar.*

This phrase translates from Angelic into English as "Cast down the Dragon and such that fall." In the Angelic Keys, the word VOVIN (Dragon) and its several variations allude to the devil and/or demonic forces, while ADRPAN, "cast down," is the best Angelic translation for "banish."

*Officiant goes to the east, takes the Fire wand H, and makes the supernal triangle facing east.*

*The Supernal triangle is made by using the weapon to tap the corners of an equilateral triangle. You start with the top point, then tap the lower right point, then tap the lower left point.*

*He or she then holds the wand above head level and circumambulates once clockwise. All participants rotate accordingly, visualizing a wall of fiery red light surrounding the temple. Attention should be directed across the altar.*

**Officiant: And when, after all the phantoms have vanished, thou shalt see that holy and formless Fire, that Fire which darts and flashes through the hidden depths of the Universe! Hear thou the Voice of Fire!**

*Officiant completes the circumambulation and then traces the Invoking Pentagram of Fire in red to the east with the wand while vibrating* **ORO IBAH AOZPI** (OH-ro EE-bah ah-oh-ZOD-pee). *The wand is then returned to the altar.*

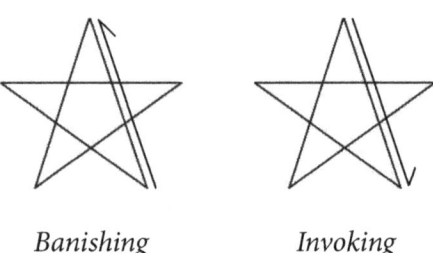

*Banishing*      *Invoking*

*Figure 86. The Pentagrams of Fire*

*Officiant next proceeds to the south, takes the Air dagger, and makes the supernal triangle facing south. He or she then holds the dagger above head level and circumambulates once clockwise. All participants rotate accordingly, visualizing a wall of bright white light surrounding the temple just inside the wall of red light. Attention should be directed across the altar.*

**Officiant: Such a Fire existeth, extending through the rushing of Air. Or even a Fire formless, whence cometh the image of a voice. Or even a flashing light, abounding, revolving, whirling forth, crying aloud!**

*Officiant completes the circumambulation and then traces the Invoking Pentagram of Air in white to the south with the dagger while vibrating* **MPH ARSL GAIOL** (MEH-peh AR-sal gah-ee-OL). *The dagger is then returned to the altar.*

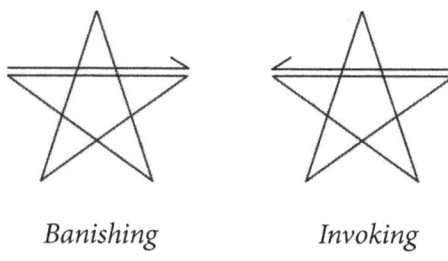

*Banishing          Invoking*

*Figure 87. The Pentagrams of Air*

*Officiant goes to the west, takes the Water cup and makes the supernal triangle facing west. He or she then holds the cup above head level and circumambulates once clockwise. All participants rotate accordingly, visualizing a wall of green light surrounding the temple just inside the wall of white light. Attention should be directed across the altar.*

**Officiant: So therefore first, the priest who governeth the works of Fire must sprinkle with the lustral Water of the loud and resounding sea!**

*Officiant completes the circumambulation and then traces the Invoking Pentagram of Water in green to the west with the cup while vibrating* **OIP TEAA PDOCE** (oh-EEP TEH-ah-ah PDO-keh). *The cup is then returned to the altar.*

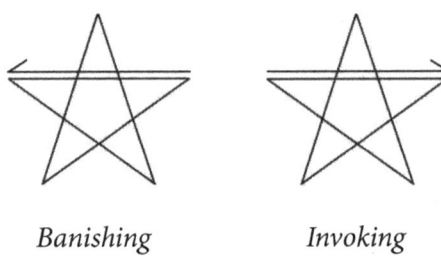

*Banishing*     *Invoking*

*Figure 88. The Pentagrams of Water*

Officiant goes to the north, takes the Earth pantacle and makes the supernal triangle facing south. He or she then holds the pantacle above head level and circumambulates once clockwise. All participants rotate accordingly, visualizing a wall of black light surrounding the temple just inside the wall of green light. Attention should be directed across the altar.

**Officiant: This Fire descendeth into that darkly splendid world, wherein continually ariseth Nature, delighting in myriad forms - precipitous, nurturing, winding, and welcoming, ever revealing a body infused with the light of the Spirit.**

Officiant completes the circumambulation and then then traces the Invoking Pentagram of Earth in black to the south with the earth pantacle while vibrating **MOR DIAL HCTGA** (MOR dee-AHL hek-TGAH). The pantacle is then returned to the altar.

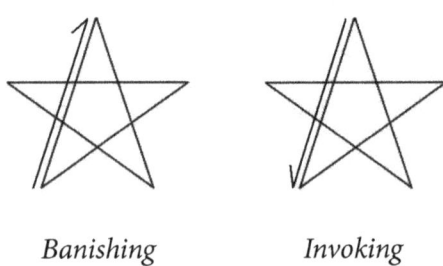

*Banishing*     *Invoking*

*Figure 89. The Pentagrams of Earth*

## II. The Vortex

*Officiant circumambulates clockwise back to the west of the altar and faces east. All participants rotate accordingly. He or she then takes the Fire or Invoking wand, traces the Invoking Pentagram of Active Spirit in bright violet above the altar, and then sweeps the wand straight down and traces the Invoking Pentagram of Passive Spirit below the altar, holding the visualization of both figures while vibrating* **EHNB** *(EH-nub).*

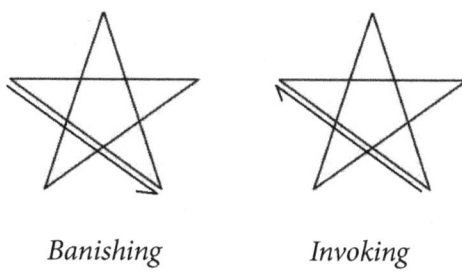

*Banishing*   *Invoking*

Figure 90. The Pentagrams of Active Spirit

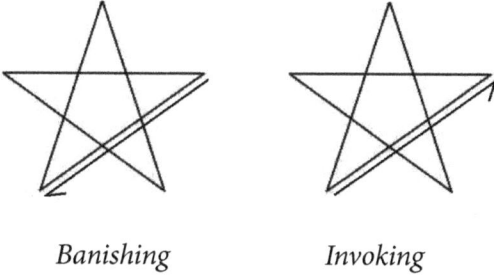

*Banishing*   *Invoking*

Figure 91. The Pentagrams of Passive Spirit

The Angelic word EHNB is formed by taking the first letters of the names of each of the four elements as they appear on the Black Cross or Tablet of Union (Exarp = Air, Hcoma = Water, Nanta = Earth, and Bitom = Fire).

The pentagram above the Holy Table should be traced as though it is set into the ceiling. This requires more skill at visualization than tracing to the directions, since the wand has to be held upward at about a 45 degree angle and the image should be slightly distorted by perspective. The Officiant may need to step back slightly to trace below the Holy Table. The pentagram will be partially obscured by the altar cloth, but it should nonetheless be visualized in full set into the floor.

*Officiant sets down the wand. All make and hold the Sign of Apophis and Typhon, with arms held up and outwards at an angle of approximately 60 degrees with the palms turned inwards.*

**All: Thee we invoke, who art universe.**
**Thee we invoke, who art in nature formed.**
**Thee we invoke, the vast and the mighty.**
**Source of darkness, source of light.**[29]

*All make the Sign of Silence, bringing the finger of the right hand or thumb to the lips. The four walls of light are now visualized melting together into grayish light and forming into a cube that surrounds the temple. Pentagrams in the appropriate colors appear on all six faces—red in the east, white in the south, green in the west, black in the north, bright violet above, and dark purple below. There is a short pause to allow for as much detail as possible.*

**Officiant: The visible Sun is the dispenser of light unto the Earth. Let us therefore form a vortex in this chamber that the invisible Sun of Spirit may shine herein.**

*All circumambulate four times, focusing on the center of the Holy Table and visualize the entire Temple rising on the planes through the four elements. On the first circumambulation, a wall of black surrounding the temple is visualized for Earth, on the second green for Water, on the third white for Air, and on the fourth red for Fire. At the conclusion of this all arrive back at their original places, with Officiant to the west of the altar. The cube surrounding the temple is then visualized as melting into a sphere of golden light encompassing the entire space.*

---

29 This invocation is adapted from the rituals of the Open Source Order of the Golden Dawn.

## III. Opening the Veil

**Officiant: Peh Resh Kaph Tau. The word is PAROKETH, which is the veil of the sanctuary. In and by that word** *(makes the Sign of Rending the Veil),* **I open the veil.**

*All make the Sign of the Enterer directed at the center of the altar.*

The Sign of the Enterer, given by advancing the hands at shoulder width, palms down, at the level of the eyes as you take a short step forward with the left foot, represents stepping through the portal, an action that all participants must perform for themselves.

**All: ABRAHADABRA**

*All then make the Sign of Osiris Risen.*

This word and sign signify arrival at the sphere of Tiphareth. The Sign of Osiris Risen is performed by crossing the arms over the chest, like the typical posture of an Egyptian mummy, with the left arm crossed over the right. The figure thus formed by the elbows, hands, and head alludes to the pentagram or blazing star.

**The Middle Pillar Ritual:** While I mentioned the Middle Pillar Ritual in my previous two books, an astute reader pointed out to me that I do not include any instructions for how to perform it. I decided to include it here because it really does go with the Lesser Ritual of the Pentagram and Lesser Ritual of the Hexagram and gives you a more generic option for a preliminary invocation form if you would rather not work with my Enochian-specific rituals.

The Middle Pillar Ritual was written by Israel Regardie and published in his book *The Middle Pillar*. Various changes to the original version have accrued over the years, some more significant than others. First of all, the original version states that you first perform the Lesser Banishing Ritual of the Pentagram and Lesser Banishing Ritual of the Hexagram. I replace this with the operant field - the Lesser Banishing Ritual of the Pentagram followed by the Lesser Invoking Ritual of the Hexagram.

Next, some modern sources instruct you to perform the ritual facing west. This is not in Regardie's original instructions, and I am not sure where it came from. It probably has to do with the Golden Dawn temple arrangement in which the flow of magical force is visualized as moving from east to west, so that you can be facing in the direction that it is perceived to be moving. I first learned this ritual according to Regardie's original instructions and have never done this.

Whether or not this is the intent behind the change, the direction makes little sense in the context of an Enochian temple. In Enochian magick, the flow of magical force is from above to below, passing directly through the Sigillum Dei Aemeth. It is my contention that for Enochian operations, you should always perform the Middle Pillar Ritual while standing in the west facing east, just like where you start your pentagram and hexagram forms. That way you are facing the column of magical force in which the Enochian entities will manifest.

Another change that many modern magicians make is to spell out the Tetragrammaton for the god-names YHVH Elohim and YHVH Eloah ve-Daath as YOD-HEH-VAV-HEH. This is also not in Regardie's original instructions. He gives "Ye-hoh-voh" as the pronunciation for YHVH, similar to Aleister Crowley's "Ye-ho-wau" in *Liber O vel Manus et Sagittae* in his instructions for the Lesser Ritual of the PentagramIn *The Middle Pillar*, The instruction to spell out the Tetragrammaton is given in a footnote to the god-name YHVH Elohim which reads as follows:

> Daath has no divine name of its own, so in the exercise of the Middle Pillar, it "borrows" the divine name for Binah which is the highest Sephirah that is close to Daath. (Since Daath is usually considered a passageway to the Supernals, Binah would be the Sephirah at its point of termination.) Although Regardie states here that YHVH is to be pronounced as "Yeh-hoh-voh" we see no reason it should be pronounced differently from the way it is pronounced in the LBRP - as «Yod-Heh-Vav-Heh.» The term Jehovoh or Jehovah is simply a transcription of the Four-lettered Name YHVH - the letters of which were merely considered as stand-ins for the actual name of God, which was unknown and unpronounceable. We believe that the divine name YHVH Elohim

should be pronounced «Yod Heh Vav Heh El-oh-heem» in all Golden Dawn rituals.

This footnote is almost certainly by Chic and Tabitha Cicero, who edited the version of *The Middle Pillar* in which I found the footnote. It was picked up by Donald Michael Kraig, who goes with «Yod-Heh-Vav-Heh» for all of the ritual instructions in *Modern Magick*, one of the best-selling occult books of all time. I find that many students perform the Lesser Ritual of the Pentagram this way and probably the Middle Pillar Ritual as well, and that they generally got it from Kraig.

But here is what I know from experimentation with different versions of these rituals - vibrating the letters of the Tetragrammaton instead of the name itself can undermine the effectiveness of your ritual work substantially. This is especially true for the Lesser Ritual of the Pentagram, in which spelling one out of the four god-names often unbalances the operation, but it applies to the Middle Pillar Ritual as well because you want each of the sephiroth to be balanced with the others.

Regardie advises students to vibrate the names of God three or four times each. The practice I have picked up lately is to vibrate them three times when performing this ritual as part of your daily practice or as part of the opening for other mystical purposes, and four times when performing it as part of the opening for a practical operation. The symbolism here is my own as far as I know, but the number three represents the sephira Binah above the Abyss, and the number four represents the sephira Chesed below the Abyss. I relate the potentiality above the Abyss to mystical operations and relate the first stirrings of manifestation below the Abyss to practical ones.

Finally, compared to how many students perform this ritual I simplify the final step of circulating the light. In *Modern Magick*, Kraig includes a complicated set of circulations involving up and down, left and right, and side-to-side motion. My version retains Regardie's original "fountain" circulation—energy moves up the body starting at the feet until it "fountains" out from the top of the head and falls back to the ground—and follows that with the microcosmic orbit, a practice adapted from Chinese Qigong. Once that is done, I join hands to seal in the energy and conclude the ritual.

With all that in mind, I perform the Middle Pillar Ritual as follows:

1. Perform the Lesser Banishing Ritual of the Pentagram followed by the Lesser Invoking Ritual of the Hexagram. The use of the operant field method here will result in your consciousness being aligned with the macrocosmic forms of the various aspects of the divine, rather than limiting yourself to the microcosmic aspects within your own mind.

2. Bring your attention to the top of your head. I like to hold my hands slightly above my head and to either side, but you can direct your attention with your mind alone if you prefer. Visualize a sphere of white brilliance forming at this point as you vibrate the name **EHEIEH** (eh-heh-yeh) three or four times.

3. Bring your attention to your throat. I like to follow my attention with my hands throughout the ritual, but you can direct your attention with your mind alone if you prefer. Visualize a sphere of bright lavender forming at this point as you vibrate the name **YHVH ELOHIM** (yah-weh el-oh-heem).

4. Bring your attention to the center of your chest, directly over the sternum. Visualize a sphere of brilliant yellow or gold light forming at this point as you vibrate the name **YHVH ELOAH VE-DAATH** (yah-weh el-oh-ah veh da-aht).

5. Bring your attention to a point about three fingers below your navel. Visualize a sphere of rich purple light forming at this point as you vibrate the name **SHADDAI EL CHAI** (shah-dye el khai). Note that "chai" is properly pronounced like the German "ch" if you are familiar with that language. For English speakers, though, the point is that it is closer to a softened "k" than it is to the English "ch" as found in "chair."

6. Bring your attention to your feet. When following my attention with my hands, for this step I simply let my arms drop to my sides. At your feet, visualize a sphere the color of the blackness of earth forming as you vibrate the name **ADONAI MELEKH** (ah-doh-nye meh-lek).

7. Perform the fountain circulation of light. Draw the energy up through the center of your body as you breathe in, and visualize it being expelled from the top of your head and falling back to earth like water in a fountain as you breathe out. For both this step and

the one following, you want to touch your tongue to the roof of your mouth and breathe through the nose if possible. I was born with a deviated septum and chronic sinus condition, so before I had that fixed with surgery I learned to do it breathing through both my open mouth and nose with my tongue touching the roof of my mouth. So, it can be done, but it is substantially more difficult. You want to breathe into your diaphragm, as deeply as you can while remaining relaxed and refraining from forcing yourself.

I find it helpful to follow the energy with my hands for this step, and it seems to make a big enough difference that I recommend trying it out to see how well it works for you. When everything is synchronized, you should start to feel a tingling sensation moving up your spine. With practice, you should be able to bring that sensation all the way to the top of your head, following the position of your hands.

For this circulation, starting with my arms at my sides, I make a motion as if lifting the energy upwards with my palms as I breathe in. I keep the tips of my middle fingers about an inch apart from each other, so that my hands do not touch. When my hands reach the top of my head, I turn my palms outward and sweep them down until they are at my sides once more. Then I start the process over.

You should perform this circulation at least four times regardless of how you are employing the ritual.

8. Perform the lesser or microcosmic orbit. This is similar to the back-to-front circulation from Kraig's version. As you breathe in, visualize energy rising from the base of your spine and up to the top of your head. Then, as you breathe out, visualize it circulating back down the front of your body until it returns to the base of the spine to start the cycle over. Again, touch your tongue to the roof of your mouth and breathe through your nose if possible, as deeply and evenly as you can while remaining relaxed.

   Following this circulation with your hands starts off just like the fountain circulation, but once your hands reach the top of your head you just bring them back down the center line of your body as you exhale. Repeat for each circulation. As with the fountain circulation, you should perform this circulation at least four times regardless of how the ritual is being employed.

9. Join hands just below your navel, take a few relaxed breaths, and visualize the energy of the fountain circulation fortifying the boundaries of your aura and the orbit circulation fortifying the energetic core of your body. Once this visualization is stable, the ritual is complete.

# Appendix B
## Comselh Ananael
## Thirty Aires Evocation Ritual

COMSELH ANANAEL IS THE NAME that my magical working group chose when we began doing group ritual work in 2002. Since that time, we have explored both the Tree of Life and the Enochian universe, and worked extensively with elemental, planetary, and zodiacal forces. Our work with the Angels of Thirty Aires was performed using the following ritual, derived from the template found in Chapter 6. The ritual has been optimized numerous times over the years and we have found this version to be quite effective for both individual and group operations.

As we work the system from the Thelemic perspective, the ritual structure reflects that rather than the Christian perspective of John Dee and Edward Kelley. Still, much of the methodology is true to the original spirit of the work, even when it incorporates modern ceremonial forms.

### 0. The Temple

*The ritual space is set up as explained in Chapter 5. A scrying stone or mirror is placed on the altar cloth above the center of the Sigillum Dei Aemeth. If possible, the four smaller Seals should be placed under each of the altar table's four legs. The closer the Temple can be to the Enochian ideal, the better the system will work.*

There are two officers in this ritual, Magus and Scryer. Magus acts as the Officiant and should wear the Enochian ring and lamen. The officers and all others present should wear white robes. Scryer attempts to contact the conjured spirit or spirits using the mirror or crystal.

The bell chime is placed on western edge of the Table. This should be a chime that can be rung easily with one hand. Scryer will be ringing it when the Angel or Angels appear, so it must not require much attention to operate. Because of this, its exact position should be left to Scryer's discretion. A low stool for Scryer is placed to the west of the altar. It should be of such a height that the stone or mirror is at Scryer's eye level.

The talisman for the Aire being opened is placed on the floor to the west of the Holy Table. This should be reasonably large, since Magus must stand upon it with both feet when reciting the conjuration. The designs for these talismans are found in Chapter 11.

## *I. Opening*

All form a circle around the altar. Magus initially stands directly west of the altar and Scryer stands directly east. Magus inhales fully, placing the banishing dagger at his or her lips. The air is then expelled as the dagger is swept backwards.

**Magus: Bahlasti! Ompehda!**

Magus then performs the AOEVEAE up to the closing as explained in Appendix A, moving around the Table and casting in the direction of Scryer who concentrates on receiving the evoked energies. All present rotate accordingly, so that the entire circle of assembled magicians turns like a wheel as Magus moves to face each quarter. The idea here is to conjure a line of force that originates with Magus, passes over or through the stone or mirror, and is received by Scryer at each of the Temple's four quarters.

The Prayer of Enoch may be inserted here, in addition to the ceremonial forms used in the opening procedure. If used, it should be followed with a knock or bell chime.

Magus: We take refuge in Nuit, the blue-lidded daughter of sunset, the naked brilliance of the voluptuous night sky, as we issue the call to the awakened nature of all beings, for every man and every woman is a star.

All: AUMGN.

Magus: We take refuge in Hadit, the secret flame that burns in every heart of man and in the core of every star, as we issue the call to our own awakened natures, arousing the coiled serpent about to spring.

All: AUMGN.

Magus: We take refuge in Heru-Ra-Ha, who wields the wand of double power, the wand of the force of Coph Nia, and whose left hand is empty for he has crushed an universe and naught remains, as we unite our awakened natures with those of all beings everywhere and everywhen, dissolving all obstacles and healing all suffering.

All: AUMGN.

Magus: For pure will, unassuaged of purpose, delivered from the lust of result, is every way perfect.

All: All is pure and present and has always been so, for existence is pure joy; all the sorrows are but as shadows; they pass and done; but there is that which remains. To this realization we commit ourselves—pure and total presence. So mote it be.[30]

## *II. The Magical Field*

*Magus performs the MADRIAX up to the closing as explained in Appendix A. As with the AOEVEAE, all present rotate accordingly.*

---

30 This section of the opening following the AOEVEAE is adapted from the Refuge and Bodhichitta practices of Vajrayana Buddhism, but has been modified so as to fit with Thelemic cosmology.

Magus: MADRIAX CARMARA, YOLCAM LONSHI!

*Magus makes the Sign of Rending the Veil, placing hands back to back and then drawing them apart as though opening a heavy curtain.*

## III. The Preliminary Invocation

*All make the Sign of Apophis and Typhon facing the center of the table.*

**Magus:** Holy art Thou, who art Universe,
Holy art Thou, who art in Nature formed,
Holy art Thou, the Vast and the Mighty,
Source of Darkness, Source of Light.[31]

*All make the Sign of Silence, then clasp hands over hearts.*

*Magus recites the Revised Oration to God as explained in Chapter 7.*

**Magus:** O Almighty and Omnipotent MAD, Lord and Creator of the universe, we devoted worshippers of the Highest most earnestly invoke and call upon your divine power, wisdom, and goodness. We humbly and faithfully seek your favor and assistance to me in all my deeds, words, and thoughts, and in the promotion, procuring, and mingling of your praise, honour, and glory. Through these, your twelve mystical Names: ORO, IBAH, AOZPI, MPH, ARSL, GAIOL, OIP, TEAA, PDOCE, MOR, DIAL, HCTGA, we conjure and pray most zealously to your divine and omnipotent majesty, that all your Angelic spirits might be called from any and all parts of the universe through the special domination and controlling power of your holy Names. Let them come most quickly to us. Let them appear visibly, friendily, and peacefully to us. Let them remain visible according to our will. Let them vanish from us and from our sight when we so request. Let them give reverence and obedience before you and your twelve mystical Names. We

---

[31] This revised wording for the Golden Dawn adoration of the Lord of the Universe is adapted from the rituals of the Open Source Order of the Golden Dawn.

command that they happily satisfy me in all things by accomplishing each and every one of my petitions, if not by one means, then by another, goodly, virtuously, and perfectly, with an excellent and thorough completeness, according to their virtues and powers, both general and unique, and by your united ministry and office, O God, Amen. So mote it be.

All: AMEN. AMEN. AMEN.

*Magus rings bell chime.*

## *IV. The Conjuration*

*Scryer moves to the west of the altar and is seated at the Holy Table, gazing into the stone or mirror. Magus stands behind Scryer and all other participants remain in a circle around the Table.*

*Magus recites the First Key, in Angelic followed by English, and Scryer then recites the Second Key, in Angelic followed by English, as explained in Chapter 9.*

*Magus performs the Greater Invoking Ritual of the Hexagram for the sign corresponding to the Angels being summoned, as explained in Chapter 10. Again, all present rotate accordingly except for Scryer, who remains seated.*

*Magus performs the Angelic Key for the Aire being opened.*

*Magus then steps onto the talisman and recites the appropriate conjuration for the angels being summoned, depending upon the objective of the rite, as explained in Chapter 11. If necessary, this action is repeated for each of the four quarters, calling upon the angels of each direction corresponding to the objective of the rite. Magus always starts conjuring to the east and ends in the north, moving clockwise and casting across the Holy Table.*

*Following the conjuration, all begin to chant the controlling names for the angels being conjured as they visualize the divine light descending into the stone or mirror. When Scryer sees a vision, he or she rings the bell chime and the chant ends.*

## V. Charge / Communication

The contents of this section depend on the nature of the ritual as explained in Chapter 12. Either questions should be asked of the summoned angels through Scryer, as Dee and Kelley did when they received the original system, or the angels should be charged with a particular task. In the latter case, be sure to make note of the exact wording of the Charge.

## VI. The License to Depart

Magus gives the License to Depart as explained in Chapter 14. This version of the License is slightly different from the one found in that chapter but will work just as well.

> **Magus:** O thou Angels of Light, because thou hast-diligently answered unto our demands, and hast been very ready and willing to come at our call, we do here license thee to depart unto thy proper place; without causing harm or danger unto man or beast. Depart, then, I say, and be thou very ready to come at our call, being duly exorcised and conjured by these sacred rites of magick. We charge thee to withdraw peaceably and quietly, and the peace of the Almighty, Eternal, True, and Living God be ever continued between us. AMEN.
>
> **All:** So mote it be!

Magus then concludes the MADRIAX as explained in Appendix A.

> **Magus:** MADRIAX CARMARA, ADRPAN LONSHI!

Magus makes the Sign of Closing the Veil, bringing both hands together with palms facing as though closing a set of heavy curtains. Scryer then rises and joins the circle, standing opposite Magus.

## *VII. Closing*

**All: May the benefit of this act and all acts be dedicated unto the complete liberation and supreme enlightenment of all beings everywhere, pervading space and time. So mote it be. May the benefits of practice, ours and others', come to fruition ultimately and immediately and we remain in a state of presence. AH!**[32]

*Magus concludes the AOEVEAE as explained in Appendix A.*

**Magus: I now declare this temple duly closed.**

*One knock with banishing dagger. The rite is at an end.*

---

32 As in the Opening, this section is adapted from Vajrayana Buddhism.

# Bibliography

Causaubon, Meric, ed. <u>A True and Faithful Relation of What Passed for Many Years Between Dr. John Dee and Some Spirits</u> (New York, NY: Magickal Childe, 1992)

Crowley, Aleister. <u>777 and Other Qabalistic Writings</u> (San Francisco, CA: Red Wheel/Weiser, 1986)

Crowley, Aleister. Magick: Book Four (San Francisco, CA: Weiser Books, 1998).

Dee, John. A True and Faithful Relation of What Passed for Many Years Between Dr. John Dee and Some Spirits (Whitefish, MT: Kessinger, 2010)

Duquette, Lon Milo. <u>Enochian Vision Magick</u> (San Francisco, CA: Weiser Books, 2008)

DuQuette, Lon Milo. <u>The Magick of Aleister Crowley</u> (San Francisco, CA: Weiser Books, 2003).

Hay, George, ed. <u>The Necronomicon: The Book of Dead Names</u> (London, UK: Skoob Books, 1993)

James, Geoffrey. <u>The Enochian Evocation of Doctor John Dee</u> (San Francisco, CA: Weiser Books, 2009)

Kraig, Donald Michael. <u>Modern Magick</u> (St. Paul, MN: Llewellyn, 1988)

Laycock, Donald C. The Complete Enochian Dictionary (San Francisco, CA: Weiser Books, 2001)

Leitch, Aaron. The Angelical Language Volumes I and II (St. Paul, MN: Llewellyn, 2010)

Peterson, Joseph, ed. John Dee's Five Books of Mystery (San Francisco, CA: Red Wheel/Weiser, 2008)

Phillips, Osborne and Denning, Melita. Mysteria Magica (St. Paul, MN: Llewellyn, 2004).

Regardie, Israel. The Golden Dawn (St. Paul, MN: Llewellyn, 2002).

Turner, Robert. Elizabethan Magic (Salisbury, UK: Element, 1990)

Tyson, Donald, ed. Agrippa's Three Books of Occult Philosophy (St. Paul, MN: Llewellyn, 1992)

Tyson, Donald. Enochian Magic for Beginners (St. Paul, MN: Llewellyn, 2008).

Tyson, Donald. Tetragrammaton (St. Paul, MN: Llewellyn, 2003).

# Index

Abaiond, 68
Abrahadabra, 184
Abriond, 68
Achaia, 58, 98
ADNI. *See* Adonai
ADRPAN, 141, 210, 213-214, 230
Advorpt, 88
Aegyptus, 38, 74, 97
Aethiopia, 63, 97, 100
Aethyr(s), 29-31, 107, 119-121, 138, 143, 157, 181, 183-186, 189-190
Affrica, 85, 98
Afghanistan, 45-46, 77, 86, 96, 101
Afnan, 86, 97, 99-101
Afnana, 98
Africa, 37, 54, 62-63, 79, 85, 100
　map (Figure 4), 90
　North, 47, 73, 85
　South, 79, 100
　West, 54
AGLA, 198
Agrippa, 33, 35, 37, 148-149, 234
AHIH, 198
Air, 7-8, 22, 124, 204, 207, 212, 214-215, 217-218, 226
　dagger, 214
　hexagram of, 202
　pentagram of, 215
Aire Key, 121, 136, 139-140, 143

ajna chakra, 212
akasha, 5
Alaska, 43, 104
Albania, 96
Algeria, 47, 88, 96, 101
Alpudus, 32, 35, 39, 42, 45, 54, 59-60, 66, 70
amber, 148, 152, 154
ambergris, 156
Ambriol, 57
America, 37, 56, 64, 83, 101
　North map (Figure 9), 94
　South map (Figure 10), 95
anahata chakra, 109, 212
Ananael, 134, 225
Andispi, 42
Andorra, 96
Angelic, 144, 204
　characters, 108-109
　First Key, 120, 136, 229
　Keys, 121, 130, 133, 141, 145, 157, 185-186, 214, 229
　Kings, 29, 32, 179
　language, 31, 140-141, 206, 214, 217, 234
　letters, 133, 135
　names, 31, 37, 39-43, 45-47, 49-52, 54-63, 65-67, 69-72, 74-79, 81-84, 86-88, 157
　script, 117
　Second Key, 120, 138

235

spirits, 131-132, 228
vowel sounds, 134
words, 2
Angels, 6, 29, 108-109, 116, 123-124, 193, 225-226, 229-230
   Enochian, 2, 116, 136, 138, 186
   Madimi, 131
   of Light, 193
Angels of the Mystical Heptarchy, 116
Angola, 96
Anguilla, 96
Ankara, 40, 87
Antarctica, 69, 89
Antigua & Barbuda, 96
AOEVEAE, 119, 122, 127, 130, 194, 204, 226-227, 231
AOIVEAE, 211
Apocalypse, 187-188
   Enochian, 186, 191
   working, 190
Apulia, 71-72
Aquarius, 6, 8, 10-11, 16, 24-26, 28, 32-33, 35, 39, 46, 49, 53, 69, 76-77, 146, 148-150, 155-156, 180
   Hexagram of (Figure 36), 155
Arabia, 96, 99-100
ARARITA, 201
Archangel, 108, 199
   Auriel, 199
   Michael, 108, 199
   Uriel, 199
Arfaolg, 35, 60, 62-63, 67, 71, 74, 79-81, 86
Argentina, 96
Aries, 6-7, 10-11, 14-16, 21, 23-24, 28, 32-33, 35, 45, 50, 58, 65, 73, 145-146, 148, 150, 156, 180
Ark of Knowledge, 137
Armenia, 58, 96
ARN, 29, 40-41, 139
   Talisman of (Figure 66), 173
Arriana, 77

ascendant
   degree of, 18, 23-27
Asher, 35
Asia
   map (Figure 5), 91
   Southeast, 57
ASP, 30, 71-72
   Talisman of (Figure 47), 164
aspects, 5-6, 14-17, 222
   final, 16
Aspiaon, 49
assafoetida, 156
Asshur, 32
Assiah, 130
Assyria, 84, 103
Astrolog, 20
Astrology, 5, 9, 13, 180
   Electional, 15-18
   Medieval, 26
   modern, 5, 10, 12
   Renaissance, 5, 11-12, 14, 17, 31
   Sidereal, 9
   Tropical, 9
   Vedic, 6, 9
ATEH, 197
Athens, 58
atlas, world, 96
Atziluth, 130
AUMGN, 227
Auriel, 199
Australia, 69, 89, 96
Austria, 52, 54, 96
autumn, 7-8
aversion, 15
Axxiarg, 44
Axziarg, 44
Aydropt, 65
Azerbaijan, 58, 96

BABALEL, 207-208
Babylon, 78, 82

Babylonians, 6
Bactra, 45, 86
Bactriane, 45, 61
Bactriani, 45, 61, 86, 101
BAG, 30, 83-84, 140, 160
   Talisman of (Figure 40), 160
Baghdad, 78
Bahamas, 96
Bahlasti, 226
Bahrain, 96
BALIGON, 207, 209
Balkh, 86
Bangladesh, 96
banishing, 119-120, 125-127, 129, 197, 199-200, 204, 206-207, 210, 226, 231
   dagger, 213
   field, 126
   hexagram, 155
   microcosmic, 194
   pentagram, 194
   ritual, 203
banner, 116-117, 119, 148, 213
Barbados, 96
Barbeau Peak, 64
BATAIVAH, 204-205
Belarus, 63, 96
Belgium, 68, 96
Belize, 96
Benin, 96
Benjamin, 32, 35
benzoin
   Siamese, 156
Bermuda, 96
Bhutan, 96
bilberry, 116
Binah, 185, 220-221
birth season, 9
Bithynia, 55, 103-104
BITOM, 204
black, 130, 193, 199, 209, 212, 216, 218
   blacke, 116

Black Cross, 5, 217
Black Sea, 40, 59, 65
blue, 111, 148, 151, 154-155, 198, 201-203
   flames, 198
   greenish blue, 148, 151, 153
   lidded daughter of sunset, 227
   robe, 199
BLUMAZA, 207, 210
BNAPSEN, 207, 209
BNASPOL, 207-208
BOBOGEL, 207
Bolivia, 96
Book Four, 203, 233
Book of Revelation, 186
Bosnia & Herzegovina, 96
Botswana, 96
Bound Lord, 23
Brazil, 96
Briah, 130
British Empire, 31, 175
British Isles, 71, 83, 89
British Museum, 140
Brunei Darussalam, 96
Brytania, 71
Brytannia, 96-97, 99-100
Bulgaria, 42, 52, 96
Burkina Faso, 96
Burundi, 97
BYNEPOR, 207-208

Cadaamp, 32, 35, 68, 71, 80
Cadamp, 57
Cairo, 38, 74
calculation grid, 18
Calzirg, 74
Cambodia, 97
Canada, 37, 43, 76, 89, 97
Cancer, 7, 9-12, 23, 25, 28, 32-33, 35, 40, 48, 75-76, 78, 82, 85, 87, 145-146, 148, 156, 180
   Hexagram of (Figure 29), 152

Cape Verde, 97
Cappadocia, 40, 104
Capricorn, 8, 10-11, 16, 20-28, 32-33, 35, 42-44, 52, 55, 58, 61, 75, 77, 83, 146, 148-149, 154, 156, 180
　Hexagram of (Figure 35), 154
Carcedonia, 70, 105
cardinal, 7, 9, 212
CARMARA, 210, 228, 230
carpet, 116
Carthage, 66
Carthago, 66, 70, 101
Caspian Sea, 42, 53, 80
Caspis, 53, 102-103
Causaubon, Meric, 233
Cayman Islands, 97
cedar, 109
Celtica, 51, 68, 96, 99
Centering Field, 126
Central African Republic, 97
Central America, 56
ceremonial forms, 123, 129, 225-226
Chad, 97
chakra, 211
　ajna, 212
　anahata, 109, 212
　muladhara, 212
　samsara, 212
　svadasthana, 212
　vishuddha, 212
Chaldea, 61, 77-78
Chaldean Order, 20, 146-147
Chaldei, 60-61, 98, 103
Charge/Communication, 230
Chart Victor, 17-18, 21-28
Chaslpo, 77
Chesed, 185, 198, 221
Chialps, 77
Chile, 97
China, 51, 61, 78, 97, 104-105
Chinese Qigong, 221

Choronzon, 185-186
　Coronzon, 185, 187, 190
CHR, 30, 69-70, 139, 164
　Talisman of (Figure 48), 164
Christian, 9, 125, 181, 193, 225
church, 13
Cicero, Chic and Tabitha, 221
Cilicia, 40, 45, 59, 103-104
Circle of Stars, 205
circumambulation, 210-211, 214-216, 218
Circniaca, 65
civet, 156
Closing the Temple, 193
Colchia, 97
Colchica, 64
Colombia, 97
Comaginen, 72
Comanan, 54
Comoros, 97
Comselh Ananael, 225
Concava Syria, 74, 103
Congo, 97
Congo River, 79, 87
conjunction, 14, 16, 205
conjuration, 229
Constantinople, 55
constellations, 9
Coph Nia, 227
correspondences, 5, 32, 145
Cousins, Robin E., 37-38, 64, 69, 73, 89
Coxlant, 66, 96, 99, 105
Cralpir, 52
Creatures, 123, 144
Creta, 88, 102
Crete, 88
crimson, 148, 153, 155
Croatia, 71, 97
Cross
　Black, 5, 217
　Qabalistic, 122, 155, 194, 198-199
cross, 198-199

Crowley, Aleister, 30, 119-120, 125, 127, 136, 143, 147, 181, 183-184, 189, 196, 203, 211, 220, 233
Crpanib, 82
Cuba, 97
Cucarpt, 62
Cucnrpt, 62
cup, 215
    water, 215
Cyprus, 47, 97
Czech Republic, 97
Czechia, 54

Da Vinci, Leonardo, 199
Daath, 220, 222
dagger, 204, 215, 226, 231
    Air, 214
    banishing, 213
Damascus, 39
Dan, 32-33, 35
Danube River, 98
David Allen Hulse, 36
debilitated, 16, 18, 21
Decan, 24-25
    Decan Lords, 24-25
    First, 24
    First Decan, 24
    Second, 24
    Third, 24
Dee, John, 1, 3, 5, 30, 74, 89, 101, 108-111, 116, 120, 123, 130, 134-135, 140, 156-157, 175, 183, 185, 187, 193, 195-196, 204, 206, 225, 230, 233-234
Democratic Republic of the Congo, 87, 97
demons, 2, 187-188
Denmark, 71, 97
Denning, Melita, 234
DEO, 29, 48-49, 139, 171
    Talisman of (Figure 61), 171
DES, 30, 79-80, 137, 140, 142, 161
    Talisman of (Figure 42), 161

Detriment, 11, 18, 21
DIAL, 130-132, 204-205, 216, 228
Dialiua, 41
Dialoia, 41
dignified, 16
Diurnal, 10-11, 145-146
divine, 33, 125, 131-132, 134, 145, 220, 222, 228-229
Divine Power, 131
Djibouti, 97
Doagnis, 40
Doanzin, 53
Docepax, 59
Dominica, 97
Dominican Republic, 97
Dongnis, 40
Doxmael, 88
Dozinal, 88
Dragon, 214
dragon's blood, 156
Drake Map, 89
DuQuette, Lon Milo, 37, 203
Dykes, Benjamin, 17

Earth, 3, 6, 9, 13, 22, 29, 31, 33, 35-38, 40, 96, 101, 104, 121, 134, 142-143, 145, 157-158, 175, 181, 198-199, 204, 207, 211-212, 217-218
    Banishing Pentagram of, 205
    hexagram of, 201
    Invoking Pentagram of Earth, 198, 206
    pantacle, 216
    Parts of, 16, 18, 179
    Pentagram of, 198, 216
    unicursal hexagram of, 207-209
Earthly Victory, 31
East, 45, 50, 58, 65, 73, 117, 149, 151, 197-201, 203-205, 207-208, 214, 217-218, 220, 226, 229

East-Northeast, 38, 41, 51, 53-54, 61
East-Southeast, 46, 48, 50, 59, 66, 69, 82
Ecuador, 97
EDLPRNAA, 204-205
Egypt, 38, 43, 73, 97, 102
Egyptian, 23-24, 201, 219
Egyptian Bounds, 23-24
EHNB, 204, 206, 212, 217
Elam, 75, 102
electional
   astrology, 15, 17
   method, 15-16
   technique, 15-16, 18
element, 5, 7, 22, 199
elemental, 3, 32, 35, 206-207, 211, 225
Elevenfold Seal, 211
Elizabethan age, 31
Elizabethan Magic, 37, 141, 234
Elizabethan script, 140
Ellesmere Island, 64
Enoch, Prayer of, 120
Enochian, 32, 34, 36, 130, 185, 187, 189, 195, 210, 219, 225
   angels, 2, 116, 136, 138, 186
   Apocalypse, 186, 191
   dictionary, 234
   elements, 211
   entities, 158, 188, 220
   evocation, 34, 189
   Golden Dawn, 31
   hexagram ritual, 206
   lamen, 108, 226
   magic, 126, 190
   magick, 2, 5, 29, 31, 107-108, 136, 183
   name, 131, 133
   neo-Enochian, 30, 107, 183
   Parts of Earth, 16, 18
   pentagram ritual, 204
   ring, 107, 119, 204, 226
   ritual, 108, 123
   rituals, opening, 127
   scrying the Aethyrs, 107
   spirits, 190
   temple, 109, 119, 123, 136, 138, 220
   universe, 1, 188, 225
Enochian Vision Magick, 37, 204, 233
Ensign, 111, 116
   of Creation, 111, 213
   of Jupiter, 114
   of Mars, 113
   of Mercury, 114
   of Moon, 115
   of Saturn, 115
   of Sun, 113
   of Venus, 112
Enterer
   sign of, 219
Ephraim, 32-33, 35
Equatorial Guinea, 97
Eritrea, 97
Estonia, 63, 97
Ethiopia, 63, 97
Euphrates, 39, 57
Euphrates River, 72
Europe, 31, 178, 189
   map (Figure 6), 92
evocation, 34, 120, 136, 138, 189
   ritual, 225
Exaltation, 11, 17-18
EXARP, 204, 206, 212

Fall, 11-12, 18
Far East, 78, 89
feet, 130, 138, 213, 221-222, 226
feminine, 7-9
Fiacim, 63
field(s), 126
   banishing, 126
   centering, 126
   invoking, 126-127
   operant, 126
fields
   magical, 211

Fiji, 97
Finland, 97
Fire, 22, 204-205, 207, 212, 214-218
   hexagram of, 201
   pentagram of, 214
   unicursal hexagram of, 208
Five Books of Mystery, 108, 234
fixed, 7-9, 30, 223
Focisni, 84
Foelix Arabia, 83, 101
forehead, 130, 183, 185, 197, 204, 206-207, 212
France, 51, 68, 97, 190
French Guiana, 97
Friday, 10, 145-146
Fundamental Obeisance, 120, 130, 132
   Revised, 131

Gabon, 97
GABRIEL, 199
Gad, 32-33, 35
galbanum, 156
Gallia, 51, 71, 97, 99-100
Ganges River, 44, 57, 105
Garamantes, 62, 97, 99, 103, 105
Garamantica, 62
garlic
   garlicke, 116
Gaul, 51
Gebabal, 32, 35, 46-47, 50, 59, 66, 69, 82
Gebal, 75
Geburah, 198
Gecaond, 58
Gedoons, 57
Gemini, 7, 10-11, 17, 20-21, 23-28, 32-33, 35, 49, 52, 56, 63, 70, 85, 88, 145-146, 148, 156, 180
   Hexagram of (Figure 28), 152
Gemnimb, 87
Genadob, 49
Genadol, 49

genitals, 207
geography, 29, 45, 64, 101
Geography, The (Claudius Potolemy), 29, 37-38, 40, 85
Georgia, 65, 97
Germania, 54, 97-100, 102
Germany, 54, 97
Getulia, 48, 97, 99-100
Ghana, 54, 98
GMICALZOMA, 141
Gmtziam, 86
Godwin's Cabalistic Encyclopedia, 184
Goetic, 2
gold, 107-108, 207, 222
Golden Dawn, 1, 31-32, 35, 107, 125, 129, 134, 136, 147, 157, 179, 186, 197, 199, 203-204, 206, 211, 221
   Angelic KIngs, 29
   Enochian, 31
   flashing color system, 117
   Israel Regardie, 234
   LBRP, 119, 122
   Open Source, 218, 228
   pronounciation system, 134-135, 144
   Scrying the Spirit, 183
   tablets, 36
   temple, 220
   tools, 213
   vowel insertions, 135
Golden Talisman, 35, 116
Gomziam, 86
Gongatha, 79, 96-101
Gorsim, 79, 101
Gosmam, 42, 64, 104
governor, 3, 29, 31-32, 35, 38, 40-43, 45-47, 49-52, 54-67, 69-72, 74-78, 80-84, 86, 88, 158, 175, 179
Graecia, 55, 104
Great Britain, 98
Great Table, 1, 3, 5, 29, 31, 34-36, 38, 74, 107, 116-117, 119, 130, 134, 179, 186, 204, 206

Great Work, iii
Greater Ritual of the Hexagram, 121, 147, 150-151, 182
Greater Ritual of the Pentagram, 147
Greece, 42, 58, 98
green, 116, 130, 151, 153, 155, 207-208, 215-216, 218
    emerald, 148
    emerald green, 148
    energy, 212
    greenish blue, 148, 151, 153
    greenish yellow, 148, 152, 155
    yellowish green, 148
Greenland, 37, 49, 83
Grenada, 98
Guadeloupe, 98
Guatemala, 98
Guinea-Bissau, 98
Guyana, 98

Hadit, 227
Haiti, 98
Hatha Yoga, 211
HCOMA, 204, 206, 212
heart, 204
heart center, 130
heavens, 124, 142, 144, 206-207, 210, 212
Hebrew, 133-134, 149-150, 184, 199
    consonant, 135
    letter names, 135
Heptarchia Mystica, 5, 157, 206
Heru-Ra-Ha, 227
hexagram, 147-148, 150, 182, 199, 207, 211, 220
    banishing, 155
    Greater Ritual of the Hexagram, 147
    Lesser Banishing Ritual of the Hexagram, 219
    Lesser Invoking Ritual of the Hexagram, 125, 222
    Lesser Ritual of the Hexagram, 150, 194, 203, 211

of Air, 202
of Aquarius, 155
of Aries, 151
of Cancer, 152
of Capricorn, 154
of Earth, 201
of Fire, 201
of Gemini, 152
of Jupiter, 154-155
of Leo, 152
of Libra, 153
of Luna (Moon), 152, 210
of Mars, 151, 153
of Mercury, 152-153
of Pisces, 155
of Sagittarius, 154
of Saturn, 154-155
of Sol (Sun), 152
of Taurus, 151
of Venus, 151, 153
of Virgo, 153
of Water, 203
planetary, 147, 207
ritual, 127, 129, 147, 205-206, 229
ritual LIRH, 120
unicursal, 207
unicursal of Air, 208
unicursal of Earth, 207-209
unicursal of Fire, 208
unicursal of Water, 208-209
highest, 131, 137, 142, 158, 220
hip, 204, 206-207
Hispania, 80, 96, 100
Holocaust, 189
holy names, 124
Holy Ones, 137
Holy Table, 107, 109-112, 116-117, 119, 121-122, 130, 136, 138, 158, 204, 207, 210, 213, 217-218, 226, 229
Honduras, 98
Hononol, 32, 35, 49, 52, 56, 63, 70, 85, 88

Horus, 125
hours, 16, 20, 28, 145-146
house, 12-13
house (Astrological), 6, 11, 18, 21-27
   eighth, 13
   fifth, 13
   first, 12
   fourth, 13
   ninth, 13
   Placidus system, 12, 14
   position, 14, 26
   second, 12
   seventh, 13
   sixth, 13
   tenth, 13
   third, 12-13
   twelfth, 13
Hulse, David Allen, 35-36
Hungary, 52, 98, 102
Hyrcania, 41, 102

Iceland, 50, 83, 98
ICH, 30, 55-56, 139, 169
   Talisman of (Figure 57), 169
ICZHIHAL, 204-205
Idumea, 67, 98
Idumian, 83, 98
Idunia, 37, 89, 97, 101
Illyria, 52, 96-100
incense, 156
   ambergris, 156
   benzoin, 156
   civet, 156
   dragon's blood, 156
   galbanum, 156
   lign-aloes, 156
   musk, 156
   olibanum, 156
   onycha, 156
   opopanax, 156
   scrammony, 156

   storax, 156
   sulphur, 156
   wormwood, 156
India, 6, 9, 44, 57, 96-101, 105
India Major, 105
indigo, 148, 156
Indonesia, 98
Idunia, 76
Indus River, 105
injunction, 131, 179, 181
intellect, 8
invocation
   preliminary, 228
invoking field, 126
invoking wand, 217
Iran, 42, 44, 48, 50, 53, 75-77, 79, 85, 98, 102-103
Iraq, 39, 57, 61, 75, 82, 85, 98, 103
   Southern, 61
Isis, 200
Israel, 32-33, 35, 67, 72, 98
Issachar, 32-33, 35
Istanbul, 55, 104
Italia, 70, 98-100
Italian Peninsula, 71
Italy, 41, 51, 71, 98, 103
Itergi, 61, 98-100, 105
Ivory Coast, 54, 98

Jamaica, 98
James, Geoffrey, 34, 109, 158, 233
Japan, 98
Jaxartes River, 52
Jordan, 67, 98
Judah, 32-33, 35
judgment, 142, 179
July, 123
Jupiter, 8, 10-11, 18, 20-28, 146, 148, 207
   Ensign, 114
   hexagram of, 155
   Hexagram of (Figure 34), 154

justice, 3, 144
juyce (juice), 116

Kalmar Union, 71
Kazakhstan, 63, 69, 83, 98, 103
Kelley, Edward, 1-3, 5-6, 12, 29, 31, 38, 64, 71, 108, 111, 116, 120, 123, 143, 193, 196, 204, 225, 230
Kenya, 98
Kether, 181, 185, 198
Keyword Analysis, 150, 200, 203
King, 32, 147, 179, 210
Kingdom, 185
Kinshasa, 87
knowledge, 31, 137, 179, 186
  undefiled, 144
Korea
  North, 99
  South, 100
Kosovo, 98
Kraig, Donald Michael, 197, 221
Krakow, 123
Kurdistan, 50, 60
Kuwait, 98
Kyrgyz Republic (Kyrgyzstan), 98

Labnixp, 83
lamen, 108, 119, 226
  Enochian, 108
Laos, 98
Laparin, 58
Latvia, 63, 98
Lauacon, 63
Lavavoh, 32
Lavavot, 35, 52, 55, 58, 61, 75, 77, 83
law, 8, 137, 178
Laxdizi, 45, 73-74, 163
Lazhiim, 80
LBRP. *See* Lesser Banishing Ritual of the Pentagram
LEA, 30, 62-63, 139
  Talisman of (Figure 52), 166

Lebanon, 72, 75, 98
legislation, 179
Leitch, Aaron, 34, 149
*Leo*, 6-7, 10-12, 19-28, 32-33, 35, 46-47, 50, 59, 66, 69, 82, 145-146, 148, 156, 180
  hexagram, 152
Lesotho, 98
Lesser Banishing Ritual of the Pentagram, 119, 122, 129, 155, 219, 222
Lesser Invoking Ritual of the Hexagram, 125, 222
Lesser Ritual of the Hexagram, 125, 127, 150, 203, 206, 211, 219
Lesser Ritual of the Pentagram, 125, 127, 129, 149-150, 197, 199-200, 203-204, 211, 219, 221
Lexarph, 53
Liber 777, 147-150, 154-155, 180-181, 184
Liber Chanokh, 136
Liber O vel Manus et Sagittae, 147, 220
*Liber Scientia*, 35-36, 38, 40-44, 48-49, 59-62, 68, 71-73, 75-77, 81-86, 88, 158
Liber V vel Reguli, 211
Liberia, 98
Libra, 7, 10-11, 23, 25, 28, 32-33, 35, 39, 42, 45, 54, 59-60, 66, 70, 146, 148, 156, 180
  Hexagram of (Figure 32), 153
Libya, 65, 98
license to depart, 156
Liechtenstein, 54, 99
lign-aloes, 156
LIL, 29, 38-39, 139, 174, 185
  Talisman of (Figure 67), 174
limitation, 179, 181
LIN, 30, 72-74, 140, 163
  Talisman of (Figure 46A), 163
  Talisman of (Figure 46B), 163
LIRH. *See* Lesser Invoking Ritual of the Hexagram
LIT, 29, 45-46, 139, 172
  Talisman of (Figure 63), 172

Lithuania, 63, 99
Living God, 193, 230
LOE, 30, 56-57, 139, 168
 Talisman of (Figure 56), 168
lot of fortune, 19, 22
 degree of, 18, 20-21, 23-27
Luna (Moon), 148
 Hexagram of (Figure 29), 152
Luxembourg, 68, 99
LVX, 201, 203
Lydia, 53, 104

Macedonia, 52, 61-62, 96, 99, 102
MAD, 131, 137, 141-142, 228
Madagascar, 99
MADRIAX, 120, 122, 127, 130, 141, 194, 205-206, 210-212, 227-228, 230
magical imagination, 183
Magickal Childe, 123, 206, 233
MAHD. *See* MAD
MAKAShANH, 184
Malawi, 99
Malaysia, 99
Maldives, 99
Mali, 54, 99, 105
Malkuth, 185, 198
Malta, 99
Manasseh, 32-33, 35
Mantiana, 50, 102
Marmara Sea, 55
Marmarica, 73-74
Mars, 10-11, 16, 18, 20-27, 145-146, 148, 207
 Ensign, 113
Martinique, 99
masculine, 6-8
*Mastering the Great Table*, 2, 35, 119, 130, 179, 186
*Mastering the Mystical Heptarchy*, 2, 119, 136
Mathers, S. L. MacGregor, 32
Mathula, 82

Mauritania, 88, 97, 99, 101
Mauritius, 99
Mayotte, 99
MAZ, 29, 46-47, 139, 171
 Talisman of (Figure 62), 171
Mazar-i-Sharif, 86, 101
Media, 76, 98
Median, 82, 98
Mediterranean, 46, 53, 65-66, 85, 101
Mercury, 7, 10-11, 17-18, 20-27, 145-146, 148, 207
 Ensign, 114
 hexagram of, 152-153
Mesopotamia, 39, 98, 103
Metagonitidim, 84, 104
Mexico, 56, 69, 99
Middle East, 31, 101
 map (Figure 7), 93
 map (Figure 8), 93
Middle Pillar Ritual, 129, 198, 211, 219-222
Mirzind, 78
Moldavia, 68
Moldova, 99
Molpand, 55
Monaco, 99
Monday, 10, 18, 20, 145
Mongolia, 61, 99, 105
Montenegro, 99
Montserrat, 99
Moon, 10-11, 15-16, 18, 20-27, 137, 145-147
 degree of, 18, 23-27
 Ensign, 115
 hexagram of, 210
MOR DIAL HCTGA, 130-132, 204-205, 216, 228
Morocco, 48, 88, 99, 104
Mountains, 51, 123
Mourning of Isis, 200
Mozambique, 99
MPH ARSL GAIOL, 130, 136, 204-205, 215

muladhara charka, 212
musk, 156
mutable, 7-9
Myanmar/Burma, 97
Mysteria Magica, 234
Mystical Heptarchy
   Angels of the, 116
Mystical Names of God, 131-132, 228
mystical operations, 181, 221

Nabaomi, 66
Names of God, 34-35
Namibi, 99
NANTA, 204, 206, 212
Naphthali, 32
Naphthalin, 35
narcissus, 156
Nasamonia, 65
NAZ OLPIRT, 120, 129, 211
Nemrodiania, 59
Nepal, 99
Neptune, 10-11
Netherlands, 68, 99
Neuburg, Victor, 185
New Guinea, 89, 99
New Moon, 20
New World, 38, 69, 179
New Zealand, 89, 99
NIA, 30, 76-77, 140, 162
   Talisman of (Figure 44), 162
Nicaragua, 99
Nigeria, 99
Nigrana, 80
Nile, 38, 73
Nocamal, 45
Nociabi, 61
Nocturnal, 10, 22, 145-146
Norse, 83
North, 40, 48, 75-76, 78, 82, 85, 87, 116, 205, 207, 211
   Africa, 73, 85

America, 49, 83, 94
Italy, 71
Korea, 99
North Africa, 85
North Pole, 64
   magnetic, 64
northern hemisphere, 6
North-Northeast, 57, 68, 72, 80
North-Northwest, 44, 47, 60, 62, 64, 67-68, 71, 73-74, 79-81, 86-87
Northwest Territories, 43
Norway, 71, 99
Notiabi, 61
Nuit, 227
Numidia, 46, 96
Nunavut, 43, 64

Oacidi, 81, 100
Oasis
   region, 81
Obert, Charles, 9, 13
Obmacas, 48
Obuaors, 78
Occodon, 38
Oddiorg, 52
Odraxti, 85
Odroxti, 85
OIP TEAA PDOCE, 130, 204-205, 215
olibanum, 156
Olpaged, 32, 35, 45, 50, 58, 65, 73
Omagrap, 68
Oman, 99
Omnipotent Creator, 131, 228
omnipotent majesty, 131-132, 228
Ompehda, 226
Onigap, 56, 69, 96-101
Onizimp, 75
onycha, 156
Ooanamb, 60
Opening by Watchtower
   revised, 213

Opening Keys, 120, 136
Opening the Temple, 119, 123
    Devotional, 120
operant field, 120, 125-126, 150, 185, 203, 219, 222
Opmacas, 48
opopanax, 156
opposition, 15-16
Orancir, 76
orange, 148, 151-152, 154, 198
    reddish, 153
Oration
    To God, Revised, 228
Orcamir, 76
Orcheny, 57, 103
Ordo Dispersi Israelis, 33-35
Ordo Templi Orientis, 125
ORO IBAH AOZPI, 130, 204-205, 214
Osidaia, 72
Osiris, 200-201, 213, 219
Ottawa, 76
Oxiana, 46, 101
Oxlopar, 84
OXO, 30, 61-62, 139, 167
    Talisman of (Figure 53), 167
Oxus River, 52
Ozidaia, 72

Pabnixp, 83
Pacasna, 40
Pacific Islands, 99
Pakistan, 44, 99, 105
Pamphilia, 80, 104
Panama, 99
pantacle, 110, 216
    of Earth, 216
Paoaoan, 73-74, 163
Paphlagonia, 59, 104
Paraguay, 99
Paraoan, 73-74
Paroketh, Veil of, 219

Parsadal, 44
Parstania, 67
Parthia, 47, 102
Parts of the Earth, 31, 104
Parva Asia, 41, 104
Parziba, 70
Pascomb, 39
Patagonia, 56
PAZ, 29, 43-44, 139, 172
    Talisman of (Figure 64), 172
pentagram, 127, 199, 213, 218
    AOEVEAE Pentagram Ritual, 119, 204
    banishing, 194
    Banishing Pentagram of Earth, 205
    Enochian Pentagram ritual, 204
    Invoking Pentagram of Earth, 206
    Lesser Banishing Ritual of the Pentagram, 119, 122, 129, 155, 219, 222
    Lesser Ritual of the Pentagram, 127, 149-150, 194, 197, 200, 203, 211, 219, 221
    of Active Spirit, 217
    of Air, 215
    of Earth, 198, 216
    of Fire, 214
    of Passive Spirit, 217
    of Water, 216
Perfect Power, 193
Persia, 78, 102
    Persian Empire, 79
    Persian Gulf, 75
personality, 5, 9, 12, 31, 125
Peterson, Joseph, iii, 234
Phalagon, 49
phases
    preliminary invocation, 129
Phasiana, 60, 104
Phenices, 71, 98, 103
Philippines, 99
Philips, Osborne, 234

Phoenicia, 72
Phrygia, 40, 87
Phyrygia, 101
Pillars of Light, 211
Pisces, 9-11, 15, 24-26, 28, 32-33, 35, 44, 47, 60, 62, 64, 67, 71-72, 74, 79-81, 86, 146, 148-150, 156, 180-181
   Hexagram of (Figure 37), 155
Placidus House System, 12, 14, 26
planetary
   day, 20
   dignities and debilities, 11
   entities, 32
   force, 225
   hexagram, 147, 207
   hours, 16, 20, 145-146
   names, 207
   operations, 32
   position, 5
   realm, 3, 207
   ruler, 10, 14, 16, 145-146, 148, 182
   spirit, 2
planets, 5-6, 10-11, 13-19, 21, 26-27, 30, 112, 146-147
Pluto, 10-11
Pocisni, 83
Poland, 54, 100
political operations, 40, 74, 180
Ponodol, 56
POP, 30, 67-68, 139
   Talisman of (Figure 49), 165
Pophand, 79
Portugal, 80, 100
Pothnir, 44
Power
   dry, 6-8
   hot, 6-7
   Moist, 7-8
practical operations, 180
Preliminary Invocation, 120, 228
prenatal lunation

   degree of, 18, 20-27
President, 178
Prince, 5-6
Pristac, 51
probability shift, 176
psychology, 5
Ptolemy, Claudius, 29, 37-38, 40, 101, 179
public opinion, 176
Puerto Rico, 100
Pyrenees Mountains, 51

Qabalistic, 122, 130, 155, 181, 184, 194, 198-199, 233
   Worlds, 130
Qabalistic Cross. *See* Cross Qabalistic,
Qatar, 100
Qigong, 211
quadrant, 117
Queen Elizabeth, 5

RAAGIOSL, 204-205
Ranglam, 79
red, 116, 130, 155, 201-203, 208, 214, 218
   banners, 117
   blanket, 116
   carpet, 116
   energy, 212
   fabric, 116
   light, 214-215
   reddish-orange, 148
   robe, 199
Red Sea, 84
Red Wheel, 37, 233-234
Regardie, Israel, 136, 219-221, 234
Renaissance, 10, 69, 176, 195
   Astrology, 5, 11-12, 14, 17, 30-31
retrograde, 27
Reuben, 32
revelation, 187-188
Rhine River, 51

RII, 30, 84-86, 140, 159
  Talisman of (Figure 39), 159
ritual, 1, 16, 116, 120, 123, 125, 129, 131, 136, 177, 187, 193, 199, 207, 210, 224
  AOEVEAE, 119, 122, 127, 204
  banishing, 203, 207
  basic forms, 197
  Comselh Ananael Thirty Aires' Evocation Ritual, 225
  Enochian, 108, 123, 127, 211
  Enochian Pentagram Ritual, 204
  Greater Invoking Ritual of the Hexagram, 229
  Greater Ritual of the Hexagram, 121, 147, 150-151, 182
  Greater Ritual of the Pentagram, 147
  hexagram, 147
  Lesser Banishing Ritual of the Hexagram, 219
  Lesser Banishing Ritual of the Pentagram, 119, 122, 129, 155, 200, 219, 222
  Lesser Invoking Ritual of the Hexagram, 120, 219, 222
  Lesser Ritual of the Hexagram, 125, 150, 194, 199, 203, 207, 211, 219
  Lesser Ritual of the Pentagram, 125, 149-150, 197, 199, 203-204, 211, 219-221
  MADRIAX, 119, 122, 127, 130, 205-206
  Middle Pillar, 129, 198, 211, 219-222
  Opening the Watchtower, 213
  pentagram, 194
  Qabalistic Cross, 122
  sequence, 132
  space, 225
  Star Ruby, 119, 194, 203
  Star Sapphire, 120, 194, 203
  Thirty Aires, 119
  timing, 28
Ritual of the Four Elements Revised, 206

Ritual of the Four Elements Revised, 206
river, 9, 73, 98, 123
  Congo, 79, 87
  Danube, 98
  Euphrates, 39, 57, 72
  Ganges, 44, 57, 105
  Indus, 105
  Jaxartes, 52
  Nile, 38, 74
  Oxus, 46
  Rhine, 51
  Tigris, 39, 57, 82, 85
robe(s), 109, 119
  black, 199
  blue, 199
  red, 199
  white, 109, 226
  yellow, 199
Robin E. Cousins. *See* Cousins, Robin E.
Romania, 52, 68, 100
Rome, 71
Ronoamb, 75
Ronoomb, 75
Round House, 35
round house, 206
Rowe, Benjamin, 185
Ruben, 35
ruler of the day, 18
  degree of, 18, 22-27
ruler of the hour, 22
  degree of, 23, 25-27
rulership, 10, 17
Russia, 63, 68
  Russian Federation, 59, 100
Rwanda, 100

Sagittarius, 8, 10-11, 23, 25, 28, 32-33, 35, 38, 41, 51, 53-54, 61, 146, 148, 156, 180
Sahara Desert, 48

Saint Augustine, 193
Saint Kitts and Nevis, 100
Saint Lucia, 100
Saint Vincent's & Grenadines, 100
Samapha, 41
Samoa, 100
samsara chakra, 212
Sands, 123
Sao Tome and Principe, 100
Saturday, 10, 146
Saturn, 8, 10-11, 16, 18, 20-27, 146-148, 207
   Ensign, 115
   Hexagram of, 154-155, 209
Saudi Arabia, 49, 100
Sauromatica, 62, 96-101, 103
Saxtomp, 46
Saziami, 81
Scale
   King, 147
   Queen, 148, 182
Scandinavia, 71
scarlet, 148, 151, 153
Scorpio, 8-11, 15-16, 23, 25, 28, 32-33, 35, 57, 68, 71, 80, 146, 148, 156, 180, 200
   Hexagram of (Figure 33), 153
scrammony, 156
Scrying the Aethyrs, 107, 119-121, 138, 143, 157, 181, 183, 186, 190
seal, 221, 225
   Elevenfold, 211
season, 6
   autumn, 7
   birth, 9
   spring, 6
   summer, 6-7
   winter, 6, 8
Sect, 10, 145
Seer, 124
self, 7, 9, 13, 123, 125, 132, 182, 186
Senegal, 100
Seniors, 179

Sephir Sephiroth, 184
Serbia, 100
Serici Populi, 78
sextile, 15
Shewstone, 116
shoulder, 198, 206-207
Siberia, 59
Sidereal Astrology, 9
Sierra Leone, 100
Sigillum Dei Aemeth, 110-112, 116, 213, 220, 225
Sigmorf, 64
Sign of
   Apophis and Typhon, 200, 218, 228
   Closing the Veil, 230
   LVX, 201, 203
   Osiris Risen, 201, 213, 219
   Osiris Slain, 200-201
   Rending the Veil, 219, 228
   Silence, 218, 228
   the Enterer, 219
   the Mourning of Isis, 200
*Sigullum Dei Aemeth*, 111
Simeon, 32-33, 35
Singapore, 100
Sloane 3191, 34, 74, 140
Slovakia, 54, 100
Slovenia, 71, 100
Soageel, 77
Sochial, 63
Sogdiana, 52, 98, 100-101
Solomon Islands, 100
Somalia, 100
Source
   of darkness, 218
   of light, 218
South, 40-41, 57, 62, 64-65, 78, 81, 84, 205
South America, 56, 69
South-Southeast, 43-44, 52, 55, 61, 77, 83
South-Southwest, 53, 55-56, 72, 84, 88
Soxia, 50, 105

Spain, 80, 100
spheres, 3, 30, 147, 185, 198
spirit, 225
   Angelic, 228
   conjured, 226
   diaries, 2, 109
   elemental, 5
   of Sun, 218
   possession, 186
   spirits, 122
   vision, 183
spring, 6
square, 15
Sri Lanka, 100
Stansfield Jones, Charles, 190
Star Ruby Ritual, 119, 122, 127, 194, 203
Star Sapphire Ritual, 120, 122, 127, 194, 203
storax, 156
Sudan, 81, 100
sulphur, 156
summer, 6-7
Sun, 5-7, 10-11, 18, 20, 22, 24, 27, 123, 137, 146, 218
   Chart Victor, 28
   degree of, 18, 23-27
   Ensign, 113
   hours, 146
   of Spirit, 218
   -rise, 20, 22, 146
   sign, 6-7
Sunday, 10, 20, 145-146
superiors, 27-28
   degree of, 18, 21-27
Supernals, 220
Supreme Court, U.S., 178
Suriname, 100
svadasthana chakra, 212
Svalbard Archipelago, 83
Swaziland, 100
Sweden, 71, 100

sweet wood, 109
Switzerland, 51, 100
Syria, 39, 72, 74, 100, 103

Taaogba, 86
Tabitom, 54
Tablet
   Of Union or Black Cross, 217
Tabula Recensa, 36-37, 40-43, 48-49, 59-62, 68, 71-77, 80, 82-83, 85-86, 88, 130, 135, 158, 204
Tahamdo, 61
Tahando, 61
Tajikstan, 52, 100
talisman, 36, 121, 181, 193, 226, 229
   ARN, 173
   ASP, 164
   BAG, 160
   CHR, 164
   DEO, 171
   DES, 161
   Ensigns of Creation, 111
   Golden, 35, 116
   ICH, 169
   LEA, 166
   LIL, 174
   LIN, 74, 163
   LIN (B), 163
   LIT, 172
   LOE, 168
   MAZ, 171
   NIA, 162
   OXO, 167
   PAZ, 172
   POP, 165
   RII, 159
   TAN, 166
   TEX, 159
   Thirty Aires, 158
   TOR, 162
   VTA, 167

VTI, 161
ZAA, 160
ZAX, 169
ZEN, 165
ZID, 170
ZIM, 168
ZIP, 170
ZOM, 173
TAN, 30, 64-65
  Talisman (Figure 51), 166
Tangiers, 84
Tanzania, 100
Taoagla, 86
Tapamal, 56
Tastoxo, 62
Tastozo, 62
Taurus, 5, 7, 10-11, 15, 23-24, 28, 32-33, 35, 40-41, 57, 62, 64-65, 78, 81, 84, 145-146, 148, 156, 180
  Hexagram of (Figure 27), 151
Tedoand, 59
Tedoond, 59
Tehran, 76
temple, 204, 210, 213-216, 218, 225-226
  arrangement, 107
  closing, 122, 193
  closing the, 231
  Enochian, 109, 119, 123, 136, 138, 220
  Golden Dawn, 220
tension, 213
Tetragrammaton, 149, 151, 182, 189, 220-221, 234
  banners of, 148
TEX, 30, 86-88
  Talisman (Figure 38), 159
Thailand, 100
The Key of it All Book Two, 36
Thebaidi, 38, 43, 102
Thebes, 38, 43
Thelema, 189-190
  Thelemite, 117

Thelemic, 107, 193
  Aeonics, 181
  cosmology, 181, 227
  current, 182
  formula, 182
  magicians, 203
  magick, 199
  perspective, 225
  text, 190
  traditions, 197, 211
Thirty Aires Conjurations, 157
Thirty Aires Ritual Template, 119
Thotanf, 43
Thotant, 43
Thrace
Thracia, 42
Three Books of Occult Philosophy (Agrippa), 234
throat, 130, 212
Thule People, 83
Thursday, 10, 146
Tiarpax, 46
Tibet, 67, 105
Tierra del Fuego, 56
Tigris River, 39, 82, 85
Timor Leste, 100
Tiphareth, 108, 198, 219
Toantom, 71
Tocarzi, 65
Todnaon, 50
Togo, 100
Tolpam, 69, 102
TOR, 30, 75-76, 140, 142
  Talisman of (Figure 45), 162
Torzoxi, 67
Totocan, 70
Tree of Life, 147, 185, 198, 225
Trenam, 54, 96, 98-100
Tribes of Israel, 32-33
trine, 15-16
Trinidad & Tobago, 101

Triplicity Lords, 22
Tropical Astrology, 9
true
    comfort, 124
    first key, 136
    God, 158, 193, 230
    lights of understanding, 124
    magick, 193
    Seal of God, 110
    will, 193
    wisdom, 123
    worshipper, 137, 158
True and Faithful Relation, 123, 131, 206, 233
Tuesday, 10, 145-146
Tuning the Space, 121, 145
Tunis, 105
Tunisia, 66, 70, 101, 105
Turkey, 40-42, 46, 53, 55-56, 59-60, 72, 87, 101, 103-104
    map (Figure 8), 93
    Turkish coast, 81
Turkmenistan, 80, 101
Turks & Caicos Islands, 101
Turner, Robert, 37, 141, 234
Tuscany, 41
Tuscia, 40, 71, 103
Tyson, Donald, 186-188, 190, 234

Uganda, 101
Ukraine, 63, 101
unicursal hexagram, 207
    of Air, 208
    of Earth, 207, 209
    of Fire, 208
    of Water, 208-209
Union
    Iberian, 56, 80
    Kalmar, 71
    Tablet of. *See* Black Cross
union, 14, 71, 207

United Arab Emirates, 101
United States of America, 37, 76, 89, 101, 178, 190
universe, 2, 131, 193, 218, 227-228
Uranus, 10-11
Uriel, 199
Uruguay, 101
Uzbekistan, 46, 52, 101

Valgars, 39
Vastrim, 84
Vauaamp, 47
Vedic Astrology, 6, 9
Venezuela, 101
Venus, 8, 10-11, 18, 20-27, 145-146, 148, 207
    Ensign, 112
Vespucci, Amerigo, 37
Victoria Island, 64
Vietnam, 101
Vinsan, 68, 103
violet, 148, 155
Virgin Islands
    U.K., 101
    U.S., 101
Virgo, 7, 10-12, 15, 23, 25, 28, 32-33, 35, 55-56, 72, 84, 88, 145, 148-150, 156, 180, 200
    Hexagram of (Figure 31), 153
Virochi, 42
Virooli, 42
virtue, 131-132, 181, 229
vishuddha chakra, 212
Vision and the Voice, The (Crowley), 31, 143-144, 183, 185
Vitruvian Man, 199
Viuipos, 60
Vixpalg, 72
Voanamb, 60
voice, 123, 215
Void of Course, 16

vowel sound(s), 134-136
   Angelic, 134
Vsnarda, 55
VTA, 30, 59-60, 139
   Talsiman of (Figure 54), 167
VTI, 30, 78-79, 140
   Talisman of (Figure 43), 161

wand, 204, 207, 214
   fire, 214
   invoking, 217
Washington D.C., 76
Watchtower, 189, 195, 206
   entities, 193
   gates, 186, 190
   Kings, 175
   Opening by, 213
   Opening by (Revised), 213
Water, 7-9, 22, 204, 207, 212, 217, 222
   cup, 215
   elemental, 218
   hexagram of, 203
   Lustral, 215
   pentagram of, 215
   unicursal hexagram of, 208-209
Wednesday, 10, 145
West, 49, 52, 56, 63, 70, 85, 88, 205, 220
Western Esoteric Tradition, 3
West-Northwest, 39, 42, 45, 54, 59-60, 67, 70
West-Southwest, 39, 46, 49, 69, 76-77
white, 130, 198, 208
   Air, 218
   banners, 117
   brilliance, 222
   energy, 212
   light, 215
   lilly white, 116
   linen robe, 109
   robe, 109, 226
   South, 215, 218

winter, 6, 8-9
wisdom, 124, 131, 228
   Chockmah, 181
   true, 123
world atlas, 96
World War, 189-190
   First, 189
   Second, 189-190
wormwood, 156

Yahweh, 148, 151
Yalpamb, 67
yellow
   robe, 199
Yemen, 101
Yesod, 198
Yetzirah, 130
*YHVH*, 131, 148-151, 198, 220, 222
Yoga
   Hatha, 211
Yugoslavia, 52
Yukon, 43

ZAA, 30, 81-82, 140
   Talisman of, 160
Zabulon, 35
Zafasai, 66
Zambia, 101
Zamfres, 50
Zarnaah, 32, 35, 40, 48, 75-76, 78, 82, 85, 87
Zarzilg, 32, 35, 38, 41, 51, 53-54, 61, 65, 84
ZAX, 30, 53-54, 139, 186
   Talisman of, 169
Zaxanin, 76
Zebulun, 32
ZEN, 30, 66-67, 139
   Talisman of, 165
ZID, 29, 50-51, 139
   Talisman of, 170
Zildron, 69

ZIM, 30, 58-59, 139
　Talisman of (Figure 55), 168
Zimbabwe, 101
Zinggen, 32, 35, 39, 46, 49, 53, 69, 76-77
ZIP, 30, 52-53, 139
　Talisman of (Figure 59), 170
Ziracah, 32, 35, 40-41, 57, 62, 64, 78, 81
Zirzird, 47
zodiac (zodiacal), 2, 6, 16, 31, 156, 181
　angels, 134
　currents, 182
　days, 28, 121
　entities, 32
　forces, 225
　governors, 33, 35, 157-158, 175, 180
　hours, 145
　operations, 17
　portions, 31
　powers, 180
　realms, 3
　scheme, 207
　signs, 5-6, 32-33, 35, 145, 147, 180
ZOM, 29, 41-42, 139
　Talisman of (Figure 65), 173
Zurchol, 32, 35, 55-56, 72, 84, 88

www.ingramcontent.com/pod-product-compliance
Lightning Source LLC
Chambersburg PA
CBHW050926240426
43670CB00022B/2943